The

EVERYTHING®
College Cookbook

Dear Reader:

When my son announced he'd decided to go away to college, I real-ized he hadn't spent enough time on kitchen duty. Whether he chose to live in a dorm or off-campus, his cooking repertoire was going to have to expand beyond nachos and microwaving the occasional leftover pizza.

Of course, not every college presents the same range of options in the cooking department. Some schools permit microwaves in individual rooms, while others limit cooking to a common dormitory kitchen. Students living off-campus may have a fully equipped kitchen at their dis-posal. But all college students share the need for tasty recipes that don't require hours of preparation.

My goal for this book is to provide nutritious, easy-to-make recipes for time-tight college students. The microwave, hot plate, and conventional oven are all put to use here. Budget conscious students will appreciate recipes featuring creative ways to use leftovers. Novice cooks will find instructions on everything from boiling eggs to frying pork chops. For stu-dents fighting the "Freshman 15," there are healthy snacks featuring easily transportable items such as granola bars and trail mix, as well as every student's favorite thirst-quencher—the smoothie.

Good luck in your college career!

Rhonda Lauret Parkinson

The EVERYTHING® Series

Editorial

Publishing Director	Gary M. Krebs
Managing Editor	Kate McBride
Copy Chief	Laura M. Daly
Acquisitions Editor	Kate Burgo
Development Editor	Karen Johnson Jacot
Production Editor	Jamie Wielgus

Production

Production Director	Susan Beale
Production Manager	Michelle Roy Kelly
Series Designers	Daria Perreault
	Colleen Cunningham
	John Paulhus
Cover Design	Paul Beatrice
	Matt LeBlanc
Layout and Graphics	Colleen Cunningham
	Rachael Eiben
	John Paulhus
	Daria Perreault
	Monica Rhines
	Erin Ring
Series Cover Artist	Barry Littmann

THE
EVERYTHING®
COLLEGE
COOKBOOK

300 hassle-free recipes
for students on the go

Rhonda Lauret Parkinson

Adams Media
Avon, Massachusetts

To my Dad, for sharing his love of cooking,
and to Robert, wishing him all the best at university.

An Everything® Series Book.
Everything® and everything.com® are registered trademarks of F+W Publications, Inc.

Published by Adams Media, an F+W Publications Company
57 Littlefield Street, Avon, MA 02322 U.S.A.
www.adamsmedia.com

ISBN 13: 978-1-59337-303-0
ISBN 10: 1-59337-303-1
Printed in the United States of America.

J I H G F E

Library of Congress Cataloging-in-Publication Data
Lauret Parkinson, Rhonda.
The everything college cookbook :
300 hassle-free recipes for students on the go / Rhonda Lauret Parkinson.
p.   cm.
An everything series book
ISBN 1-59337-303-1
1. Quick and easy cookery. I. Title. II. Series.
TX833.5.L38 2005
641.5'55—dc22
2004026502

This publication is designed to provide accurate and authoritative information with regard to the subject matter covered. It is sold with the understanding that the publisher is not engaged in rendering legal, accounting, or other professional advice. If legal advice or other expert assistance is required, the services of a competent professional person should be sought.
—From a *Declaration of Principles* jointly adopted by a Committee of the American Bar Association and a Committee of Publishers and Associations

Many of the designations used by manufacturers and sellers to distinguish their products are claimed as trademarks. Where those designations appear in this book and Adams Media was aware of a trademark claim, the designations have been printed with initial capital letters.

This book is available at quantity discounts for bulk purchases.
For information, please call 1-800-289-0963.

Contents

cknowledgments

For all their advice and support throughout this project, I would like to thank my fellow About Guides, especially Paula Ford-Martin. I would like to thank my agent, Barb Doyen, for her hard work, and my editor, Kate Burgo, at Adams Media for her guidance.

Introduction

▶ EVERY FALL, thousands of students begin their first year of college or university. New students face numerous challenges, both academic and nonacademic. Along with quizzes and finals, many must tackle the challenges and responsibilities that come with living on their own for the first time, from handling a budget to doing their own laundry.

With all these obstacles to overcome, it's easy for harried students to conclude that taking the time to learn how to cook just isn't worth the effort. But there are several reasons students should take the time to learn a few skills in the kitchen.

First and foremost is the fact that cooking is cheaper than eating out. Studies indicate that food is the second biggest expense for college students, second only to accommodations. The majority of students can expect to spend at least $2,000 annually on food. Being dependent on restaurants, fast-food kiosks, or even the college dining hall for every meal will push that amount even higher. Even students who live at home while attending a local college will find that their hectic schedule doesn't fit with family mealtimes. Since most parents aren't willing to go on kitchen duty at midnight, students will need to start preparing their own meals and late-night snacks.

Believe it or not, cooking saves time. In the time it takes to walk to a fast-food restaurant or make your way through the buffet line at the college dining hall, you could have prepared a simple dinner of stir-fried chicken with steamed vegetables and rice. Heating up leftovers is even quicker. And you can study in the comfort of your dorm or apartment while eating. True, some dishes—such as Chili con Carne—take longer. But most of that time the food is simmering; all you need to do is look up from your books occasionally and give the dish a quick stir.

Cooking your own food is healthier. Why is eating healthy so important? It's not just about establishing healthy eating patterns that will help ward off disease in later life (although that's also important). A balanced diet increases your ability to handle the stresses of college life. Eating nutritious meals at regular times helps you sleep better, gives you more stamina, and makes it easier to resist sugar-loaded snacks that temporarily raise your blood sugar levels but leave you feeling more tired than ever an hour later. It will also help you avoid the weight gain many students experience in their first year of college or university.

Finally, cooking is fun! Spending Sunday afternoon in the kitchen is a great way to unwind after a hectic week of studying. And mastering new skills gives you a sense of accomplishment. Furthermore, cooking involves building on previously learned skills. For example, once you've mastered the basic technique of making a simple white sauce, you'll find it easy to prepare variations, such as Florentine sauce.

Of course, this doesn't mean you need to avoid the residence dining room or campus food courts completely. Across the country, colleges and universities are responding to student demands for healthier menu options. On many campuses, tofu and tempeh can be found alongside the pasta, and stir-fries are dominating the menu. Still, planning to cook at least some of your meals makes it easier to control your food intake and stay within a budget.

Note to readers: Recipes that are vegetarian are indicated by a carrot symbol after the name.

Chapter 1

You Will Be Tested: Getting Started

Leaving home for college presents challenges as well as opportunities. For students whose kitchen know-how doesn't extend beyond the reheat setting on the microwave, the idea of having to learn basic cooking skills along with calculus can seem overwhelming. It's all too easy to give in to the lure of the dining hall or food court. However, these basic tips will help turn cooking from a chore into a creative, stress-free break from studying.

The ABCs of Stocking the Kitchen

There are a few basic pieces of equipment that every well-equipped kitchen should have. Of course, whether or not you bring all of them to college will depend on your specific circumstances. For example, residences with communal kitchens often provide pots, pans, and other cooking essentials for residents. And there is no point in bringing a heavy-duty frying pan if you're going to be relying on a microwave oven as your primary heat source. Here is a basic list of items for setting up a kitchen, which you can add to or subtract from based on your own needs.

There are a few basic utensils you will need to stock your kitchen area. Fortunately, most are quite inexpensive and can frequently be found at discount stores. Items you absolutely need for cooking include:

- Plastic mixing bowls for mixing ingredients and serving noodle and salad dishes
- Wooden spoons for stirring and mixing
- A heatproof rubber spatula for mixing ingredients and turning food during cooking
- A plastic or metal colander for draining washed, blanched, and boiled food
- Knives, particularly a good French knife for cutting meat
- A plastic or wooden cutting board for cutting, chopping, and mincing food
- Measuring spoons and a plastic measuring cup
- A vegetable peeler and a can opener
- A grater for grating, shredding, and slicing cheese and other foods
- A pastry brush for basting food
- A wire whisk for whisking sauces and eggs

Mix It Up!

Many recipes call for food to be beaten, blended, whipped, processed, or crushed. If your budget is limited, hand tools can perform many of these functions. For example, an egg beater (also called a hand mixer) is fine for beating eggs and whipping cream. And nothing beats a mortar and pestle for grinding and crushing nuts, herbs, spices, crackers, soft fruit, and almost any food that will fit into the bowl-shaped mortar.

However, if your budget permits, you may want to explore some higher-tech options for blending and mixing. The ultimate timesaving device, a blender is perfect for harried but health-conscious students. Compact, inexpensive, and easy to clean, a blender will do everything from liquefying smoothie ingredients to puréeing vegetables. Even if your cooking requirements don't extend beyond hastily throwing together breakfast on busy weekdays, a blender will help you put together a tasty and nutritious meal in mere minutes. (You may have to drink it while walking to class, but that's okay!)

Blender or Food Processor?

Besides the basic blender, another option for mixing food is a food processor. A food processor performs all of the functions of a blender and more. Besides grating cheese and making pastry dough, higher-end models can even be used to make bread dough.

However, for most students, these extra options don't justify the food processor's higher-end price tag. Furthermore, the blender's tall shape means it can hold more liquid, which makes it a better choice for preparing smoothies and other drinks. If you have the space and can afford it, a food processor is a useful addition to your kitchen, but not essential.

Electrical Extras

Some college residences allow students to keep small electrical appliances in the dorm or the residence kitchen. A coffeemaker allows you to have a cup of java ready as soon as you wake up in the morning. Tea drinkers will want a kettle for boiling water. Along with a toaster or toaster oven, these items will help make your living quarters seem more like home.

When it comes to larger appliances, definitely consider a microwave oven or a hot plate if your budget and college regulations permit it. Basically, a hot plate performs all the functions of a stovetop heating element, while taking up considerably less space than a conventional stove. A hot plate can be used for everything from cooking soup to frying pork chops. Although it can't completely replace a standard electric oven, a microwave oven can be used for everything from making popcorn and reheating leftovers to preparing an entire meal. Today, compact microwave and refrigerator combinations, designed specifically for dormitories, are available. Some even come with a small freezer attached.

Another handy device for dorm cooking is a rice cooker/steamer combination. Compact and inexpensive, this appliance steams meat, seafood, and vegetables, and it cooks rice and beans more quickly than the standard stovetop heating element. As an added bonus, it has a plastic surface that makes cleaning easy. For students who have a microwave, the addition of a rice cooker/steamer can provide some of the advantages of stovetop cooking, making it unnecessary to purchase a hot plate.

Equipment for the Stovetop

A few good pots are essential for stovetop cooking. Ideally, you should have three different sizes: a smaller pot for sauces, a medium-sized pot for soups and single-serving meals, and a large pot for boiling noodles, potatoes, and cooking for a group. However, if money is an issue, it's better to purchase one pot made of quality material rather than several inexpensive pots that may not heat properly or may be hard to clean. In that case, a medium-sized pot is the most practical choice.

Make sure the saucepan is made of a heavy material that conducts heat evenly. While cast-iron and copper pots are heavier than you need (and probably beyond your budget), stainless steel wrapped in aluminum or copper is a good choice. While you can always wear oven mitts, cooking will be easier if the handles are made of a material that won't heat up during cooking, such as wood, plastic, or rubber. Finally, test the lid to make sure it fits tightly.

Not surprisingly, quality frying pans are made of the same type of material as saucepans because both are designed for stovetop cooking. A medium-sized, 12-inch frying pan will meet all your needs for sautéing, braising meat, and cooking eggs. As with a saucepan, it's important to make sure the frying pan comes with a tight-fitting lid.

Oven Cooking

Oven cooking requires its own special equipment that can take the high heats needed for baking, broiling, and roasting. A large, rectangular-shaped metal baking sheet is used for making cookies, while a square, deep-sided metal baking pan is used for baking bars and desserts such as Classic Brown Betty Dessert (page 233) and Easy Apple Crisp (page 234). When it comes to muffins, there is no substitute for a standard muffin pan—consider getting more than one to prevent having to cook in batches. A glass baking dish is used for main dishes such as fish fillets and marinated chicken breasts that don't need a rack to let the fat drip off. Finally, a deep-sided casserole dish is used for one-pot meals such as rice and noodle-based casseroles.

Kitchen Staples

Once you've purchased the basic tools needed for cooking, it's tempting to start filling up the refrigerator. Hold off until you've purchased a few dry staple ingredients. A pantry stocked with basic ingredients—such as flour—will keep you from having to make repeat emergency trips to the local grocery store every time you cook a meal. Here are the essentials:

- *Flour:* As its name implies, all-purpose flour is used for almost every type of baking.
- *Sugar:* Regular granulated white sugar is used both as a sweetener at the table and in cooking.
- *Brown sugar:* Molasses-based brown sugar is used in baking, sauces, and wherever a recipe calls for a stronger flavor agent than granulated sugar.
- *Olive oil:* Olive oil is used for sautéing and frying, and as a salad dressing and in marinades.
- *Instant broth:* Chicken, beef, and vegetable broth are used in soups, casseroles, and other dishes.
- *Dried herbs and spices:* Dried herbs and spices lend flavor to soups, stews, and other slow-cooked dishes.

- *Salt and pepper:* Standard table salt should meet all your cooking needs, but you may want to consider purchasing a pepper mill to grind your own peppercorns.
- *Noodles:* No, they don't need to be ramen! Italian pasta noodles like linguine, penne, or even standard spaghetti are a quick and easy source of protein.
- *Rice:* For variety, experiment with different types such as brown and scented rice.
- *Miscellaneous flavoring agents:* Lemon juice, tomato sauce, and soy sauce will allow you to create a number of different dishes.

FACT

Not only is olive oil healthier than vegetable oil—scientists believe its monounsaturated fats can help ward off heart disease—it's also much more versatile. Besides being an excellent cooking oil, olive oil lends a delicate flavor to salad dressings and marinades, and can even serve as a low-fat substitute for butter on toasted bread.

Timesaving Ingredients

While nothing beats the flavor of fresh herbs or chicken broth prepared from scratch by slowly simmering a whole chicken in water, packaged and instant ingredients will save you time on busy weeknights. For example, don't let recipes that call for lemon juice put you off—most supermarkets carry lemon juice in a handy plastic lemon. Made with oregano, basil, and other seasonings, canned tomato sauce saves you from the work of having to boil and crush tomatoes. Stored in a cool, dry place, a can of unopened tomato sauce will keep for several months.

Instant broth comes in many forms, including cubes, powdered mix, cans, and ready-to-use cartons. All are equally convenient. However, the carton types need to be refrigerated and used within two weeks after they are opened.

When it comes to noodles, many types of Asian noodles—such as rice noodles—don't even need to be boiled. Just soak them in hot or warm water until they soften. And precooked (also called "oven-ready") lasagna noodles can go straight from the package to the frying pan or casserole dish.

QUESTION?

Which dried spices should you choose?
There are literally hundreds of spices. However, for those on a limited budget, a good tip is to think Italian. Nothing beats dried oregano, basil, and parsley for bringing out the flavor of simmered and slow-cooked dishes. Garlic powder and onion powder make a convenient substitute for actual onion and garlic on nights that you don't feel up to peeling, mincing, and chopping.

Shelf Life

Even dry ingredients go stale eventually. Expect flour, baking powder, and baking soda to last for up to one year. White granulated sugar has a longer shelf life than other dry ingredients—it will last up to eighteen months. On the other hand, brown sugar lasts for only six months.

Of course, improper storage will cause ingredients to go stale more quickly. Worse, certain types of small bugs—such as the flour beetle—feed on dry ingredients. For best results, store your staples in tightly sealed canisters. Don't worry about blowing your budget on a matching set of fancy chrome or other metal canisters. Plastic is fine, as long as it has a tight seal. Don't have room in your dorm for a full set of canisters? Set one canister aside to serve as a storage space for smaller amounts of various ingredients. Store each ingredient in a plastic bag, seal it, and place the bag in the canister.

Meal Planning 101

Preparing a detailed grocery list makes it much easier to stick to a budget. But where do you begin? The best way is to start by preparing a meal plan for one or two weeks. Try to pick more than one recipe that uses the same ingredients so that you can save money by purchasing in bulk. Let's say, for example, that you decide to cook Chili con Carne (page 97) and Spanish

Rice (page 96). Including both recipes in the same grocery shopping trip lets you purchase larger portions of everything from ground beef to tomato sauce.

Of course, you'll want to incorporate leftovers into your meal plan. But refrigerated leftovers have to be eaten within days, and eating the same meal twice in one week can get a little boring. Fortunately, there are ways around this problem.

For recipes designed to provide two or more servings, one option is to cook two half-portions of the recipe, slightly altering the ingredients for each half. For example, with Chili con Carne you could prepare a half-portion, cutting the ingredients in half but otherwise following the recipe exactly. Then prepare a second half-portion, but substitute chickpeas for the kidney beans and replace the beef with ground turkey or chicken. This gives you more variety, making it easier to resist the temptation to skip dinner in favor of the snack machine conveniently located just down the hall.

When halving or doubling a recipe, it's helpful to know how to convert cups into tablespoons, tablespoons into teaspoons, and vice versa. The following table contains several conversions.

Equivalent Measures	
Measurement	**Equivalent Measure**
3 teaspoons	1 tablespoon
4 tablespoons	¼ cup
5 tablespoons plus 1 teaspoon	⅓ cup
8 tablespoons	½ cup
10 tablespoons plus 2 teaspoons	⅔ cup
12 tablespoons	¾ cup
16 tablespoons	1 cup
48 teaspoons	1 cup
1 cup	8 ounces
1 quart	32 ounces

Shopping Tips

When writing up a grocery list, many people find it helps to organize ingredients in the same way that items are organized in the grocery store. Fresh vegetables are categorized together, as are canned vegetables, frozen foods, and meat products. Items located at either end of the store are either first or last on the list. Organizing the grocery list in this way ensures that you're moving in an organized fashion from one end of the store to the other, instead of wandering back and forth between aisles.

Here are a few tips for cutting costs at the grocery store:

- Never shop when you're tired or hungry. This makes it easier to avoid expensive "impulse buying."
- Always bring a list and stick to it.
- Check the "sell by" and "use by" dates on perishable items such as milk and meat. Always purchase food with the most recent date so that it will last longer.
- Be sure to ask for a rain check if the store is out of an advertised special.
- Always store perishable goods in the refrigerator or freezer as soon as possible so there is no danger of spoilage.
- Many larger supermarkets have frequent-shopper programs that give substantial discounts to regular customers. Check to see if you are eligible for a frequent-shopper card.

Finally, if your refrigerator comes with a freezer compartment, be sure to use it. This will give you more variety—even if you live far from the ocean, shrimp and other types of shellfish are readily available frozen. A freezer also allows you to buy fresh meat and seafood in bulk and freeze individual portions.

The Freshman Weight Gain

Statistics show that approximately half of all students put on between ten and fifteen pounds during their first year of college and university. It's easy to fall victim to the "Freshman 15" when you're living on your own for the first time, trying to adjust to a busy schedule, and fast-food vendors are scattered across campus. However, putting on weight will just increase the stress that you're already feeling from academic pressures, and it can be hard to take off later.

FACT

The benefits of a vigorous exercise session go beyond the calories expended during the workout. Exercising increases the body's metabolic rate, causing you to burn up calories at a faster rate even after you've finished your workout. The effect can last for up to two full days.

Here are a few tips for keeping the pounds away: First and foremost, stick to a regular meal schedule. If you are planning a lengthy study session away from the dorm, prepare healthy snacks to take with you. Simple snacks such as granola bars, cheese and crackers, and trail mix all provide energy without the fat and calories in potato chips and chocolate.

Plan your meals at least one week in advance. One option is to cook ahead, making all your weekly meals on the weekend. It's much easier to stick to a healthy meal plan on a busy weeknight when all you need to do is heat up dinner instead of cooking it. Finally, take time to exercise. Many colleges and universities have excellent exercise facilities right on campus that are free for students. With a little planning, you can fit an exercise session into your daily schedule. A daily swim or aerobics workout makes it easier to control your weight, and it also lifts your spirits by releasing endorphins, giving you a much-needed boost of energy.

Chapter 2

Wake-Up Call: Breakfast

Basic Bagel with Cream Cheese

1 bagel, any flavor
2 teaspoons raisins
2 teaspoons chopped walnuts

2 tablespoons plain cream cheese
½ teaspoon (or to taste) ground cinnamon

Cut the bagel in half and place in toaster. While the bagel is toasting, chop the raisins. Mix together the raisins, walnuts, and cream cheese. Stir in the ground cinnamon. Spread the cream cheese mixture on the toasted bagel.

Garlic Cheese Toast

2 teaspoons (or to taste) margarine
2 small slices crusty rye bread

¼ teaspoon garlic powder
2 tablespoons ricotta cheese

Spread the margarine on the bread. Mix the garlic powder into the ricotta cheese. Spread onto the bread. Broil in the oven until the toast is lightly browned and the cheese is softened (but not completely melted). Serve warm.

More Tips on Egg Peeling

Never try hard-boiling a fresh egg. Eggs fresh from the hen are frequently difficult to peel, no matter what method of hard-boiling is used. After a few days, eggs develop a gas layer between the shell and skin that makes for easier peeling.

Cheesy English Muffins

4 English muffins
⅛ teaspoon garlic powder
2 teaspoons lemon juice

¼ cup canned tuna
3 ounces plain cream
*   cheese*

1. Split the English muffins in half and toast.
2. While the muffins are toasting, stir the garlic powder and lemon juice into the tuna in a small bowl. Add the cream cheese, mashing to mix it in thoroughly.
3. Spoon a heaping tablespoon of the mixture onto each toasted muffin half. Serve cold. Store the unused portion of the tuna and cream cheese mixture in a sealed container in the refrigerator. (It will last for 2 to 3 days.)

Serves 4

If you like the Asian appetizer Crab Rangoon (page 158), this recipe is sure to please. You can substitute canned crab-meat for the tuna, or spice up the flavor by adding a teaspoon of chopped onion.

Broiled English Muffins

6 English muffins
¼ teaspoon garlic powder
1 tablespoon lemon juice
2 tablespoons mayonnaise
½ cup canned tuna, drained

½ cup shredded Cheddar or
*   Monterey jack cheese*
2 tablespoons Worcestershire
*   sauce*

1. Split the English muffins in half and place in toaster.
2. While the muffins are toasting, stir the garlic powder, lemon juice, and mayonnaise into the tuna in a small bowl. Stir in the shredded cheese and the Worcestershire sauce.
3. Spoon a heaping tablespoon of the mixture onto each toasted muffin half. Broil briefly in the oven until the cheese is melted and the tuna is heated through. Store the unused portion of the tuna and cream cheese mixture in a sealed container in the refrigerator. (It will last for 2 to 3 days.)

Serves 6

These taste delicious served on sourdough English muffins. Feel free to increase the amount of shredded cheese, if desired.

Hard-Boiled Eggs

2 eggs, any size

Serves 1–2

The trick is to start with cold water, and then remove the eggs from the burner as soon as the water reaches a rolling boil. This prevents the eggs from tasting rubbery.

∾

1. Place the eggs in a saucepan and cover with cold water to at least ½ inch above the eggs. Cover the pot with the lid and bring to a rolling boil over high heat.
2. As soon as the water is boiling, remove from heat. Let the eggs stand in the hot water for 17 to 20 minutes. Remove the eggs from the saucepan and place in a bowl filled with cold water for at least 2 minutes, or until cool enough to handle. Peel off the shells. These will keep in the refrigerator for about 1 week.

Soft-Boiled Eggs

2 pasteurized eggs, any size

Serves 1–2

These taste delicious sprinkled with salt and pepper and served with toast or a good crusty bread.

∾

1. Fill a pot with enough cold water so that there will be at least ½ inch of water above the eggs. Bring the water to a rolling boil. Place the eggs in the pot and cook for 3 to 5 minutes (depending on your own preference for soft-boiled eggs).
2. Remove the eggs from the pot and place in cold water until cool enough to handle. Peel off the shells. These will keep in the refrigerator for up to 1 week.

Basic Poached Egg

1 egg, any size   *Pinch salt*

1. In a medium-sized saucepan, bring 3 inches of water to a boil. Add the salt to help the water boil faster. While waiting for the water to boil, break the egg into a small bowl.
2. When the water reaches a boil, turn the heat down until it is just simmering. Gently slide the egg into the simmering water and cook for 3 to 5 minutes, depending on how firm you like the yolk.
3. Remove the egg with a slotted spoon, letting any excess water drain into the saucepan. Use the slotted spoon to gently push aside any "threads" from the egg white. Serve plain or on toast.

Serves 1

For best results, use the freshest eggs possible. To add extra flavor, try poaching the eggs in milk or broth instead of water.

∾

Perfect Scrambled Eggs

2 eggs   *Paprika, to taste*
2 tablespoons milk   *2 tablespoons butter*
Salt and pepper, to taste   *or margarine*

1. Break the eggs into a small bowl. Add the milk, salt and pepper, and paprika. Beat the eggs until they are an even color throughout.
2. In a small skillet, melt the butter or margarine over low heat. Increase heat to medium-low and add the eggs.
3. Cook the eggs, using a spatula to turn sections of the egg from time to time so that the uncooked egg on top flows underneath. Adjust the heat up or down as needed. For best results, remove the scrambled eggs from the pan when they are firm but still a bit moist (about 6 to 8 minutes).

Serves 1–2

The trick to making scrambled eggs is an evenly heated skillet and eggs that are at room temperature before cooking.

∾

Savory Scrambled Eggs

Serves 1–2

For extra flavor, stir in 2 tablespoons of sweet salsa just before removing the scrambled eggs from the pan.

2 eggs
2 tablespoons milk
Salt and pepper, to taste
10 capers

4 tablespoons butter or
margarine, divided
½ tomato, chopped
1 green onion, chopped

1. Break the eggs into a small bowl. Add the milk, salt and pepper, and capers. Beat until the eggs are an even color throughout.
2. In a small frying pan, melt 2 tablespoons of the butter or margarine on low heat. Add the tomato and green onion. Cook until the tomato is tender but still firm. Remove from pan and set aside. Clean the pan.
3. Melt the remaining 2 tablespoons of butter or margarine in the pan on low heat. Turn the heat up to medium-low and add the eggs.
4. Cook the eggs, using a spatula to turn sections of the egg from time to time so that the uncooked egg on top flows underneath. Adjust the heat up or down as needed to cook the eggs.
5. When the eggs are nearly cooked, return the tomato and green onion to the pan. Cook the scrambled eggs until they are firm but still a bit moist (about 6 to 8 minutes).

Peeling Hard-Boiled Eggs

First, never cook an egg by letting it sit in boiling water for several minutes—this will make it much harder to peel. Instead, follow the instructions in Hard-Boiled Eggs (page 14). To peel the egg, crack both ends on the countertop and roll it in your hands to loosen the shell. Then remove the shell, starting with the larger end.

Cinnamon Toast with Ricotta and Raisin Spread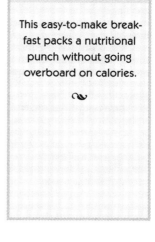

*⅛ teaspoon (or to taste)
    ground cinnamon
2 teaspoons orange marmalade*

*3 tablespoons ricotta cheese
2 teaspoons (or to taste) raisins
1 slice bread*

1. Preheat oven to 180°. Spray a baking sheet with cooking spray.
2. In a small bowl, mash the ground cinnamon and marmalade into the ricotta cheese. Stir in the raisins. When thoroughly mixed, spread over the bread.
3. Place the bread on the prepared baking sheet. Bake for 15 minutes.
4. Increase temperature to 200° and bake for 5 more minutes. Serve warm.

Serves 1

This easy-to-make breakfast packs a nutritional punch without going overboard on calories.

ᔜ

French Toast

*2 eggs
Salt, to taste
¼ cup milk
2 tablespoons butter or
    margarine*

*2 slices bread
½ teaspoon sugar, optional
¼ teaspoon cinnamon,
    optional*

1. In a small bowl, lightly beat the eggs. Add the salt and milk.
2. Heat the butter or margarine in a frying pan over medium-low heat.
3. Take a slice of bread and dip one side into the beaten egg, letting it sit for a few seconds to soak up the egg mixture. Turn the bread over and repeat with the other side. Lay the bread flat in the frying pan. Repeat with the other slice of bread.
4. Cook until the bread is browned on the bottom, then turn over and repeat with the other side. Remove from the frying pan and sprinkle with sugar and/or the cinnamon, if using. Serve with syrup.

Serves 1–2

Have some beaten egg and milk mixture left over? Scramble it in the frying pan and serve it with the French toast.

ᔜ

Italian-Style French Toast

¼ cup milk or cream

1 cinnamon stick

2 eggs

1 teaspoon granulated sugar

1 tablespoon brown sugar

2 tablespoons butter or
  margarine

2 slices bread

1. Pour the milk or cream into a small saucepan and add the cinnamon stick. Heat on low. In a small bowl, lightly beat the eggs with the white and brown sugar.
2. Heat the butter or margarine in a frying pan over medium-low heat.
3. Remove the cinnamon stick from the milk and combine the milk with the egg mixture. Take a slice of bread and dip one side into the beaten egg, letting it sit for a few seconds to soak up the egg mixture. Turn the bread over and repeat with the other side. Lay the bread flat in the frying pan. Repeat with the other slice of bread.
4. Cook until the bread is browned on the bottom, then turn over and repeat with the other side. Make sure the bread is cooked through and not soggy. Serve hot.

Avoiding Soggy French Toast

It all comes down to how you dip the bread in the egg. For best results, hold the bread in the mixture for a few seconds and then remove it. Laying the bread right down in the egg mixture will cause it to soak up more liquid. Also, only soak as many pieces of bread at a time as you will be cooking.

Simple Welsh Rarebit

2 slices French or Italian bread
2 tablespoons nonalcoholic
    beer
1 teaspoon butter or margarine
¼ cup grated Cheddar cheese
1 egg

½ teaspoon (or to taste)
    Worcestershire sauce
⅛ teaspoon (or to taste)
    cayenne pepper
Salt and pepper, to taste

Serves 1

For best results, use aged Cheddar cheese and serve on crusty bread.

∾

1. Toast the bread. Fill a saucepan halfway with water and bring to a low simmer. Place a metal bowl over the saucepan and add the beer and butter to the bowl. Heat until warm.

2. Add the cheese to the warmed beer. Heat on low until the cheese melts, stirring and making sure the water doesn't boil.

3. Add the egg. Stir gently so that the egg is mixed in but the mixture doesn't begin to scramble. When the mixture has thickened, stir in the Worcestershire sauce, cayenne pepper, and salt and pepper. Spoon the rarebit over the toasted bread.

Welsh Rarebit Origins

Although it makes a great breakfast, Welsh Rarebit originated in British taverns. Originally called Welsh Rabbit, the authentic dish consists of Cheddar cheese, ale, and seasonings that are baked and served on toast.

Tomato Rarebit

Serves 1

This is a great breakfast for cold winter days. Use the leftover stewed tomatoes to make Warming Herbed Tomato Soup (page 45).

∾

2 slices crusty bread
4 slices tomato
2 tablespoons nonalcoholic beer
2 tablespoons juice from canned stewed tomatoes
1 teaspoon butter or margarine
¼ cup grated Cheddar cheese
1 egg
½ teaspoon Worcestershire sauce
⅛ teaspoon (or to taste) cayenne pepper

1. Toast the bread. Lay 2 tomato slices flat on each slice of bread and set aside.
2. Fill a saucepan halfway with water and bring to a low simmer. Place a metal bowl over the saucepan and add the beer, canned stewed tomato juice, and butter to the bowl. Heat until warm.
3. Add the cheese to the warmed beer. Heat on low until the cheese melts, stirring and making sure the water doesn't boil.
4. Add the egg. Stir gently so that the egg is mixed but the mixture doesn't begin to scramble. When the mixture has thickened, stir in the Worcestershire sauce and cayenne pepper.
5. Spoon the Tomato Rarebit over the toasted bread and tomatoes. Serve open-faced.

Salmonella Risk in Soft-Boiled Eggs

Unfortunately, soft-boiled eggs aren't cooked long enough to completely remove the risk of salmonella poisoning. The best way to solve the problem (other than giving them up altogether), is to use pasteurized eggs. By heat-treating the eggs, pasteurization kills any salmonella bacteria that may have infected the raw egg.

Simple Eggs Benedict

1 Basic Poached Egg (page 15)
1 English muffin
1 tablespoon (or to taste) butter
   or margarine

2 tablespoons plain yogurt
1 teaspoon prepared mustard

Split the English muffin in half, toast, and butter both halves. Mix together the yogurt and mustard. Spread the yogurt and mustard mixture on 1 muffin half, and place the poached egg on the other half.

Serves 1

This simplified version of authentic Eggs Benedict makes a quick and easy recipe for busy weekdays.

❧

Eggs Benedict with Mock Hollandaise Sauce

1 or 2 slices bacon, as desired
1 English muffin
1 tablespoon (or to taste),
   plus 1 teaspoon butter or
   margarine

2 teaspoons egg substitute
2 tablespoons mayonnaise
1 teaspoon lemon juice
Pinch cayenne pepper
1 Basic Poached Egg (page 15)

1. Cook the bacon until crisp and drain on paper towels. Split the English muffin in half, toast, and butter both halves.
2. Heat the egg substitute, mayonnaise, lemon juice, cayenne pepper, and the 1 teaspoon butter or margarine in a small saucepan until the mixture thickens, whisking constantly.
3. Lay the bacon on one muffin half and place the poached egg on top. Spoon the Mock Hollandaise sauce over the egg. Eat the other muffin half separately or place on top to close the muffin.

Serves 1

This quick and easy recipe gives you the flavor of hollandaise sauce without all the work. You can also use packaged hollandaise sauce mix.

❧

Basic Cheese Omelet

2 eggs
2 tablespoons milk
Salt and pepper, to taste
¼ teaspoon (or to taste) chili powder

1 tablespoon butter or margarine
¼ cup grated cheese
Salsa, optional

1. Lightly beat the eggs with the milk. Stir in the salt, pepper, and chili powder.
2. Melt the butter or margarine in a frying pan over low heat. Swirl the butter around to coat the pan entirely.
3. Pour the egg mixture into the pan. Cook over low heat. After the omelet has been cooking for a few minutes, sprinkle the grated cheese over half of the omelet.
4. Tilt the pan occasionally or lift the edges of the omelet with a spatula so that the uncooked egg runs underneath.
5. When the omelet is cooked evenly throughout, loosen the edges of the omelet with a spatula. Carefully slide the spatula underneath the omelet and fold it in half. Slide the omelet onto a plate. Garnish with salsa if desired.

Omelet Origins

Contrary to popular opinion, the popular dish combining cooked egg with seasonings and various filling ingredients did not originate in France. Instead, its origins probably date back to ancient times, when kookoo, a Persian dish consisting of fried egg and chopped fresh herbs, was first eaten.

Western Omelet

3 large eggs
3 tablespoons milk
Salt and pepper, to taste
⅛ teaspoon (or to taste)
* paprika*
3 tablespoons diced ham

3 tablespoons diced onion
3 tablespoons diced green bell
* pepper*
2 tablespoons butter or
* margarine*
Ketchup, optional

> **Serves 1–2**
>
> In a western omelet, the vegetables are added to the egg mixture before the egg is fried in the pan.
>
> ∾

1. Lightly beat the eggs with the milk. Stir in the salt, pepper, and paprika. Mix in the ham, onion, and green pepper.

2. Melt the butter or margarine in a frying pan over low heat. Swirl the butter around to coat the pan entirely.

3. Pour the egg mixture into the pan. Cook over low heat. After the omelet has been cooking for a few minutes, tilt the pan occasionally or lift the edges of the omelet with a spatula so that the uncooked egg runs underneath.

4. When the omelet is cooked evenly throughout, loosen the edges of the omelet with a spatula. Carefully slide the spatula underneath the omelet and fold it in half. If desired, fold 2 more times so that it forms a triangular shape. Slide the omelet onto a plate. Serve with ketchup, if desired.

Fabulous Frittata

Like Egg Foo Yung, Italian Frittata is a combination of an omelet and a pancake, filled with sautéed meat, cheese, or vegetables. Like the omelet, a frittata can be a hearty lunch or dinner as well as a breakfast dish. When preparing frittata, feel free to experiment with using different types of cheese, such as Swiss, Gruyère, or Emmental.

Cheese and Mushroom Frittata

Serves 4–8

Don't worry if the frittata falls apart the first few times you try to make it. It can take a few tries to know when it's firm enough to turn over. Besides, a little breakage won't affect the taste!

❧

4 tablespoons olive oil, divided
6 large mushrooms, sliced (about 1¼ cups)
¼ cup chopped onion
3 large eggs
½ cup milk
⅛ teaspoon nutmeg
Salt and fresh-cracked pepper, to taste
1 small tomato, chopped
¾ cup grated cheese, such as Cheddar
4–8 slices French bread, toasted

1. Heat 2 tablespoons of the olive oil in a frying pan over medium-low heat. Add the mushrooms and onion. Cook until the onion is tender. Remove from pan and set aside. Clean the pan.
2. Lightly beat the eggs with the milk. Stir in the nutmeg, salt, and pepper. Stir in the cooked mushrooms and onion, the tomato, and ½ cup of the grated cheese.
3. Heat the remaining 2 tablespoons olive oil in the frying pan on medium-low heat. Swirl the oil around the pan to coat the pan entirely. Pour the egg mixture into the pan. Move the vegetables around if necessary to make sure they are evenly mixed throughout the egg. Cook the frittata over medium-low heat. Tilt the pan occasionally or lift edges of the frittata with a spatula so that the uncooked egg runs underneath.
4. When the frittata is firm on top, cover the frying pan with a lid or plate. Turn the pan over so that the frittata falls onto the lid. Return the pan to the stovetop and slide the frittata back into the pan, so that the bottom of the frittata is on top. Sprinkle the remaining ¼ cup of grated cheese over the frittata. Cook over medium-low heat until the cheese is melted and the frittata is cooked through.
5. To serve, cut the frittata pizza-style into wedges and serve on top of the toasted French bread.

Easy Pancake Roll-Ups

2 teaspoons baking powder
⅛ teaspoon salt
1 cup all-purpose flour
2 tablespoons granulated sugar
1 egg

1½ tablespoons vegetable oil,
  plus extra for greasing
1 cup milk
6 tablespoons (or to taste)
  peanut butter

> **Yields 3 large
> or 6 small pancakes**
>
> These taste delicious
> served cold, with each
> rolled-up pancake cut
> into 1-inch pieces.
>
> ∾

1. Heat a griddle or heavy skillet, making sure it is very hot (a drop of water should sizzle when dropped on it).
2. In a medium-sized bowl, stir the baking powder and salt into the flour, blending thoroughly. Stir in the sugar. In a small bowl, lightly beat the egg and add the vegetable oil and milk.
3. Add the egg mixture to the dry ingredients. Do not overmix. (Don't worry about lumps.) The batter should be runny.
4. Grease the griddle or skillet with oil as needed. Pour the batter into the pan in ½-cup portions for each pancake (or ¼-cup portions for smaller pancakes). Cook until the pancakes are browned on the bottom and bubbling on top. Flip over and cook the other side until browned. Remove the pancakes from the skillet or griddle.
5. Spread the peanut butter on the pancakes and roll up. Serve as is, or topped with butter and syrup or dusted with powdered sugar.

Leftover Pancakes and Batter?

Leftover batter will usually keep for a day in a sealed container in the refrigerator. Just add a bit of milk before reusing. However, leftover pancakes should be frozen.

Buckwheat Pancakes

Yields 12 pancakes

A smaller size helps keep these blueberry-filled pancakes from breaking apart during cooking.

ॐ

¾ cup all-purpose flour
¼ cup buckwheat flour
2 teaspoons baking powder
1 teaspoon baking soda
⅛ teaspoon salt
3 tablespoons granulated sugar
1 egg

1½ tablespoons vegetable oil,
  plus extra for greasing
1 cup buttermilk
¾ cup frozen blueberries
1 tablespoon sesame seeds,
  optional

1. Heat a griddle or heavy skillet, making sure it is very hot (water should sizzle when dropped on it).
2. In a medium-sized bowl, mix together the all-purpose and buckwheat flour. Stir the baking powder, baking soda, and salt into the flour, blending thoroughly. Stir in the sugar. In a small bowl, lightly beat the egg and add the vegetable oil and buttermilk.
3. Add the egg and milk mixture to the dry ingredients. Do not overmix. (Don't worry about lumps.) The batter should be runny. Gently stir in the blueberries.
4. Grease the griddle or skillet with oil as needed. Pour the batter into the pan in 2-tablespoon portions. Sprinkle about ¼ teaspoon of sesame seeds on top of each pancake, if using. Cook until the pancakes are browned on the bottom and bubbling on top. Flip over and cook the other side until browned. Remove the pancakes from the skillet or griddle. Repeat with the remaining pancake batter. Serve warm with maple syrup.

How to Freeze Pancakes

For best results, cool the cooked pancakes before freezing. Don't stack them during cooling, as the heat won't escape from the pancakes in the middle of the stack. Once the pancakes have cooled, stack them by placing a layer of wax paper between each pancake. Place the stacked pancakes in the freezer. Once they are frozen, remove the pile of pancakes, place them in a resealable plastic bag, and return to the freezer. Frozen pancakes will keep for 1 to 2 months.

Healthy Honey Crepes

2½ tablespoons honey
2 teaspoons baking powder
⅛ teaspoon salt
1 cup whole-wheat flour
3 eggs
1 cup buttermilk

⅓ cup water
1½ tablespoons vegetable oil,
*   or as needed*
2 tablespoons toasted wheat
*   germ or powdered sugar,*
*   optional*

> **Yields 16 small or 8 regular crepes**
>
> Leftover crepes make a great lunch—just fill with meat and cheese and wrap.
>
> ∾

1. Melt the honey in a small saucepan over low heat.
2. In a medium-sized bowl, stir the baking powder and salt into the flour, blending thoroughly. In a small bowl, beat the eggs with the buttermilk, water, 1 tablespoon vegetable oil, and melted honey.
3. Make a "well" in the middle of the dry ingredients and add the egg mixture. Stir until smooth. (If you have a blender or food processor, blend all the ingredients at medium speed.) Let the batter rest for at least 1 hour.
4. In a heavy skillet over medium heat, warm just enough vegetable oil to coat the bottom of the pan. Pour ¼ cup of the batter into the skillet. Rotate the pan so that the batter flows toward the edges and covers the bottom of the entire pan. Cook until browned on the bottom, turn over, and cook on the other side. Sprinkle with the toasted wheat germ or powdered sugar, if desired. Repeat with the remaining batter.

Crepe Batter Tips

Don't have time to let the crepe batter rest for 1 hour? Make it the night before and refrigerate. Just be sure to let the batter come back to room temperature before using in the recipe.

Basic Waffle Recipe

1 egg, separated
¼ cup melted butter
¾ cup, plus 2 tablespoons milk
1½ teaspoons baking powder

⅛ teaspoon salt
2 tablespoons granulated sugar
½ teaspoon ground cinnamon
1 cup all-purpose flour

1. Preheat waffle iron. In a small bowl, use an electric mixer to beat the egg white until stiff. In another bowl, beat the egg yolk well and mix in the melted butter and milk.
2. In a medium-sized bowl, stir the baking powder, salt, sugar, and cinnamon into the flour, blending thoroughly.
3. Make a "well" in the middle of the flour mixture. Pour the beaten egg mixture into the well and stir into the dry ingredients. The batter should resemble a muffin batter. Gently fold in the egg white.
4. Cook the waffles according to the instructions on the waffle iron. Serve topped with sugar, fresh fruit, or syrup.

Fresh Fruit Granola

½ apple
¼ cup dried dates
1 cup Cinnamon and Raisin Granola (page 56) or store-bought granola

½ cup milk or light cream
1 tablespoon liquid honey, optional

Chop the apple and dried dates. Combine the dry ingredients in a bowl and pour the milk over the top. Drizzle the honey over the granola and fruit, if desired.

Rolled Oats FAQs

Recipes frequently call for "rolled oats." If you're having trouble finding them in the supermarket, try looking for "old-fashioned oats" or "oatflakes" instead. Quick-cooking oats are also a type of rolled oat, and can usually be substituted for regular rolled oats in a recipe.

Hawaiian Waffles with Macadamia Nuts

1 egg, separated
¼ cup melted butter
¾ cup, plus 2 tablespoons
    buttermilk
1½ teaspoons baking powder
⅛ teaspoon salt

2½ tablespoons brown sugar
1 cup all-purpose flour
¼ cup chopped macadamia
    nuts
½ cup pineapple chunks,
    canned or fresh

1. Preheat waffle iron.
2. In a small bowl, use an electric mixer to beat the egg white until it is stiff. In a separate bowl, beat the egg yolk well and mix in the melted butter and buttermilk.
3. In a medium-sized bowl, stir the baking powder, salt, and brown sugar into the flour, blending thoroughly.
4. Make a "well" in the middle of the flour mixture. Pour the beaten egg mixture into the well and stir into the dry ingredients. The batter should resemble a muffin batter. Gently fold in the egg white. Gently stir in the macadamia nuts and pineapple.
5. Cook the waffles according to the instructions on the waffle iron.

Yields 4–6 waffles

To enhance the tropical flavor, serve topped with toasted coconut flakes and banana and pineapple slices.

❧

Waffle FAQs

The waffle's distinctive honeycombed shape immediately sets it apart from a pancake. However, differences between them can also be found in the batter. Waffle batters are normally high in butter, removing any need to grease a waffle pan before cooking. Egg whites make the batter light and fluffy.

Yogurt Surprise

¾ cup Cinnamon and Raisin
   Granola (page 56) or store-
   bought granola

¾ cup low-fat vanilla yogurt
¼ small banana, sliced

Place 2 tablespoons of the granola in the bottom of a tall glass. Add 3 tablespoons of the yogurt. Continue layering by alternating even portions of the granola and yogurt. Top with the banana slices.

Which Yogurt to Use?

Not all yogurts are created equal. Made with low-fat milk, low-fat yogurt has a fat content between 0.5 and 2 percent, while skim milk keeps the fat content of nonfat yogurt below 0.5 percent. Plain yogurt is both unflavored and unsweetened. However, its fat content will depend on the type of milk used.

Oatmeal with a Twist

1 cup water
½ cup rolled oats (not the
   quick-cooking type)
3 teaspoons apple juice

3 tablespoons ricotta cheese
2 tablespoons raisins
1 teaspoon granulated sugar
Ground cinnamon, to taste

1. Bring the water to a boil. Stir in the oats. Cover, reduce heat to low, and let the oats simmer for 10 to 15 minutes or until the water is nearly evaporated.
2. While the oats are cooking, stir the apple juice into the ricotta cheese, and then stir in the raisins.
3. Transfer the porridge to a large serving bowl. Stir in the ricotta cheese mixture and the sugar. Sprinkle with cinnamon, if desired. Serve hot.

Chapter 3

Is It Noon Already? Lunch

Baked Pita Chips with Yogurt Dressing

2 pita pockets
Olive oil, as needed
½ cup plain yogurt
¼ teaspoon (or to taste) garlic salt
1 teaspoon lemon juice
1 tablespoon chopped red onion
2 sprigs fresh parsley, finely chopped
Salt and pepper, to taste

1. Preheat oven to 350°.
2. Cut the pitas in half, and cut each half into 3 wedges. Brush both sides of each wedge with the olive oil. (It takes about 1½ teaspoons olive oil to cover both sides of all 6 wedges.)
3. Place the pita wedges on a baking sheet and bake for 8 to 10 minutes, turning over once halfway through the cooking time.
4. Combine the yogurt, garlic salt, lemon juice, chopped red onion, and parsley. Season with salt and pepper to taste. Spoon a heaping tablespoon of the mixture on each pita chip, or serve the dip on the side.

Flatbread FAQs

Many cuisines have a special type of flatbread, from Middle Eastern pita to Indian naan, and Mexican tortillas. Despite their flat shape, some flatbreads contain a leavener (an ingredient to make the dough or batter rise). Double-layered breads (such as pita) may use either sourdough as a leavener, while single-layered Italian focaccia is always made with yeast.

Asian Lettuce Wrap Sandwich

2 teaspoons rice vinegar
2 teaspoons soy sauce
1 teaspoon granulated sugar
1 teaspoon cornstarch
2 teaspoons water
1 (4- to 6-ounce) boneless,
*   skinless chicken breast*
3–4 tablespoons vegetable oil,
*   or as needed*
1 garlic clove, smashed and
*   peeled*

3 tablespoons chopped onion
⅓ cup chopped red bell pepper
¼ cup bean sprouts
3–4 drops sesame seed oil, or
*   to taste*
1 romaine or iceberg lettuce leaf,
*   shredded*
4 tortilla wraps or 4 pita pocket
*   halves*

Serves 1–2

You can use leftover cooked chicken in this recipe. Just chop the chicken into bite-sized pieces and add to the frying pan during the final stages of cooking to heat through.

1. In a small bowl, combine the rice vinegar, soy sauce, and sugar, and set aside. Mix together the cornstarch and water, and set aside in a separate small bowl. Chop the chicken into bite-sized pieces.
2. Add 2 tablespoons of the vegetable oil to a frying pan and heat on medium-high heat. When the oil is hot, add the garlic. Fry briefly, using a spatula to move the garlic through the oil. Add the chicken and stir-fry until white and nearly cooked, stirring constantly. Remove from the pan and set aside.
3. Add 1 to 2 more tablespoons of the vegetable oil to the pan. Add the onion and stir-fry for about 1 minute. Add the red pepper and stir-fry for another minute. Add the bean sprouts.
4. Add the rice vinegar mixture to the pan, pouring it in the middle of the vegetables. Give the cornstarch and water mixture a quick restir. Turn the heat up to medium high and add the cornstarch mixture. Cook, stirring constantly, until it boils and thickens. Add the chicken and mix with the vegetables and sauce. Sprinkle the sesame seed oil over the top.
5. If using tortilla wraps, place a few pieces of shredded lettuce on each wrap, spoon ¼ of the chicken and sauce mixture over the top of each, and roll up. If using pita pocket halves, place the shredded lettuce and ¼ of the chicken mixture inside each half. If using a tortilla wrap, roll it up.

Denver Sandwich

Serves 1

The Denver sandwich is simply a western omelet transformed into a sandwich, with cheese added for extra protein.

❧

1 large egg
1 tablespoon milk
Salt and pepper, to taste
⅛ teaspoon (or to taste) paprika
2 tablespoons diced ham
1 tablespoon diced onion
1 tablespoon diced green bell pepper
1 tablespoon butter or margarine
2 slices bread
2 lettuce leaves
2 slices processed Swiss cheese

1. In a small bowl, lightly beat the egg with the milk. Stir in the salt, pepper, and paprika. Mix in the ham, onion, and green pepper.
2. Melt the butter or margarine in a frying pan over low heat. Swirl the butter around to make sure the pan is entirely coated.
3. Place the egg mixture in the pan. Brown on the bottom, then turn over and cook on the other side.
4. Toast the bread. Add 1 lettuce leaf and 1 slice Swiss cheese on each piece of toast. Use a spatula to place the egg mixture on the sandwich. Close up the sandwich.

Sandwich History

Nearly everyone knows that the modern sandwich—consisting of 2 pieces of bread with a meat and cheese filling—was invented by the Earl of Sandwich. (The earl wanted something that he could hold in his hand and eat while gambling.) Fewer people are aware that the idea of combining bread with other ingredients dates back to Roman times, when a Jewish rabbi wrote about combining dried fruit, nuts, and spices between pieces of flatbread.

Mu Shu Wraps

*½ boneless, skinless, chicken
    breast (about 3 ounces)*
4 teaspoons hoisin sauce
4 teaspoons chicken broth

½ teaspoon granulated sugar
2 teaspoons olive oil
¼ cup shredded napa cabbage
2 soft tortilla wraps

1. Cut the chicken breast into thin slices. In a small bowl, combine the hoisin sauce, chicken broth, and sugar, and set aside.
2. Heat the olive oil in a frying pan. Add the chicken and cook on medium heat until browned on both sides.
3. Push the chicken to the sides of the frying pan. Add the shredded cabbage. Cook for about 1 minute, stirring constantly. Increase heat to high, and add the sauce. Mix the sauce with the cabbage and chicken. Remove the frying pan from the heat and let cool slightly.
4. Lay 1 tortilla wrap flat on a plate. Spoon ½ cup of filling onto the bottom half of the wrap, spreading it toward the edges. Fold over the right side of the wrap. Fold the bottom of the wrap over the food, and continue rolling up the wrap. Repeat with the other tortilla.

Yields 2 wraps

For added flavor, replace the napa cabbage with a coleslaw mixture and use a flavored tortilla wrap, such as spinach or red pepper.

∾

Instant Ramen Noodles

Despite their popularity in Japanese cooking, ramen noodles originated in China. However, the Japanese first saw the potential of ramen noodles as an instant food. In 1958, Nissin Foods introduced chicken ramen in Japan, and the rest is history. Ramen noodles have been a staple in college diets since 1970, when Nissin brought them to the United States.

Greek Salad Pita Pockets

1 pita pocket
½ tomato
2 romaine lettuce leaves
8 cucumber slices (preferably English cucumber)
¼ cup crumbled feta cheese

6 whole olives, chopped
2 tablespoons extra-virgin olive oil
Salt and freshly cracked black pepper, to taste

1. Cut the pita pocket in half. Cut the tomato into thin wedges. Shred the romaine lettuce leaves. In a medium-sized bowl, toss the lettuce and tomato with the cucumber.
2. Add the feta cheese, chopped olives, and olive oil, and toss again. Sprinkle with the salt and freshly cracked black pepper.
3. Fill each pita pocket with half of the salad, and serve.

Classic BLT

2 slices bacon
2 lettuce leaves
2 slices bread

1 tablespoon (or to taste) mayonnaise
4 slices tomato

1. Cook the bacon in a frying pan or broiler until crisp. Drain the bacon slices on paper towels and cut into strips about 3 inches long.
2. Wash the lettuce leaves and drain thoroughly. Break into bite-sized pieces. Toast the bread.
3. Spread the mayonnaise on one side of each slice of bread. Lay the bacon strips horizontally on 1 slice of bread on top of the mayonnaise. Lay the tomato slices on top, and then the lettuce. Close the sandwich and cut in half.

Baked Tortilla Wraps

3½ ounces beef round steak
2 teaspoons olive oil
3 tablespoons chopped red
  onion
¼ small green bell pepper,
  finely chopped

1 tablespoon red wine vinegar
2 cheese-flavored soft tortilla
  wraps
2–4 tablespoons peanut butter

Yields 2 Wraps

Peanut butter fans
will like this recipe.
However, if you prefer
something more conven-
tional, use regular butter
(or margarine) instead.

1. Preheat oven to 350°. Spray a baking sheet with cooking spray.
2. Cut the beef into thin strips. Heat the olive oil in a frying pan over medium heat. Add the onion and cook until tender. Add the green pepper and cook for 1 or 2 minutes.
3. Push the vegetables off to the side of the pan and add the beef in the middle, laying the strips out flat. Splash the red wine vinegar over the beef. Cook until the beef is browned on both sides, turning over once. Mix the vegetables in with the beef and vinegar. Remove from heat and let cool briefly.
4. Lay 1 tortilla wrap flat on a plate and spread 1 or 2 tablespoons peanut butter, as desired, on the inside. Add half the meat and vegetable mixture on the bottom of the wrap, making sure the filling isn't too close to the edges. Fold in the right and left sides of the wrap. Roll up and tuck in the edges. Repeat with the other tortilla wrap.
5. Place both wraps on the prepared baking sheet. Bake for 15 minutes or until heated through.

Bell Pepper Types

Ever wonder what the difference is between green, orange, and red bell peppers? Actually, all 3 come from the same plant. The main difference is that red and orange bell peppers have been allowed to ripen longer on the vine. The extra ripening time gives red bell peppers a sweeter flavor than green bell peppers, making them a popular salad ingredient.

Grilled Cheese Sandwich

About 2½ tablespoons softened butter or margarine
2 slices bread

2 teaspoons (or to taste) mustard
2 slices processed cheese

1. Spread about 2 teaspoons butter or margarine over one side of a slice of bread. Spread the mustard over one side of the other slice. Place the cheese slices in the middle and close the sandwich, dry sides out.
2. Heat a frying pan over medium heat for about 1 minute. When the frying pan is hot, melt 1 tablespoon of butter in the frying pan (it should be sizzling).
3. Add the sandwich to the frying pan. Cook until the bottom is golden brown, about 3 to 4 minutes. Press down gently on the sandwich with a spatula while it is cooking.
4. Push the sandwich to the side and add about 2 teaspoons of butter to the pan. Turn the sandwich over and cook on the other side until browned and the cheese is nearly melted, about 3 to 4 minutes. Remove the sandwich from the pan and cut in half.

Grilled Cheese Sandwich—the American Quesadilla

The classic grilled cheese sandwich is really just a quesadilla minus the sour cream dip, and with bread replacing the flour tortilla. The main difference between them is the greater variety of ingredients that find their way into a quesadilla—everything from goat cheese to cream cheese may be used. And, while most of us would balk at the idea of serving a grilled cheese sandwich to guests, quesadillas cut into wedges are a popular appetizer.

Hearty Grilled Cheese Sandwich

Serves 1

2 slices bacon
About 2 teaspoons butter or
margarine
2 slices bread

Pinch paprika
¼ cup grated Cheddar cheese
2 teaspoons (or to taste)
mustard

Grating the Cheddar cheese before cooking keeps it from over-flowing the sandwich and forming a sticky mess in the frying pan.

1. Cook the bacon in a frying pan until crisp. Drain on paper towels. Do not clean out the pan.
2. Spread the butter or margarine over one side of a slice of bread. Sprinkle with the paprika and add the grated cheese on top. Lay the bacon slices over the top. Spread the mustard over one side of the other slice of bread. Close the sandwich.
3. Return the frying pan to the stovetop and heat on medium. Add the sandwich to the frying pan. Cook until the bottom is golden brown, about 1 to 2 minutes. Press down gently on the sandwich with a spatula while it is cooking.
4. Turn the sandwich over and cook on the other side until browned and the cheese is nearly melted, about 1 to 2 minutes. Remove the sandwich from the pan and cut in half.

Calorie-Cutting Tip

For a leaner sandwich, instead of butter or margarine, try spreading the juice from a freshly cut tomato on your bread. You won't miss the extra fat and calories, and the juice from the tomato gives the bread extra flavor. This works best with toast or crusty bread, such as French bread or a baguette.

Jazzed-Up Chicken Sandwiches

2 tablespoons honey mustard
1 tablespoon mayonnaise
½ teaspoon soy sauce
½ teaspoon granulated sugar
2 teaspoons finely chopped red onion
2 tablespoons finely chopped red bell pepper

Pinch (or to taste) mild curry powder
½ cup chopped cooked chicken breast
2 pita pocket halves

1. Mix together the honey mustard, mayonnaise, soy sauce, sugar, onion, red pepper, and curry powder. Add the chicken breast and mix thoroughly. Refrigerate in a sealed container for 2 hours before using.
2. Fill each pita half with an equal amount of filling, and serve.

Simple Stuffed Pita Sandwiches

½ small Spartan apple
½ celery stalk
1 leaf romaine lettuce
2 processed cheese slices
3 teaspoons low-calorie Caesar or Thousand Island dressing

1 tablespoon chopped walnuts, optional
1 pita pocket

1. Wash and dry the apple, celery, and lettuce. Cut the celery into thin slices. Core the apple and chop finely. Shred the lettuce. Cut the cheese first horizontally and then vertically into tiny pieces.
2. Mix together the apple, celery, lettuce, cheese, salad dressing, and chopped walnuts. Refrigerate in a sealed container for at least 2 hours to give the flavors a chance to combine.
3. Cut the pita in half. Stuff half the filling into each pita pocket.

Hearty Mexican Taco Salad

2 lettuce leaves
½ red bell pepper
½ green bell pepper
1 small tomato

1 cup grated cheese
3 tablespoons (or to taste)
    salsa
Taco chips

Wash and dry the vegetables. Shred the lettuce leaves. Seed the red and green peppers and chop. Chop the tomato. Combine the vegetables and grated cheese in a small salad bowl. Stir in the salsa. Serve with the taco chips.

Serves 1–2

This version of taco salad replaces the ground beef with extra cheese. A combination of grated Cheddar and Monterey jack cheese works very well in this recipe.

Deviled Egg Sandwiches

2 Hard-Boiled Eggs (page 14)
3 teaspoons mayonnaise
2 teaspoons Dijon mustard
⅛ teaspoon (or to taste)
    paprika

Salt and pepper, to taste
1 lettuce leaf
¼ small tomato
4 slices crusty bread or 2 pita
    pocket halves

1. Peel the eggs, chop, and place in a small bowl. Mash the eggs with the mayonnaise and the Dijon mustard. Stir in the paprika, salt, and pepper.
2. Shred the lettuce leaf. Finely chop the tomato to yield about 2 heaping tablespoons. Stir the lettuce and tomato into the egg mixture.
3. If using crusty bread, spread half of the mixture on 1 slice of bread. Place the other slice on top and close. If using pita pockets, stuff half of the egg mixture into each pocket. If not eating immediately, store in a resealable plastic bag or a plastic container until ready to eat.

Yields 2 sandwiches

Dieters take note: Regular mayonnaise is high in fat and calories. For a healthier meal, use low-fat mayonnaise or substitute plain yogurt.

Flatbread with Ham and Roasted Red Peppers

Serves 1

Not sure which mustard brand to use? Sweet prepared mustards—such as honey mustard—make a nice contrast with the smoky flavor of the roasted red pepper in this recipe.

1 pita pocket
1 tablespoon light mayonnaise, optional
Freshly cracked black pepper to taste, optional
2 romaine lettuce leaves
½ roasted red bell pepper (see below)
2 slices cooked ham
1 tablespoon (or to taste) prepared mustard

1. Cut around the edges of the pita to separate the pita into 2 rounds. If using the mayonnaise, spread it over the inside of each pita half. Sprinkle with pepper, if desired.
2. Wash the lettuce leaves and drain. Cut the roasted red pepper into bite-sized pieces.
3. Lay a lettuce leaf on 1 of the pita halves. Lay 1 slice of the ham on top of the lettuce and spread some of the mustard on top. Place a few pieces of red pepper on top of the ham, add another piece of lettuce, and the final piece of ham. Spread the remaining mustard on the final ham slice. Lay the other pita half on top of the ingredients and close up the sandwich. Cut the sandwich into 4 quarters.

How to Roast a Bell Pepper

Place the pepper side down (not standing up) on a broiling pan. Brush the top side of the pepper with balsamic vinegar. Turn over and brush the other side with olive oil. Broil the pepper for about 15 to 20 minutes, turning frequently, until the skin is blackened and charred. Then place the pepper in a sealed plastic bag, and leave it in the bag for at least 10 minutes. Remove from the bag and peel off the skin. Remove the stem and the seeds. To serve, cut into cubes or lengthwise into strips.

Corn Tortilla

1 large fresh button mushroom
½ green onion
3½ ounces cooked chicken
⅛ teaspoon chili powder
1 tablespoon butter or
    margarine

1 flour tortilla
½ cup grated Cheddar cheese
2 olives, sliced
2 tablespoons sour cream or
    salsa, optional

Serves 1

Canned chicken works very well in this recipe. For extra flavor, toss the chicken with salsa before placing it on top of the tortilla.

∾

1. Wipe the mushroom clean with a damp cloth and slice. Wash the green onion in hot water, drain, and dice. Toss the chicken with the chili powder.
2. Melt the butter or margarine in a frying pan. Add the tortilla. Cook for 1 minute, then sprinkle ¼ cup of the grated cheese on half of the tortilla. Heat until the cheese melts, then add the chicken on top. Lay the mushroom slices on top of the chicken and add the green onion and olives. Fold the tortilla in half.
3. Cook the tortilla until it is browned on the bottom. Turn over and cook the other side. Sprinkle the remaining ¼ cup of grated cheese over the folded tortilla during the last minute of cooking. Serve hot with sour cream or salsa on the side for dipping, if desired.

Blanching Vegetables Ahead of Time

Busy cooks may want to shorten meal preparation time by blanching vegetables earlier in the day. For best results, always plunge the blanched vegetables into ice-cold water immediately after blanching to stop the cooking process. Remove the vegetables when they are cool to the touch. Cover and refrigerate until ready to use.

Ultimate Submarine Sandwich

1 (8-inch) whole-wheat sub bun
1 tablespoon mustard
1 tablespoon mayonnaise
1½ tablespoons finely chopped red onion
1 romaine lettuce leaf
2 slices cooked ham

2 ounces Cheddar cheese, thinly sliced
2 slices turkey
2 ounces mozzarella cheese, thinly sliced
½ tomato, sliced
4–5 pickles

Slice the sub bun in half lengthwise. Spread the mustard on the inside of one half. Spread the mayonnaise on the inside of the other half. Fill with the red onion, lettuce leaf, sliced ham, Cheddar cheese, sliced turkey, mozzarella cheese, sliced tomato, and pickles.

Bruschetta with Tomatoes

1 garlic clove
1 medium tomato
Salt and pepper, to taste
4 slices French or other crusty bread

1 tablespoon extra-virgin olive oil
½ teaspoon dried basil, optional

1. Smash the garlic clove, peel, and cut in half. Wash the tomato and chop. Sprinkle the chopped tomato with salt and pepper and set aside.
2. Toast the bread slices. Rub the garlic over one side of each toasted bread slice. Spread the chopped tomato on top. Drizzle with the olive oil.
3. Sprinkle with the dried basil, if using, and add a bit of salt and pepper if desired.

Warming Herbed Tomato Soup

½ small green bell pepper
½ celery stalk
½ white onion
2 tablespoons olive oil, butter,
    or margarine
1 cup stewed tomatoes, with
    juice

¼ teaspoon celery salt
¼ teaspoon dried thyme
¼ bay leaf, optional
1 cup chicken broth
½ cup water
Salt and pepper, to taste

> **Yields 2½ cups**
>
> Don't let the lengthy ingredient list throw you! This dish is quick and easy. For even quicker preparation, cut extra green pepper and onion while preparing dinner the night before, and set aside to use in the soup.
>
> ∽

1. Remove the core and seeds from the green pepper and chop. Cut the celery on the diagonal into thin slices. Peel and chop the white onion.
2. In a heavy saucepan, heat the olive oil. Add the chopped onion. Cook for 1 to 2 minutes. Add the green pepper. Cook over medium-low heat until the onion is soft and translucent but not browned.
3. Add the stewed tomatoes, celery, celery salt, thyme, and bay leaf. Simmer for 5 minutes.
4. Add the chicken broth and water. Bring to a boil, reduce heat, and simmer for 5 to 10 minutes. Add the salt and pepper to taste. Remove the bay leaf before ladling out the soup.

Prepared Mustard FAQs

It can be very confusing when a recipe simply calls for "prepared mustard" without any clarification. Should you use the same sharp mustard that goes on hot dogs, a more subtly flavored French Dijon, or something else altogether? The term "prepared mustard" refers to all types of mustard made from dry mustard seeds. If the recipe doesn't elaborate further, feel free to use your favorite.

Middle Eastern Hummus

2 large garlic cloves
1 (19-ounce) can chickpeas
4 tablespoons reserved juice
from chickpeas
2 tablespoons, plus 1 teaspoon
lemon juice

2 tablespoons tahini or peanut
butter
¼ teaspoon (or to taste)
ground cumin
1–2 pita pockets

1. Preheat oven to 350°.
2. Smash, peel, and finely chop the garlic cloves. Drain the chickpeas and mash them, reserving the juice from the can.
3. In a small bowl, blend together the chopped garlic, mashed chickpeas, chickpea juice, lemon juice, tahini, and cumin.
4. Cut 1 or 2 pita pockets into 6 wedges each. Place on a baking sheet and toast in the oven for 8 to 10 minutes, until crispy. Spread a heaping tablespoon of hummus on each pita wedge. Store the remainder of the hummus in a sealed container in the refrigerator until ready to use.

Replacing Tahini with Peanut Butter

Peanut butter makes a handy (and less expensive!) alternative to tahini in recipes. Both are made from nuts (tahini is made by grinding raw or toasted sesame seeds) and lend a creamy texture and nutty flavor to dishes such as Middle Eastern Hummus. However, tahini is the winner in the nutrition department. While their fat and calorie content are nearly identical, tahini is loaded with vitamins and minerals such as calcium and lecithin.

Portobello Mushroom Burger

1 English muffin, cut in half
4 teaspoons low-fat margarine
1 large Portobello mushroom
1 romaine lettuce leaf
1 tablespoon olive oil

3 tablespoons (or to taste)
  chopped onion
1 tomato slice
2 tablespoons grated cheese,
  such as Swiss or Cheddar

> **Serves 1**
>
> Earthy-flavored Portobello mushrooms are frequently used as a meat substitute by vegetarians. This recipe makes either a filling lunch or a light dinner.
>
> ∾

1. Toast the English muffin halves. Spread 1 teaspoon of margarine on each half while still warm, and set aside. Wipe the Portobello mushroom with a damp cloth and cut into thin slices. Wash the lettuce leaf, dry, and tear into pieces.

2. Heat the olive oil on medium in a skillet. Add the chopped onion and cook on medium-low heat until tender.

3. Add the remaining 2 teaspoons margarine to the frying pan. Push the onion to the side and lay the Portobello mushroom slices flat in the pan. Cook until browned on the bottom, about 2 minutes. Turn over and cook the other side until browned. Add the tomato slice to the pan while the mushroom is cooking.

4. When the mushroom slices are browned on both sides, sprinkle the grated cheese on top. Cook briefly until the cheese is melted.

5. To make the burger, lay the tomato on 1 muffin half and place the cooked onion on the other half. Lay the mushroom and melted cheese mixture on top of both halves. Serve open-faced, garnished with the lettuce.

Cooking with Bay Leaves

While bay leaves add a pungent flavor to everything from soups to cheese fondue, their sharp, pointy edges can be dangerous if eaten. Always be sure to remove bay leaves before serving a dish.

Chapter 4

Crunch Time:
Simple Snacks on the Go

Breadsticks with Cheese and Fruit

½ tomato
4 tablespoons light cream cheese
2 tablespoons milk

½ teaspoon dried parsley flakes
12 sesame breadsticks

Chop the tomato finely. Mix together the cream cheese, chopped tomato, milk, and parsley flakes to make a dip for the breadsticks. Serve as is, or purée the cream cheese in the blender for a smoother dip.

Supreme Pizza Crackers

3 tablespoons tomato sauce
1 pita pocket
2 slices ham, salami, or other sliced meat

2 large mushrooms, sliced
2 tablespoons sliced olives
⅓ cup grated Cheddar or Parmesan cheese

Spread the tomato sauce on the pita pocket. Lay the meat slices on top. Add the mushroom slices and the olives. Sprinkle the cheese over the top. Broil for about 2 to 3 minutes, until the cheese melts. Cut into wedges.

Banana Muffins

1 egg
1 cup milk
¼ cup vegetable oil
¾ teaspoon baking soda
¾ teaspoon baking powder
⅛ teaspoon salt

1½ cups all-purpose flour
3 tablespoons liquid honey
1 cup mashed banana (about 2 bananas)
¼ teaspoon ground cinnamon

Yields 12–15 muffins

For added protein, cut the muffin in half and spread with your favorite flavored cream cheese.

∾

---

1. Preheat oven to 375°. Grease a muffin pan.
2. In a small bowl, add the egg to the milk and beat lightly. Add the vegetable oil and stir to combine.
3. In a large bowl, stir the baking soda, baking powder, and salt into the flour until well blended.
4. Add the egg mixture to the flour mixture and stir to form a batter. Stir in the honey, banana, and ground cinnamon. Stir until combined but do not beat.
5. Spoon the batter into the muffin tins so that they are about ⅔ full. Bake for 20 to 25 minutes or until a toothpick inserted into the middle of a muffin comes out clean. Let cool for 5 minutes before serving. Store the muffins in a sealed tin.

Freezing Canned Fruit for Smoothies

Using canned fruit gives you more options when making a smoothie. Prepare the fruit by puréeing it in a blender. Place the puréed fruit in ice cube trays and freeze. If not using immediately, transfer the frozen cubes to a resealable plastic bag for storage.

Blueberry Muffins

Yields about 12 muffins

Don't have buttermilk?
Add 1 tablespoon lemon
juice to 1 cup of regular
milk and let it sit for a
minute before adding
the egg.

1 egg
1 cup buttermilk
3 tablespoons vegetable oil
¾ cup all-purpose flour
¾ cup whole-wheat flour
¼ cup oat bran

¾ teaspoon baking powder
½ teaspoon baking soda
⅛ teaspoon salt
⅓ cup brown sugar
1 cup blueberries, frozen or
*   fresh*

1. Preheat oven to 375°. Grease a muffin pan.
2. In a small bowl, add the egg to the buttermilk and beat lightly. Add the vegetable oil and stir to combine.
3. In a large bowl, combine the all-purpose flour, whole-wheat flour, and oat bran. Stir in the baking powder, baking soda, salt, and brown sugar until well blended.
4. Add the egg mixture to the flour mixture and stir to form a batter. Be careful not to overmix the batter; don't worry if there are still lumps. Gently stir in the blueberries.
5. Spoon the batter into the muffin tins so that they are between ½ to ⅔ full. Bake for 20 to 25 minutes or until a toothpick inserted into the middle of a muffin comes out clean. Let cool for 5 minutes before eating. Store the muffins in a sealed tin.

Minute Muffins

Few baked goods are as easy to make as muffins. Simply combine the dry ingredients and the wet ingredients in separate bowls, stir briefly to combine, and bake in greased pans. The entire process, from mixing bowl to oven, takes about 30 minutes.

Apple and Cinnamon Muffins

1 egg
1 teaspoon vanilla extract
1 cup buttermilk
¼ cup vegetable oil
1½ teaspoons baking powder
½ teaspoon baking soda

Pinch salt
½ cup granulated sugar
1¾ cups all-purpose flour
¾ teaspoon ground cinnamon
½ teaspoon ground nutmeg
1½ cups diced apple

> **Yields 12 muffins**
>
> Sweet cinnamon and tart apple make an excellent combination. For even more flavor, add frozen or fresh cranberries.
>
> ❧

1. Preheat oven to 375°. Grease a muffin pan.
2. In a small bowl, add the egg and vanilla extract to the buttermilk and beat lightly. Add the vegetable oil and mix to combine.
3. In a large bowl, stir the baking powder, baking soda, salt, and sugar into the flour and blend well. Stir in the cinnamon and nutmeg.
4. Add the egg mixture to the flour mixture and stir to form a batter. Be careful not to overmix the batter; don't worry if there are still lumps. Stir in the diced apples.
5. Spoon the batter into the prepared muffin tins so that they are between ½ to ⅔ full. Bake for 20 minutes or until a toothpick inserted into the middle of a muffin comes out clean. Let cool for 5 minutes before serving. Store the muffins in a sealed tin.

It's All in the Baking Powder

Muffins get their distinctive domed shape from the addition of baking powder. When baking powder comes into contact with wet ingredients, carbon dioxide gas is released. This causes the batter to expand. The reaction is quick, so it's important to get muffins in the oven as quickly as possible after making the batter. Otherwise, too much gas escapes before they're heated, leading to flat-topped muffins.

Marvelous Mango Muffins

Yields about 15 muffins

Canned mango is available throughout the year in Asian markets.

1¾ cups canned mango, diced
4 tablespoons reserved mango juice
1 egg
1 cup sour cream
¼ cup vegetable oil
1½ teaspoons baking powder
⅛ teaspoon salt
1 cup granulated sugar
1½ cups all-purpose flour
½ teaspoon ground allspice
¼ cup sweetened coconut flakes

1. Preheat oven to 375°. Grease a muffin pan. Mash the mango into a soft pulp. Reserve 4 tablespoons juice.
2. In a small bowl, beat together the egg, vegetable oil, and sour cream. Combine thoroughly.
3. In a large bowl, stir the baking powder, salt, and sugar into the flour until well blended. Stir in the ground allspice.
4. Add the egg mixture to the flour and stir to form a batter. Be careful not to overmix the batter; don't worry if there are still lumps. Stir in the reserved mango juice. Stir in the mango and the coconut flakes.
5. Spoon the batter into the prepared muffin tins so that they are between ½ to ⅔ full. Bake for 25 minutes or until a toothpick inserted into the middle of a muffin comes out clean. Let cool for 5 minutes before serving. Store the muffins in a sealed tin.

Freezing Muffins

Got extra muffins? To freeze, wrap tightly in aluminum foil or place in a resealable plastic bag. To reheat, microwave briefly on high heat or warm in a 300° oven for 15 to 20 minutes.

Pineapple Surprise

1 stick unsalted butter
1 egg
1 tablespoon vanilla extract
1 cup milk
1½ teaspoons baking powder
½ teaspoon baking soda
⅛ teaspoon salt
½ cup brown sugar

1 cup all-purpose flour
¾ cup rolled oats
1 cup canned crushed
pineapple, drained
½ cup plain yogurt
½ cup sweetened shredded
coconut

Yields about 16 muffins

These taste delicious served warm with extra yogurt spread in the middle. Feel free to increase or decrease the amount of brown sugar as desired.

1. Preheat oven to 375°. Grease a muffin pan. Melt the unsalted butter in a small saucepan over low heat.

2. In a small bowl, add the egg and vanilla extract to the milk and beat lightly.

3. In a large bowl, stir the baking powder, baking soda, salt, and brown sugar into the flour and rolled oats until well blended. Stir in the melted butter.

4. Add the egg mixture to the flour mixture. Stir until the mixture is just combined, without beating. Gently stir in the pineapple, yogurt, and shredded coconut.

5. Spoon the batter into the prepared muffin tins so that they are between ½ to ⅔ full. Bake for 20 minutes or until a toothpick inserted into the middle of a muffin comes out clean. Let cool for 5 minutes before serving. Store the muffins in a sealed tin.

How to Make a Smoothie

Smoothies are easy to make. All you need is frozen fruit and a dairy product. Fruit juice can be added or left out as desired. While not essential, crushed ice or ice cubes give the smoothie a texture similar to a milk shake. To heighten the effect, serve the smoothie in a frosted glass.

Cinnamon and Raisin Granola

Yields about 3 cups

This tastes delicious topped with applesauce and heated in the microwave. Be sure to use at least 1 cup of dried fruit (such as raisins) to balance the strong taste of the wheat germ.

2 cups rolled oats
2½ tablespoons toasted wheat germ
1 teaspoon ground cinnamon
6 tablespoons apple juice

2 tablespoons canola oil
1 tablespoon butter or margarine, softened
2 tablespoons brown sugar
1 cup raisins

1. Preheat oven to 250°.
2. In a large bowl, mix together the rolled oats and wheat germ. Stir in the ground cinnamon. Stir in the apple juice, canola oil, and margarine, blending thoroughly.
3. Spread out the mixture on a baking sheet. Bake for 15 minutes, stirring regularly. Remove the baking sheet from the oven.
4. Pour the granola back into the mixing bowl. Stir in the brown sugar and raisins. Spread the mixture back onto the baking sheet. Cook for another 15 to 20 minutes or until the granola is golden brown. Let cool. Store in a sealed container.

What Makes Wheat Germ So Great?

Made from the kernel of the wheat berry, wheat germ is a concentrated source of all the nutrients found in wheat, including vitamin E, B vitamins, iron, and potassium.

Chewy Granola Bars

1 stick unsalted butter
¼ cup, plus 2 tablespoons
   liquid honey
¼ cup brown sugar
2 cups rolled oats
2 tablespoons wheat germ

¾ teaspoon ground cinnamon
1 tablespoon sesame seeds
2 eggs
½ cup raisins
½ cup chopped peanuts

1. Preheat oven to 300°.
2. Melt the butter with the honey and brown sugar in a small saucepan on low heat, stirring continuously.
3. In a large bowl, combine the rolled oats, wheat germ, ground cinnamon, and sesame seeds.
4. Add the melted butter, honey, and brown sugar to the dry ingredients, and stir to mix. Lightly beat the eggs and add them to the mixture, stirring to combine. Stir in the raisins and chopped peanuts.
5. Spread the mixture in a 9" × 9" inch pan, pressing it down with a spatula to spread it out evenly. Bake for 15 minutes or until golden brown. Let cool and cut into bars.

> **Yields about 16 bars**
>
> Having trouble getting the granola bars to hold their shape after baking? Let the bars cool, cut lightly with a knife while still in the pan, and freeze for about 30 minutes, until they are firm but not frozen.
>
> ∾

Choosing Smoothie Ingredients

The only limit is your imagination! Skim or whole milk, yogurt, or even buttermilk can make up the dairy portion. Frozen blueberries, strawberries, and raspberries are all good choices for frozen fruit, and are readily available throughout the year. Seasonal fresh fruits such as peaches, honeydew, kiwi, and cantaloupe are good candidates for a smoothie. Just cut the fruit into chunks, place in a resealable plastic bag, and freeze for up to 2 hours before using. Want to add fruit juice? Apple juice, cranberry juice, and orange juice all work well.

Granola Biscotti

4 eggs
1 teaspoon vanilla extract
½ teaspoon almond extract
1½ cups all-purpose flour
1 cup rolled oats
½ teaspoon baking powder
⅛ teaspoon salt

1 tablespoon toasted wheat germ
½ cup brown sugar
½ cup granulated sugar
½ cup toasted almonds
½ cup chopped dates
⅓ cup liquid honey, optional

1. Preheat oven to 325°. Grease a large baking sheet.
2. In a small bowl, lightly beat the eggs with the vanilla and almond extract. In a large bowl, combine the flour, rolled oats, baking powder, salt, toasted wheat germ, brown sugar, and granulated sugar. Blend thoroughly. Add the beaten eggs and blend to form a sticky dough. Stir in the toasted almonds and chopped dates.
3. Cut the dough in half. Flour your hands and shape each half into a 14-inch log. Place the logs on the prepared baking sheet and bake for 30 minutes or until a toothpick inserted into the center comes out clean. Let cool for 10 minutes.
4. Cut the dough diagonally into slices about ½ inch thick. Place the biscotti cut-side down on 2 ungreased baking sheets. Bake for a total of 15 minutes, removing the baking sheets from the oven at the halfway point and turning the biscotti over. If using the liquid honey, drizzle it over the tops of the biscotti.
5. Return the biscotti to the oven, moving the baking sheet that was on the top rack to the bottom rack and vice versa (to ensure the cookies cook evenly). Let cool. Store the biscotti in a cookie tin or other airtight container.

Mushroom-Flavored Popcorn

3 tablespoons margarine
3 tablespoons condensed
  mushroom soup
1 tablespoon brown sugar
¼ teaspoon (or to taste) dried
  parsley flakes

¼ teaspoon (or to taste) dried
  thyme
¼ teaspoon (or to taste) red
  pepper flakes
5–6 cups popped popcorn

1. Preheat oven to 325°.
2. Place the margarine in a small saucepan over low heat. When it begins to melt, stir in the soup, brown sugar, parsley, thyme, and red pepper flakes. Continue melting, stirring so that the sugar dissolves.
3. Spread the popcorn out on a large baking sheet. Pour the sauce over the popcorn, stirring to make sure it is evenly mixed.
4. Bake the popcorn for 8 to 10 minutes. Check once and stir the popcorn around if necessary to make sure it is evenly mixed. Let cool. Store in an airtight container.

Yields about 1 cup

Savory mushroom soup and spices lend flavor to plain popcorn in this recipe.

∾

Stuffed Celery Snacks

The firm texture and "hollowed-log" shape of celery make it perfect for filling. Peanut butter and semifirm cheeses such as blue cheese, cream cheese, and even Cheese Whiz are all good filling choices. For extra protein, add granola, raisins, nuts, sunflower or pumpkin seeds to the filling before spreading on the celery stalk.

Healthy Popcorn with Yogurt

1½ cups popped popcorn
3 tablespoons low-fat yogurt
1 tablespoon liquid honey
¼ teaspoon nutmeg

Place the popcorn in a small bowl. Combine the yogurt and honey. Add to the popcorn, tossing to mix. Sprinkle with the nutmeg.

Did You Know?

Since 1988, the blueberry muffin has been the official muffin of Minnesota.

Yields 1½ cups

Use unbuttered popcorn and your favorite flavor of low-fat yogurt in this recipe.

ल

Italian Pesto Popcorn

⅓ cup butter or margarine
1 teaspoon dried basil or parsley flakes
¼ teaspoon garlic salt
2 teaspoons grated Parmesan cheese
15 cups popped popcorn

1. In a small saucepan, melt the butter over low heat. Stir in the basil, garlic salt, and Parmesan cheese.
2. Spread the popcorn out on a large tray. Slowly pour the melted butter mixture over the popcorn, stirring to make sure it is mixed thoroughly.

Yields 15 cups

Looking for a quick and easy snack to sustain you and your roommates through a long night of studying? This recipe transforms pesto, a popular Italian pasta sauce, into a flavorful popcorn topping.

ल

Low-Cal Blueberry Smoothie

⅔ cup frozen, unsweetened
    blueberries
1 banana

½ cup plain, low-fat yogurt
½ cup skim milk
1 teaspoon liquid honey

1. Wash and drain the blueberries. Peel and slice the banana.
2. Process the blueberries in a food processor or blender. Add the yogurt and milk and process again. Add the sliced banana and honey and process again. Serve in a tall glass.

> **Yields 2 cups**
>
> The texture and tart flavor of blueberries make a nice combination with sweet banana. Enjoy as is, or add crushed ice during the final stage of blending.
>
> ∾

Tropical Pineapple Smoothie

1 banana
8 ounces frozen strawberries
1 cup milk
1 cup canned crushed
    pineapple, with juice
2 tablespoons sweetened
    shredded coconut

1 teaspoon (or to taste) lime
    juice
¼ teaspoon (or to taste)
    cinnamon
2 crushed ice cubes

1. Peel the banana, slice, and chill in the freezer for about 15 minutes.
2. Slice the frozen strawberries.
3. Process the strawberries in a blender or food processor. Add the milk and pineapple, and process again. Add the banana, coconut, lime juice, cinnamon, and ice cubes, and process again. Serve in a chilled glass.

> **Yields 3½ cups**
>
> Pamper yourself by serving this smoothie in a tall chilled glass, garnished with a wedge of lime and a few banana slices.
>
> ∾

Instant Smoothie

Yields 2½ cups

If using unsweetened fruit cocktail, add 1 tablespoon (or to taste) granulated sugar, brown sugar, or liquid honey.

1 (14-ounce) can fruit cocktail
1 cup milk

1 banana, optional
3 cubes crushed ice

Chill the fruit cocktail in the freezer for at least 30 minutes, until crystals begin to form. In a food processor or blender, process the fruit cocktail with the milk. If using the banana, add and process. Add the crushed ice and process again. Drink immediately.

Homemade Trail Mix

Yields 1¾ cups

Sweet chocolate and salty peanuts combine with healthy granola to make a healthful and tasty backpack snack. Feel free to substitute coconut flakes or sunflower seeds for the banana chips.

1 cup Cinnamon and Raisin
  Granola (page 56)
¼ cup salted peanuts
¼ cup semisweet chocolate
  chips

¼ cup dehydrated banana
  chips
2 tablespoons hazelnuts,
  optional

Combine all the ingredients in a medium-sized bowl. Pack in a resealable plastic bag or container for easy carrying. If not using immediately, store in an airtight container.

Satisfying Smoothies

With their smooth, icy texture and sharp taste, smoothies are like a fruit-flavored milkshake without the excess sugar and calories.

Lemony Oatmeal Drop Cookies

½ cup butter or margarine
1 cup granulated sugar
1 egg
1 teaspoon vanilla extract
1 teaspoon lemon extract
½ teaspoon baking soda

½ teaspoon baking powder
½ teaspoon salt
1 cup all-purpose flour
½ cup sweetened shredded coconut
1 cup quick-cooking oats

Yields about 50 cookies

This makes a lighter, crisper cookie than other cookie recipes. Quick-cooking oatmeal can be found with other types of oatmeal in the supermarket. Don't use instant oatmeal in its place.

1. Preheat oven to 350°. Grease a baking sheet well.
2. Cream together the butter and sugar. Beat the egg with the vanilla and lemon extract. Beat into the butter and sugar mixture until creamy.
3. Sift the baking soda, baking powder, and salt into the flour. Add to the butter mixture and beat until well blended. Stir in the coconut and the oats.
4. Use a teaspoon to drop the dough onto the baking tray, placing them well apart (about 15 cookies per tray). For best results, don't drop more than a level teaspoon, as the cookies expand quite a bit. Bake for about 6 minutes, until lightly browned around the edges. Let cool. Store in an airtight container.

Terrific Trail Mix

The gourmet version of granola, trail mixes typically include exotic nuts such as brazil nuts and cashews, along with various combinations of dried fruits and seeds. To satisfy the sweet tooth, chocolate chips, M&Ms, or other goodies are frequently sprinkled among the healthier ingredients. When preparing recipes such as Homemade Trail Mix (page 62), feel free to load it up with your own favorite fruit and nut combinations.

Supersized Oatmeal Cookies

½ cup shortening
¼ cup butter or margarine
1 cup brown sugar
1 egg
1 teaspoon vanilla extract
½ teaspoon baking soda
½ teaspoon salt

1 cup all-purpose flour
1 teaspoon ground cinnamon
1 cup quick-cooking oats
¾ cup semisweet chocolate
    chips
¼ cup chopped walnuts,
    optional

1. Preheat oven to 350°. Cream together the shortening, butter, and brown sugar well. Beat in the egg and vanilla extract.
2. Sift the baking soda and salt into the flour. Add the ground cinnamon and blend well. Stir in the oats and chocolate chips.
3. Shape 3 to 4 tablespoons of the dough into a ball about 2 inches in diameter. Place on the baking sheet, set well apart (6 balls to a tray). Press down gently with a fork. Press in a few walnut pieces in the middle, if desired.
4. Bake for 13 to 15 minutes or until done. Let cool. Store in an airtight container.

Biscotti

An Italian creation, biscotti are oblong-shaped, crunchy biscuits that are perfect for dunking in tea or coffee. The secret to biscotti lies in baking the dough twice: first to cook it through, and then a second time to add extra crispness. (The word biscotti means "twice-baked" in Italian.)

Fruity Rice Pudding

1½ cups apple juice
1 cup long-grain rice
¼ teaspoon ground nutmeg
⅛ teaspoon ground allspice
½ teaspoon lemon extract

1 teaspoon vanilla extract
1 cup milk
½ cup raisins
¾ cup plain yogurt

1. In a medium-sized saucepan, combine the apple juice and the rice. Stir in the nutmeg and allspice.
2. Bring the rice to a boil, uncovered, over medium heat. Cover, reduce heat, and simmer for about 20 minutes, until cooked through, stirring occasionally.
3. Remove the rice from the heat. Stir the lemon extract and vanilla extract into the milk. Stir the milk into the rice. Stir in the raisins. Whisk in the yogurt. Spoon the rice pudding into dessert dishes. Serve warm.

Yields 3½ cups

This recipe makes 2 to 3 servings. If not serving immediately, store in a sealed container in the refrigerator until ready to use. Serve cold, or warm briefly before serving.

ॐ

Creamy Tofu Shake

10½ ounces soft, silken tofu
1 cup frozen, unsweetened
    blueberries
1 cup canned crushed
    pineapple, with juice

2 tablespoons liquid honey
½ teaspoon vanilla extract
⅓ cup soy milk

1. Drain any excess water from the tofu and cut into chunks. If using home frozen blueberries instead of commercially bought frozen berries, wash before using.
2. Process the tofu and crushed pineapple along with the pineapple juice from the can until smooth. Add the blueberries and process until smooth. Add the honey, vanilla extract, and soy milk, and process again. Chill the shake in the refrigerator until ready to serve.

Yields 3 cups

This protein-packed snack can be made at breakfast and refrigerated in a sealed container until you need it later in the day. For extra protein, add a few drops of wheat germ, soy powder, or other protein supplement.

ॐ

Low-Cal Banana Sundae

Serves 1

Did you know? A teaspoon of honey has only 21 calories and nearly twice as much sweetening power as sugar.

∾

2 large bananas
¼ teaspoon ground cinnamon
1 teaspoon cornstarch
2 teaspoons pineapple juice

¼ cup low-fat vanilla yogurt
¼ cup canned crushed
* pineapple*
2 teaspoons liquid honey

1. Peel the bananas and slice lengthwise. Sprinkle ground cinnamon over the bananas. Mix the cornstarch into the pineapple juice and set aside.
2. In a small saucepan over medium-low heat, whisk together the yogurt, pineapple, and honey.
3. Increase heat to medium-high and add the cornstarch and pineapple juice mixture, whisking constantly until thickened.
4. Spoon the mixture over the bananas. Sprinkle extra cinnamon over the top if desired.

Stuffed Celery Sticks

Serves 1

Remember "Ants on a Log"—the kids' snack made by stuffing celery sticks with peanut butter and raisins? This version uses granola and processed cheese.

∾

2 celery stalks
3 tablespoons Cheese Whiz or
* plain cream cheese*

3 tablespoons Cinnamon and
* Raisin Granola (page 56)*

Wash and dry the celery stalks and remove any leaves. Cut each stalk into 3 equal pieces. Mash together the Cheese Whiz or cream cheese and the granola. Use a knife to spread the mixture on each celery stalk.

Basic Picante Sauce

1 large white onion
1 fresh jalapeño pepper or ¼
*   cup canned jalapeños*
6 medium-sized ripe tomatoes
6 tablespoons vegetable oil

1 teaspoon salt
¼ teaspoon granulated sugar
1 tablespoon fresh, crushed
*   cilantro or 1 teaspoon dried*
*   cilantro*

1. Remove the skin from the onion and chop into ¼-inch pieces.
2. Remove the stems from the jalapeño (if using fresh) and tomatoes and chop into ¼-inch pieces.
3. Preheat the oil to medium temperature in a large frying pan. Add the onions and sauté for about 10 minutes or until tender but not brown.
4. Add the remaining ingredients. Turn heat to medium-low and simmer for about 10 minutes.

Yields about 3 cups

For a less spicy sauce, keep the jalapeño whole and remove it after simmering the mixture.

∾

Guacamole

2 large, ripe avocados
1 medium-sized red tomato
1 small yellow onion
½ cup canned jalapeño
*   peppers*

1 tablespoon lime juice
1 teaspoon salt
½ teaspoon ground black
*   pepper*

1. Cut the avocados in half lengthwise and pry out the pits. Remove the peels and cut the avocados into 1-inch pieces. Mash with a fork.
2. Cut the tomato into ½-inch pieces. Remove the skin from the onion and cut into ¼-inch pieces. Drain off the liquid from the jalapeño peppers and cut the peppers into ¼-inch pieces.
3. Combine all the ingredients; mix well.

Serves 8

This is a wonderful topping for potatoes and meat dishes as well as a popular dip for tostadas and raw vegetables.

∾

Chapter 5

Survival of the Fittest: Healthy Dishes

Easy Eggs Florentine

2 cups fresh-packed spinach
    leaves
2 eggs
¼ teaspoon salt
2 teaspoons olive oil

2 slices crusty rye bread
2 tablespoons ricotta cheese
¼ teaspoon (or to taste)
    cayenne pepper

1. Wash the spinach leaves in cold water and drain thoroughly. Lay the leaves out on paper towels and pat dry. Chop roughly.
2. Fill a medium-sized saucepan with 3 inches of water, add the salt, and bring to a boil. While waiting for the water to boil, break each egg into separate small bowls.
3. When the water reaches a boil, turn the heat down until it is just simmering. Gently slide 1 egg into the simmering water. Cook for 3 to 5 minutes, depending on how firm you want the yolk. Remove the egg with a slotted spoon to drain off any excess water. Repeat with the second egg.
4. Heat the oil in a frying pan. Add the spinach leaves and cook briefly, until they wilt and turn dark green (less than 1 minute).
5. Toast the bread. Spread 1 tablespoon of ricotta cheese on each slice and sprinkle with a bit of the cayenne pepper. Place half the sautéed spinach leaves on each slice of bread, lay a poached egg on top of each, and sprinkle with cayenne pepper. Enjoy hot.

Don't Skimp on the Spinach

It can be hard to believe that the small pile of cooked spinach on your plate came from several cups of fresh leaves. But it's true. Spinach retains a lot of water, which is released during cooking, reducing its size. As a rule, when cooking with spinach, count on using at least 1 cup of freshly packed spinach leaves per person.

Easy Egg Drop Soup for One

1 green onion
1 egg
2 cups chicken broth

White pepper, to taste
⅛ teaspoon salt

1. Wash the green onion, pat dry, and cut diagonally into 1-inch pieces. In a small bowl, lightly beat the egg and set aside.
2. Bring the chicken broth to a boil. Stir in the white pepper and salt.
3. Remove the saucepan from the heat. Slowly pour in the beaten egg, stirring rapidly clockwise to form thin shreds. Stir in the green onion. Serve immediately.

> **Serves 1**
>
> Feel free to load up this basic recipe with frozen spinach for extra iron. Serve with the Hearty Grilled Cheese Sandwich (page 39) for a nutritious and filling lunch.
>
> ✾

Easy Hot Chicken Salad

About 4 cups water
1 (5- to 6-ounce) skinless,
    boneless chicken breast
¼ cup low-fat plain or vanilla
    yogurt

1 teaspoon honey
1 cup cooked vegetable pasta,
    such as fusilli
1 tablespoon toasted sesame
    seeds, optional

1. In a large saucepan, heat the water until just simmering. While the water is heating, rinse the chicken, cut off any fat, and pat dry with paper towels.
2. Poach the chicken in the simmering water until it is white and cooked through, about 10 minutes. Turn off the heat and let the chicken sit in the broth for another 20 minutes. Remove and cut into thin slices.
3. Mix together the yogurt and the honey. Toss the poached chicken with the yogurt and honey mixture. Lay the chicken slices on top of the pasta. Sprinkle with the toasted sesame seeds, if desired.

> **Serves 1**
>
> Vegetable pasta makes a colorful contrast to the poached chicken. For a bit of extra flavor, try replacing half of the poaching water with chicken broth.
>
> ✾

Roasted Pepper Soup

1 tablespoon olive oil
1 garlic clove, smashed, peeled, and chopped
¼ cup chopped white onion
½ cup sliced fresh mushrooms
2½ cups chicken broth
2 small or medium-sized roasted red bell peppers,
roughly chopped (see sidebar, page 42)
¾ cup chickpeas
¼ teaspoon salt
Black or white pepper, to taste
¼ teaspoon (or to taste) parsley flakes

1. Heat the oil in a medium-sized saucepan. Add the garlic and onion. Cook over low-medium heat until the onion is tender. Add the mushrooms and cook for 1 to 2 minutes, stirring occasionally.
2. Add the chicken broth and bring to a boil. Add the roasted peppers chunks and the chickpeas. Bring the soup back to a boil and stir in the salt, pepper, and parsley. Serve hot.

Garden Salad

4 iceberg lettuce leaves
½ tomato
2 celery stalks
½ cup sliced mushrooms
½ cup baby carrots
3 tablespoons low-calorie salad dressing, any flavor

Wash the lettuce leaves, tomato, and celery stalks, and slice. Wipe the mushrooms with a damp cloth. Chop the baby carrots in half. Combine the salad ingredients and toss with the salad dressing.

Tips for Toasting Nuts

Toasting nuts is a great way to bring out their flavor. To toast, simply spread the nuts out on an ungreased baking sheet and bake at 300°, turning the nuts frequently, until they are browned (different nuts will have different cooking times). Watch them carefully to be sure they don't burn or overcook.

Healthy Stuffed Potato

2 potatoes
4 tablespoons plain yogurt,
    divided
¼ teaspoon cayenne pepper
1 teaspoon tomato sauce

1 canned artichoke heart, finely
    chopped
Salt and pepper, to taste
1 tablespoon soy cheese,
    optional

Serves 2

When scooping out the pulp, be sure to leave about ¼ inch around the skin so that it doesn't fall apart.

1. Preheat oven to 400°.
2. Wash the potatoes and scrub to remove any dirt. Poke a few holes in each potato. Place directly on the middle oven rack.
3. Bake the potatoes for 45 minutes, or until done. To test for doneness, pierce the potatoes with a fork. It should go through easily. Remove from the oven. Cut each potato in half lengthwise while still hot.
4. Remove the pulp from the potatoes and set aside the skins. Place the pulp in a bowl and add 2 tablespoons of the yogurt, cayenne pepper, tomato sauce, artichoke, and salt and pepper. Use a fork to whip the potatoes until fluffy. Add as much of the remaining 2 tablespoons yogurt as needed while whipping to reach desired consistency. Stir in the salt and pepper.
5. Scoop the potato mixture into the reserved potato skins. Sprinkle with the soy cheese, if desired. Bake for about 15 minutes or until the cheese melts. Serve hot.

How to Toast Sesame Seeds

To toast sesame seeds, spread the seeds out in a heavy frying pan and cook on medium heat, shaking the pan occasionally, until they turn golden brown and are aromatic. Cool before using.

Rainbow Salad with Fennel

Serves 2

Fennel adds a distinct licorice flavor to this standard coleslaw recipe. If you can't find fennel, parsley can stand in as a substitute garnish, but the dish won't have the same flavor.

1 carrot
1 red bell pepper
2 cups shredded red cabbage

2 tablespoons, plus 2 teaspoons
* low-fat mayonnaise*
3 teaspoons liquid honey
1 fennel bulb

1. Wash the carrot and red pepper. Grate the carrot (there should be ½ to ⅔ cup of grated carrot). Cut the red pepper into thin strips.
2. Mix together the carrot, red pepper, and cabbage in a bowl. Mix the mayonnaise with the honey. Toss the vegetables with the mayonnaise mixture.
3. Rinse the fennel under running water and pat dry. Trim off the top and bottom of the fennel bulb. Cut the fennel into quarters, remove the core in the middle, and cut into thin slices. Garnish the coleslaw with the fennel.

Apple and Walnut Salad

Serves 1–2

Feel free to experiment by using your favorite fla-vored vanilla yogurt, such as vanilla with peaches. For added pro-tein, serve with Cheddar cheese slices.

1 celery stalk
1 cup chopped apple (about 1
* small apple)*

⅓ cup walnut pieces
2 tablespoons vanilla yogurt

Wash the celery and cut on the diagonal into 1-inch pieces. In a small bowl, combine the celery with the chopped apple and walnut pieces. Toss with the yogurt. Serve immediately, or cover and chill.

Vegetable-Cleaning Tip

Always wash fresh produce just before serving or eating, not when you first store the food in the crisper section of the refrigerator.

Simple Caesar Salad

¾ head romaine lettuce
1 cup plain croutons
¼ cup bacon bits
¼ cup grated Parmesan cheese

3 tablespoons Caesar salad
   dressing
Black pepper, to taste

Serves 3–4

Feel free to substitute toasted French or Italian bread cubes for the croutons. Either regular or creamy Caesar salad dressing can be used in this recipe.

∽

1. Wash the lettuce and pat dry. Tear the leaves into strips approximately 1 inch wide.
2. Mix together the croutons, bacon bits, Parmesan cheese, and lettuce. Just before serving, toss with the Caesar salad dressing and sprinkle with black pepper.

Whole-Wheat Pasta with Basil and Tomato Pesto

1½ cups rigatoni pasta
1 ounce fresh basil leaves
3 garlic cloves
1 large tomato

⅓ cup pine nuts
½ cup grated Parmesan cheese
½ cup olive oil

Serves 2

This recipe is designed to make extra sauce to save and serve with pasta on another night. To turn this into a dish for 4, increase the amount of rigatoni to 3 cups and use all the sauce.

∽

1. Cook the pasta in boiling salted water until tender but still firm (al dente). Drain.
2. Chop the basil leaves to make 1 cup. Smash, peel, and chop the garlic. Wash and chop the tomato, reserving the juice.
3. Process the garlic and pine nuts in a food processor. One at a time, add and process the tomato and basil leaves. Slowly add the olive oil and keep processing until the pesto is creamy. Add the grated Parmesan cheese. Pour half the pesto sauce over the cooked pasta. Store the remaining pesto sauce in a sealed container in the refrigerator for up to 7 days.

Speedy Chop Suey for Four

Serves 4

Can't find prepackaged chop suey mix? Use frozen stir-fry vegetables, or any assortment of cut-up vegetables, such as snow peas, onion, carrots, and broccoli.

∾

1½ cups, plus 4 teaspoons water
1¼ cups short-grain white rice
2 pounds flank steak
¾ pound prepackaged chop suey mix

2 teaspoons cornstarch
2 tablespoons, plus 2 teaspoons vegetable oil
½ cup prepared stir-fry sauce

1. Bring the rice and 1½ cups water to a boil over medium heat. Reduce heat to low and cover tightly. Simmer until all the water is absorbed and the rice is cooked, about 15 to 20 minutes. Remove from heat and let stand for 10 to 15 minutes. Do not stir.
2. Meanwhile, cut the steak into thin strips, about 2 inches long. Rinse the chop suey vegetables and drain. In a small bowl, mix the cornstarch with the 4 teaspoons water and set aside.
3. Heat 2 tablespoons of the oil on medium-high in a frying pan. Add half the steak strips, laying them flat down in the frying pan. Let the meat cook for 1 minute, then stir with a spatula. Cook the steak until it changes color and is nearly cooked, stirring frequently. Remove from the frying pan and cook the remaining steak, adding more oil if necessary.
4. Clean out the frying pan and add the remaining 2 teaspoons oil. When the oil is hot, add the chop suey vegetable mix, stirring. Cook for 2 to 3 minutes, and add ¼ cup of the stir-fry sauce. Mix well and cook for another 1 to 2 minutes, until the sauce is heated through. Add the steak and the remaining ¼ cup stir-fry sauce, and mix thoroughly.
5. Push the mixture to the sides of the frying pan. Turn up the heat. Give the cornstarch and water mixture a quick restir and add it to the middle of the pan and stir until it thickens. Mix with the meat and vegetables.
6. Fluff the rice with a fork. Serve the chop suey hot over the rice.

Easy Steamed Turkey Breast for One

2 (3-ounce) boneless turkey
   breast fillets
1 cup chicken broth

1 cup water
1 teaspoon dried rosemary
½ cup baby carrots

1. Rinse the turkey fillets under running water and pat dry.
2. Fill the steamer section of the cooker with the chicken broth and water. Add the turkey fillets to the steamer bowl. Place the dried rosemary in the section provided for herbs if your steamer has one. If not, lay the rosemary around the turkey fillets.
3. Set the timer for 25 minutes. After 5 minutes, add the baby carrots to the steamer bowl with the turkey. When the timer shuts off, remove the steamed turkey and carrots, taking care to wear oven mitts and standing back to avoid any excess steam.

Serves 1

This dish takes less than 30 minutes to make and leaves only one appliance to clean up afterward. The amount of liquid required may vary depending on your specific make and model of rice cooker/steamer.

❧

Marinated Artichoke Hearts

4 canned artichoke hearts
½ tomato
⅓ cup extra-virgin olive oil
1 tablespoon lemon juice

⅛ teaspoon garlic powder
Salt and freshly cracked black
   pepper, to taste

1. Squeeze any excess juice from the canned artichokes. Wash the tomato, pat dry, and slice.
2. In a small bowl, combine the olive oil, lemon juice, garlic powder, and salt and pepper.
3. Pour the marinade into a resealable plastic bag. Add the artichokes and tomatoes and seal the bag. Refrigerate overnight to give the flavors a chance to blend.

Serves 1–2

Serve the marinated artichoke hearts and tomato in a salad, pasta dish, or on top of crusty French or Italian bread. If you prefer to leave out the tomato, reduce the olive oil to ¼ cup.

❧

Unstuffed Cabbage Roll Casserole

1 head green cabbage
2 tablespoons butter or margarine
1 pound ground beef
½ onion, chopped

Salt and pepper, to taste
1½ cups cooked brown rice
2 cups tomato sauce
4 tablespoons white vinegar
4 teaspoons granulated sugar

1. Preheat oven to 325°.
2. Boil the cabbage in a large pot of salted water. Drain and chop into pieces to yield approximately 3 cups.
3. Heat the butter or margarine on medium in a frying pan. Add the ground beef. When the pink color is nearly gone and the beef is nearly cooked through, add the onion. Continue cooking until the onion is tender. Drain the excess fat from the pan.
4. Stir in the salt and pepper, rice, tomato sauce, white vinegar, and sugar. Cook for a few minutes to heat through.
5. Line the bottom of a casserole dish with the chopped cabbage. Pour the ground beef mixture on top. Bake for 1 to 1½ hours, until the cabbage is tender.

Cabbage—a Nutritional Powerhouse

Nutritionists believe that cabbage—particularly raw cabbage—is one of the healthiest vegetables. Besides being rich in vitamin C, cabbage contains vitamin A, vitamin E, calcium, and folic acid. To gain the greatest nutritional value from cabbage, enjoy it raw. Dieters have no fear—1 cup of shredded cabbage contains less than 25 calories.

Chicken with Marinated Artichoke Hearts

2 (5-ounce) boneless chicken
thighs
⅛ teaspoon salt
⅛ teaspoon pepper
1 recipe Marinated Artichoke
Hearts (page 77)

⅓ cup chicken broth
¼ cup tomato sauce
2 teaspoons granulated sugar
1 cup cooked rice or pasta

Serves 1–2

Prepare the artichoke hearts a day in advance. For a one-dish meal, substitute boiled potatoes for the cooked rice. Chop the boiled potatoes into chunks and add to the frying pan during the final stages of cooking.

∾

1. Rinse the chicken thighs and pat dry. Remove the skin and any excess fat. Rub the salt and pepper over the chicken.
2. Heat 2 tablespoons of the olive oil marinade from the Marinated Artichoke Hearts in a deep-sided frying pan over medium heat. Add the chicken thighs and cook on medium heat until browned on both sides.
3. Drain any excess fat out of the frying pan. Add the chicken broth, tomato sauce, sugar, and the Marinated Artichoke Hearts (including the tomatoes and marinade). Cover and simmer for 15 minutes. Make sure the chicken thighs are fully cooked through. Serve with the cooked rice or pasta.

Jazzed-Up Hot Chicken Salad

When serving Easy Hot Chicken Salad (page 71) to guests, feel free to jazz it up by serving it on a bed of romaine lettuce or fresh spinach leaves. Another option is to garnish the salad with fresh fruit—Asian pears, grapes, or even tomatoes are all good choices.

Basic Steamed Chicken with Carrots

Serves 2

While they are not always allowed in dorms, many colleges allow students to keep cooking equipment such as a steamer in the residence kitchen. An electric steaming unit makes a nutritious and easy-to-use alternative to a stove.

∾

*2 (5-ounce) boneless, skinless
    chicken breasts*
½ cup baby carrots
1 tablespoon fresh rosemary

⅛ teaspoon (or to taste) salt
*⅛ teaspoon freshly cracked
    black pepper*

1. Rinse the chicken breasts and pat dry. Cut off any excess fat. Wash the baby carrots and dry. Leave whole or cut in half.
2. Lay the chicken breasts flat in the top part of the steamer. If your steaming unit has a screen for herbs, lay the rosemary on it. If not, lay the rosemary around the chicken breasts.
3. Set the steaming unit's timer according to the manufacturer's instructions. After the chicken has been steaming for 5 minutes, open the lid and add the baby carrots. Steam until the chicken is cooked through and the carrots are tender. (The exact time will vary according to the steaming model, but boneless chicken is normally steamed for 20 to 25 minutes, and carrots for 15 to 20 minutes.) Add salt and pepper to taste.

Preparing Potato Salad

Many recipes call for the mayonnaise, mustard, and other seasonings to be added individually to the salad. Instead, try combining the dressing ingredients ahead of time. That way, you can do a taste test before mixing the dressing with the other ingredients and make any adjustments that are necessary.

Creamy Open Artichoke Sandwich

½ recipe Marinated Artichoke
    Hearts (page 77)
¼ cup plain cream cheese
1 tablespoon chopped red
    onion, optional

¼ teaspoon red pepper flakes
4–6 slices crusty rye bread

Serves 2–4

This tasty spread can be enjoyed cold or heated. To heat, place in a micro-wave-safe dish and cover with plastic wrap. Cook on low heat for 1 to 2 minutes.

∾

1. Chop the artichoke hearts and the tomato slices prepared from the Marinated Artichoke Hearts recipe. Stir in the cream cheese, chopped red onion, and red pepper flakes. Process in a food processor or blender until the mixture is smooth but still a bit chunky.
2. Spread approximately 2 heaping tablespoons of the cream cheese and artichoke mixture on each slice of bread. Broil for 3 to 5 minutes, until the spread is heated through. Store any leftover spread in a sealed container in the refrigerator.

Steamed Jasmine Rice

1¼ cups jasmine rice

1½ cups water

Yields 3 cups

Scented jasmine rice is a long-grain rice from Thailand that has a soft texture and a flavor similar to roasted nuts. Use it as a flavorful alternative to regular white rice.

∾

1. Rinse the rice, running your fingers through it to mix it around, until the water runs clear.
2. Bring the rice and water to a boil over medium heat. Reduce heat to low and cover tightly. Simmer until all the water is absorbed and the rice is cooked, 15 to 20 minutes.
3. Remove the pot from the heat. Do not remove the cover. Let the rice stand for 10 to 15 minutes. Fluff up the rice with a fork and serve.

Mock Oyster Stew

1 cup canned or fresh mushrooms
2 cups chicken broth

¼ cup milk
1 teaspoon soy sauce
Black pepper, to taste

1. If using fresh mushrooms, wipe clean with a damp cloth. Slice the mushrooms.
2. Bring the chicken broth and milk to a boil in a medium-sized saucepan. Add the mushrooms. Bring back to a boil, and stir in the soy sauce and black pepper. Taste and adjust the seasoning if desired.

Hearty Vegetarian Egg Drop Soup

1 garlic clove
1 zucchini
2 roma tomatoes
1 teaspoon olive oil
4 cups low-sodium vegetable broth

¼ teaspoon salt
⅛ teaspoon (or to taste) black pepper
½ teaspoon dried basil
2 tablespoons egg substitute

1. Smash, peel, and chop the garlic clove. Wash the zucchini, peel, and cut into thin slices. Wash and dice the tomatoes.
2. Heat the olive oil in a medium-sized saucepan over medium-low to medium heat. Add the garlic and the diced tomato, stirring. Cook for a few minutes, then add the zucchini.
3. Add the broth and bring to a boil. Stir in the salt, pepper, and dried basil. Cook for another 2 to 3 minutes. Turn off the heat, stir in the egg substitute, and serve.

Roasted Pepper Medley

1 red bell pepper
1 orange bell pepper
3 packed cups fresh spinach
leaves
2 tomatoes
1 cup canned chickpeas,
drained

4 tablespoons red wine vinegar
2 teaspoons lemon juice
1 teaspoon extra-virgin olive oil
⅛ teaspoon (or to taste) garlic
powder

Serves 1–2

Letting the roasted pepper sit for several hours drains off the excess moisture. For best results, do this whenever you want to use roasted red pepper in a salad.

1. Wash the bell peppers and pat dry. Wash the spinach leaves and drain thoroughly. Wash the tomatoes and slice.
2. Place a sheet of aluminum foil on a roasting pan. Broil the peppers for 10 minutes or until the skins are blackened. Turn the peppers over after 5 minutes so that both sides blacken. Remove from oven, place in a plastic bag, and seal. Leave the peppers in the bag for at least 10 minutes. Remove the skin from the blackened peppers, cut them in half, and remove the seeds. Cut the peppers into long strips and let sit for 2 to 3 hours. Wipe the strips dry and cut into cubes.
3. Toss the chickpeas with the red wine vinegar, lemon juice, olive oil, and garlic powder. Add the roasted pepper cubes, spinach, and sliced tomatoes. Serve immediately.

Wash Your Fruit and Vegetables!

According to a recent statistic, up to 20 strangers may have handled a tomato by the time it reaches your kitchen. That's 20 opportunities for the fruit to pick up illness-producing bacteria or germs through improper handling. Even fresh produce that is properly handled may carry dirt or pesticides. Always wash fresh fruit and vegetables in cold drinking water before eating or serving in a recipe. An added tip: Before cleaning the produce, make sure to wash your hands in soapy water so that you don't accidentally pass on unwanted germs.

Spring Roll Salad

1 cup mung bean sprouts
1 carrot
1 red bell pepper
1 (14-ounce) can baby corn

2 teaspoons olive oil
3 teaspoons soy sauce
1 tablespoon red wine vinegar
1 teaspoon granulated sugar

1. Wash the vegetables. Drain the mung bean sprouts thoroughly. Peel the carrot and cut into thin strips about 2 inches long. Cut the red pepper in half, remove the seeds, and cut into thin strips about 2 inches long. Rinse the baby corn in warm water and drain thoroughly.
2. Combine the olive oil, soy sauce, red wine vinegar, and sugar in a jar and shake well. Toss the salad with the dressing. Wait about 30 minutes to serve to give the flavors a chance to blend.

Festive Fruit Salad

2 apples
2 bananas
1 orange

1¾ cups canned pineapple chunks, with juice
2 tablespoons sweetened coconut flakes, optional

1. Wash the apples and cut into slices. Peel the bananas and cut diagonally into 1-inch pieces. Peel the orange and separate into segments.
2. Place the fruit in a large bowl with the pineapple chunks and juice. Cover and refrigerate until ready to serve. Sprinkle with the sweetened coconut flakes, if desired.

Three-Bean Cassoulet

1 garlic clove
4 ounces fresh snap beans or
    other green beans
1 zucchini
⅓ cup chopped white onion
1 cup Romano beans (also
    called Italian flat beans)

¾ cup black-eyed peas
1 cup tomato sauce
1 cup chicken broth or water
1 teaspoon dried parsley flakes
½ teaspoon dried basil
⅛ teaspoon (or to taste) salt

> **Serves 1–2**
>
> To make a more filling dish, cut up 2 or 3 left-over cooked sausages and stir them into the cassoulet during the final 15 minutes of cooking.
>
> ∾

1. Preheat oven to 350°.
2. Smash, peel, and chop the garlic clove. Wash the snap beans and drain. Trim the ends and cut off any brown spots. Wash, peel, and slice the zucchini.
3. Bring a pot of water to a boil. Blanch the snap beans in the boiling water for about 3 minutes, until they turn bright green.
4. Combine the garlic, snap beans, zucchini, onion, Romano beans, black-eyed peas, tomato sauce, and chicken broth or water in an ungreased 1½- or 2-quart casserole dish. Stir in the dried parsley, dried basil, and the salt.
5. Bake for 2 to 2½ hours, stirring occasionally, until the vegetables are tender and the cassoulet has thickened.

Having Fun with Pasta

Tired of spaghetti or linguine? Pasta comes in a number of intriguing shapes and sizes. For example, fusilli are shaped like short "springs," while gnocchi resemble a stuffed shell. And then there are tube-shaped pastas such as penne, manicotti, and rigatoni. The next time you have a yen for pasta, try experimenting with different types.

Vegetarian Cabbage Rolls

Yields 8–10 cabbage rolls

For directions on boiling cabbage leaves, see Cabbage Rolls with Spanish Rice (page 144).

6 ounces firm tofu
2 teaspoons olive oil
1 garlic clove
½ red onion
1 cup crushed tomatoes
½ green bell pepper
½ teaspoon ground cumin

⅛ teaspoon (or to taste) paprika
8–10 boiled cabbage leaves
6 ounces tomato sauce
3 ounces water
2 tablespoons white vinegar
2 teaspoons granulated sugar

1. Preheat oven to 350°. Spray a large baking sheet with nonstick cooking spray.
2. Drain the tofu and dice into small pieces. Heat the olive oil in a medium-sized frying pan. Add the garlic and red onion. Sauté until the onion is tender. Crumble the tofu into the frying pan. Add the tomatoes and green pepper, mashing the tomatoes with a spatula to break them up slightly. Stir in the ground cumin and paprika.
3. Lay a cabbage leaf flat on the counter. Spread 2 heaping tablespoons of filling in the middle (the exact amount needed will depend on the size of the cabbage leaf). Roll up the bottom, tuck in the sides, and continue rolling up to the top. Place the roll in the baking dish, with the seamed section on the bottom.
4. In a small bowl, mix together the tomato sauce, water, white vinegar, and sugar. Pour over the cabbage rolls. Place the dish in the oven and bake the cabbage rolls for 40 to 45 minutes.

Freezing Cabbage Rolls

Frozen cabbage rolls reheat very nicely, making a quick and easy dinner for busy weeknights. Allow the cooked cabbage rolls to cool and place in resealable plastic freezer bags with a small amount of tomato sauce. Thaw before reheating.

Easy Eggplant Parmigiana

1 medium eggplant
½ teaspoon dried basil
½ teaspoon dried oregano
⅛ teaspoon (or to taste) garlic salt

1 cup spaghetti sauce
6 slices soy mozzarella cheese
¼ cup grated soy Parmesan cheese

Serves 2–4

This quick and easy version of the Italian classic is made with soy cheese for vegetarians who don't eat dairy products. Unfortunately, melted soy cheese can have a slightly rubbery texture, so vegetarians who do consume dairy may want to stick with regular mozzarella.

1. Preheat oven to 350°. Spray an 8" × 8" baking pan with nonstick cooking spray.
2. Wash the eggplant and cut into slices about ¼ inch thick. Stir the dried basil, dried oregano, and garlic salt into the spaghetti sauce.
3. Lay out half the eggplant slices flat on the prepared baking pan. Spoon the spaghetti sauce over the top.
4. Cover the eggplant with foil and bake for 20 minutes or until tender. Remove from the oven. Uncover and lay the soy mozzarella slices on top.
5. Bake for another 3 to 5 minutes, until the cheese melts. Sprinkle with the Parmesan cheese and serve.

Chicken with Marinated Artichoke Hearts—for Four

It's easy to adjust the recipe for Chicken with Marinated Artichoke Hearts (page 79) to serve 4 people. Replace the chicken thighs with 4 boneless chicken breasts, approximately 7 ounces each, and cook according to the recipe instructions. In addition to the tomato sauce and vegetables, add 1 can condensed cream of mushroom soup to the cooked chicken. Simmer, covered, for 30 to 35 minutes. Serve over 3 cups of cooked rice or noodles.

Chili Bean Soup

Serves 6

Heat up the leftovers from this recipe for a perfect late-night snack for you and your friends.

1 pound dried pink beans
6–8 cups water
1 teaspoon garlic salt
1 teaspoon onion salt
¼ teaspoon dried thyme
¼ teaspoon dried marjoram

1¼ cups reduced-sodium, fat-free beef or chicken broth
1 (16-ounce) can chopped tomatoes
1 packet chili seasoning mix
1 cup hot water

1. Rinse the beans and soak them overnight in cold water to cover. Drain.
2. Place the beans in a large pot and add the water, garlic salt, onion salt, thyme, and marjoram. Bring to a boil, reduce the heat to low, and cover; simmer for 2½ to 3 hours until tender. Add hot water if necessary to keep the beans from boiling dry.
3. Spoon out 1 cup of the beans and about ½ cup of liquid from the pot; using a potato masher, mash them thoroughly. Return them to the pot, along with the broth, tomatoes, chili mix, and the 1 cup hot water. Stir well and heat for at least 10 minutes to blend the flavors. Ladle into soup bowls and serve.

Turkey Chili

1 pound uncooked turkey
½ onion
2 cloves garlic
2 tablespoons chopped
    jalapeño chilies
1 (15- to 16-ounce can) white
    beans
1 (15- to 16-ounce can)
    chickpeas (garbanzo beans)
2 tablespoons olive oil

4 teaspoons ground cumin
1 teaspoon summer savory
1 teaspoon marjoram
½ pound ground turkey
4 cups chicken broth
¼ cup pearl barley
Hot sauce
Salt and pepper
Cheddar cheese, grated

Serves 4

This protein-packed chili
makes a great meal
during exam period!

∾

1. Cut the turkey into ½-inch cubes. Mince the onion and garlic. Seed and chop the jalapeños. Drain and rinse the beans.
2. In a soup pot, heat the oil. Sauté the onion and garlic on medium heat for 3 minutes. Stir in the cumin, savory, and marjoram and cook for half a minute. Add both kinds of turkey, sautéing them until browned slightly. Pour in the broth and stir in the barley and the jalapeños. Bring to a boil, reduce to a simmer, and cook for 30 minutes.
3. Add the beans and a dash of hot sauce, and salt and pepper to taste; simmer for another 10 minutes. Top with the grated cheese and serve.

Chapter 6

Beat the Heat: What to Make with a Hot Plate

Pan-Fried "French" Fries

2 slices bacon
1 baking potato

2 tablespoons olive oil, or more
as needed
Salt, to taste

1. Cook the bacon on low heat until crispy. Remove from the frying pan and set aside. Do not clean out the pan.
2. While the bacon is cooking, wash and peel the potato. Cut lengthwise into pieces about ¼ to ½ inch thick.
3. Place the olive oil in a small bowl. Toss the potato slices in the oil.
4. Lay the potato slices in the frying pan, reserving any oil left in the bowl. Cook on medium heat for 10 minutes or until browned on one side. Turn over and add the reserved olive oil. Cook for another 10 minutes or until browned, adding more oil if necessary. Remove the fries and drain on paper towels. Sprinkle with salt before serving. Serve the bacon with the fries, either whole or chopped.

Protein-Packed Potato

The skyrocketing popularity of low-carbohydrate diets has caused pota-toes sales to drop recently. That's too bad, because the common spud is really a dieter's friend. Besides being an excellent source of vitamin C and potassium, potatoes are fat-free and low in calories. A medium-sized baked potato contains a mere 100 calories and enough energy to see you through a long afternoon of classes.

Basic Mashed Potatoes for One

1 large potato
1 tablespoon butter or
    margarine

1½ teaspoons milk, or as
    needed
Salt and pepper, to taste

1. Wash and peel the potato, and cut into quarters. Fill a medium-sized saucepan with enough salted water to cover the potato and bring to a boil.
2. Cook the potato in the boiling water until tender and easily pierced with a fork (about 5 minutes). Drain.
3. Place the potato in a bowl and add the butter or margarine. Mash using a fork or a potato masher. Add the milk a bit at a time as you are mashing, being sure not to add more than is needed. Mash until the potato is fluffy. Stir in the salt and pepper.

> **Serves 1**
>
> You can spice up this basic recipe by adding paprika, garlic powder, nutmeg, or other seasonings with the salt and pepper.
>
> ❧

Basic Cooked Pasta

8 ounces dried pasta
About 8 cups water

1 tablespoon salt

1. Rinse the pasta and drain.
2. Bring the water to boil in a large saucepan, making sure there is enough water to cover the pasta. Add the salt to make it boil faster.
3. Add the pasta to the boiling water. Stir with a wooden spoon, separating the individual pieces. Cook the pasta until tender but still firm (al dente).
4. Drain the pasta in a colander in the sink, being sure to lift the colander to get rid of all excess water. If using the pasta in a cold salad, rinse it in cold water and drain. Otherwise, do not rinse the pasta, and serve immediately.

> **Yields about 2 cups**
>
> The trick to making pasta is to make sure there is enough water for the pasta to move around while cooking, and to separate the pasta strands immediately after adding them to the boiling water.
>
> ❧

Coconut Risotto

1 tablespoon olive oil	¾ cup chicken broth
½ cup arborio rice	1 cup coconut milk
¼ cup water	Salt and pepper, to taste

1. Heat the olive oil in a medium-sized saucepan. Add the rice, stirring until the grains become shiny and translucent. Add the water. Cook on medium heat, stirring constantly, until the water is nearly absorbed, approximately 20 minutes.
2. Slowly add the chicken broth, ¼ cup at a time, stirring constantly and adding more as the liquid is absorbed. When the broth is nearly absorbed, repeat the process with the coconut milk. Stir in the salt and pepper, and serve.

Basic Cooked Converted Rice

1 cup converted rice	1 tablespoon butter or
2 cups water	margarine

In a medium-sized saucepan, bring the rice and water to a boil, uncovered, on medium heat. Let the mixture boil until holes, or "craters," appear in the rice. Cover tightly, reduce heat to low, and simmer until all the water has evaporated (20 to 25 minutes). Add the butter, fluff up the rice, and serve.

Dry Rice Problems

Find that your rice is turning out dry, even though you're using the same amount of water as usual? Check the date on the bag. Like flour, rice dries out as it ages. Try adding a bit more water during cooking.

Basic Cooked Long-Grain Rice

1 cup long-grain rice   *1½ cups water*

In a medium-sized saucepan, bring the rice and water to a boil. Partially cover the pot, reduce heat to low, and cook until you see holes, or "craters," in the rice. Cover tightly and simmer until the water has evaporated, about 20 minutes. Fluff up the rice and serve.

Pasta-Cooking Tips

To prevent overcooked pasta, be sure the water has come to a full boil before adding the pasta to the pot. To see if the pasta is cooked, fish 1 piece out of the pot and check. Cooked pasta will be a solid color throughout, with no white in the middle.

Chicken-Flavored Risotto Side Dish

2 carrots   *¼ teaspoon salt*
2 tablespoons olive oil   *⅛ teaspoon pepper*
½ cup chopped onion   *2 cups chicken broth*
1 cup arborio or short-grain rice *1 tablespoon grated Parmesan*
½ cup water   *cheese, optional*

1. Wash, peel, and dice the carrots.
2. Heat the olive oil in a medium-sized saucepan. Add the onion and cook until tender. Stir in the rice so that the grains are mixed with the olive oil. Cook for 3 to 4 minutes, until the grains turn shiny.
3. Add the water. Cook until it is nearly absorbed. Stir in the salt and pepper, and add the carrots. Stir in ½ cup of chicken broth. Continue adding the broth, ½ cup at a time, stirring constantly. The rice is cooked when it is rich and creamy (about 25 minutes). Stir in the Parmesan cheese, if desired.

Yields 3 cups

The extra starch in long-grain rice makes it cook up nice and fluffy.

❧

Serves 2–4

This recipe can easily be doubled or halved to serve more or fewer people, as needed. Feel free to replace 1 cup of the chicken broth with 1 cup of milk for a creamier risotto.

❧

Spanish Rice

½ red onion
½ green bell pepper
2 teaspoons olive oil
1 pound ground beef
1½ cups crushed tomatoes
1½ cups water

2 cups cooked white rice
Salt and pepper, to taste
¼ teaspoon ground cumin
¼ teaspoon (or to taste)
   cayenne pepper

1. Peel and chop the red onion. Wash the green bell pepper, remove the seeds, and dice.
2. Heat the olive oil in a frying pan. Add the onion and cook on medium-low heat until tender. Add the green pepper.
3. Spoon the vegetables into a bowl and add the ground beef to the pan. Brown the ground beef and drain off most of the fat. Add the crushed tomatoes, water, and cooked rice. Stir in the salt and pepper, ground cumin, and cayenne pepper. Cover and simmer for another 20 minutes, or until the water is absorbed. Serve hot.

Cooking Brown Rice

Cooking instructions for brown rice are nearly identical to those for long-grain white rice. Use 1½ cups of water for every cup of rice. Bring the water to a boil, cover the saucepan tightly with a lid, and let the rice simmer for 30 minutes or until the water has evaporated. Turn off the heat and let stand, covered, for another 10 minutes. Do not stir.

Chili con Carne

*2 tablespoons butter or
    margarine*
1 pound ground beef
½ red onion, chopped
½ green bell pepper, chopped
*1 tablespoon (or to taste) chili
    powder*
½ teaspoon (or to taste) cumin

*½ teaspoon (or to taste) garlic
    powder*
1 tablespoon granulated sugar
*2 cups canned kidney beans,
    with liquid*
*2 cups canned crushed
    tomatoes*

> **Serves 4**
>
> Feel free to adjust the
> seasonings to make this
> dish as spicy or as mild
> as you like.
>
> ∾

1. Melt the butter in a frying pan over medium heat. Add the ground beef. When the pink color is nearly gone and the ground beef is nearly cooked through, add the onion and green pepper. Cook for another couple of minutes until the ground beef is fully cooked. Drain excess fat from the pan.
2. Stir in the chili powder, cumin, garlic powder, and sugar. Add the kidney beans and crushed tomatoes. Mix thoroughly.
3. Cover and simmer the chili on low heat for at least 30 minutes. Taste and add more seasonings if desired. Serve hot.

How to Store Excess Ground Beef

Have more fresh ground beef than you need for one meal, no access to a freezer, and no desire to dine on ground beef two nights in a row? The solution: Cook the entire amount and store what you don't need in a sealed container in the refrigerator immediately after cooking (this helps prevent bacteria growth). Use within 3 or 4 days.

Ground Beef Stroganoff

16 ounces egg noodles
2 tablespoons butter or margarine
½ red onion, chopped
1 cup canned sliced mushrooms, drained
1¼ pounds ground beef

⅛ teaspoon (or to taste) salt
⅛ teaspoon (or to taste) black pepper
½ teaspoon (or to taste) dried parsley flakes
½ cup beef broth
¼ cup (or to taste) sour cream

1. Cook the egg noodles according to the package directions. Drain and set aside.
2. Melt the butter or margarine in a frying pan over medium heat. Add the chopped onion and the mushrooms. Sauté until the onion is tender. Remove the onion and mushrooms from the pan.
3. Add the ground beef to the pan. Cook on medium heat until browned. Drain off any excess fat. Stir in the salt, pepper, and dried parsley.
4. Add the onion and mushrooms back to the pan. Add the beef broth. Heat through, and stir in the sour cream. Heat for a few more minutes, and serve over the noodles.

Leftover Ground Beef?

How long can uncooked ground beef be refrigerated? Refrigerate the ground beef immediately after arriving home from the store. Use within 2 days. For longer storage, the meat needs to be frozen.

Steak for Roommates

Serves 4

This is a great recipe for nights when you and your roommates want something that's quick to make but also filling.

∾

2 pounds round steak
½ teaspoon mild curry powder
4 tablespoons all-purpose flour
2–3 tablespoons oil, as needed
1 small onion, peeled and
   chopped

1 (10¾-ounce) can condensed
   cream of celery soup, plus
   1 can water
2 tablespoons Worcestershire
   sauce

1. Cut the beef across the grain (see "How to Cut Beef Across the Grain"), and remove any excess fat. Blend the curry powder into the flour. Dredge the beef in the flour.
2. Heat the oil in a heavy skillet. When the oil is hot, cook the meat on medium to medium-high heat until browned. Push the meat off to the sides and add the onion in the middle of the pan. Cook until the onion is tender.
3. Add the soup, water, and Worcestershire sauce. Cover and cook for 20 minutes on medium heat. Turn the heat up to medium-high and cook for another 10 minutes. Serve hot over rice.

How to Cut Beef Across the Grain

If you look at a piece of flank steak, you will see lines running across it. These are the muscle fibers, or "grains." To cut beef across the grain, simply cut across—and not parallel to—the muscle fibers. This helps tenderize the beef by shocking the muscle fibers.

Easy Pork Chops for a Crowd

Serves 4–8

Turn the heat up or down on this dish by using mild or strong curry power as desired. Serve with Basic Mashed Potatoes for One (page 93) (adjusted to serve more people as required) for a complete meal.

2 pounds boneless, center-cut loin pork chops (about 8 chops)
1 teaspoon curry powder
1 tablespoon vegetable oil
2 slices fresh ginger
1 (10¾-ounce) can condensed tomato soup, plus 1 can water
1 tablespoon, plus 1 teaspoon Worcestershire sauce
2 teaspoons granulated sugar
½ white onion, chopped

1. Preheat oven to 350°.
2. Wash the pork chops and pat dry. Trim off the fat. Rub the curry powder lightly over both sides.
3. Heat the oil in a large nonstick frying pan on medium heat. Lay the chops flat in the pan. Cook for a total of 15 minutes over medium heat, turning over once, until both sides are browned. Add the ginger slices and cook for another minute. Drain off excess fat.
4. Transfer the pork chops to a 9" × 13" casserole dish, removing the ginger. Combine the tomato soup, water, Worcestershire sauce, sugar, and onion. Pour over the chops. Bake for 1 hour, or until the pork chops are tender and cooked through.

Baking Potatoes

"Baking Potatoes" is the name commonly given to russet (also called Idaho) potatoes. Large, brown-skinned, and long or oblong-shaped, the high starch and low moisture content of russets make them an excellent choice for French fries (see French Fries from Scratch, page 110) or baking (see Basic Baked Potato, page 201).

Sweet-and-Sour Pork

1 pound lean boneless pork
½ large green or red bell
pepper
¼ cup baby carrots
1 green onion, optional
⅓ cup white vinegar

2 tablespoons ketchup
3 tablespoons granulated sugar
⅓ cup, plus 2 tablespoons
water
2 tablespoons vegetable oil
1 tablespoon cornstarch

> **Serves 2–4**
>
> Adding cornstarch and water is a quick way to thicken the sauce. Always mix the cornstarch with water in a small bowl first. Never try adding the cornstarch directly to the sauce.
>
> ❧

1. Cut the pork into cubes. Wash and drain all the vegetables. Cut the bell pepper into cubes, and cut the baby carrots in half. Dice the green onion, if using.
2. In a small bowl, combine the vinegar, ketchup, sugar, and ⅓ cup water, and set aside.
3. Heat the oil in a frying pan on medium to medium-high heat. When the oil is hot, add the pork cubes and brown. Drain off the fat from the pan and add the sauce. Reduce heat to medium-low, cover, and simmer for 45 minutes or until tender.
4. Combine the cornstarch and 2 tablespoons water in a small bowl. Increase heat to high and add the cornstarch mixture, stirring to thicken. Reduce heat to medium and add the green pepper and carrots. Cover and simmer for 10 minutes or until the vegetables are tender. Stir in the green onion if using. Serve hot over rice.

Frying Meat First

Many recipes such as Simple Pepper Steak (page 103) call for the meat to be fried first, then removed from the pan and added back in the final stages of cooking. This cooking technique serves 2 purposes. Besides ensuring that everything is thoroughly cooked, it keeps the meat from overpowering the other ingredients, so that all the flavors come through.

Chicken in Walnut Sauce

4 chicken thighs
1½ teaspoons olive oil
1 ounce (or more to taste) snow
  peas
¼ small white onion
1 garlic clove
½ cup chicken broth

2 tablespoons walnut crumbs
¼ teaspoon (or to taste) chili
  sauce or other hot sauce
½ cup cooked rice, using Basic
  Cooked Long-Grain Rice
  recipe (page 95)

1. Wash the chicken thighs and pat dry. Remove the skin and any large pieces of fat.
2. Heat the olive oil in a deep-sided frying pan. Add the chicken thighs and cook over medium heat until browned on both sides. Transfer to a plate covered with a paper towel to drain. Do not clean out the frying pan.
3. While the chicken is cooking, wash the snow peas, blanch, and drain (see Appendix A for blanching instructions). Peel and chop the onion. Smash, peel, and chop the garlic.
4. Add the onion and garlic to the frying pan. Cook over low heat until the onion is tender. Add the chicken broth, walnut crumbs, and chili sauce. Increase heat to medium to medium-high and bring to a boil, stirring constantly. Add the snow peas.
5. Add the chicken thighs. Reduce heat to medium low, cover, and simmer for about 15 minutes, stirring occasionally. Make sure the thighs are fully cooked. Prepare the rice while the chicken is cooking. Serve hot.

Rice Types

Ever wonder what the difference is between long-grain, medium, and short-grain rice? It all comes down to starch. Long-grain rice has more of a type of starch called amylase, which makes it fluff up nicely. At the other end, short-grain rice has a starch called amolypectin, which makes it sticky. Medium-grain rice is a combination of short and long grain.

Simple Pepper Steak

12 ounces beef round steak
2 tablespoons soy sauce,
divided
1 teaspoon cornstarch
1 green bell pepper
¼ cup chopped onion

1 garlic clove
2 tablespoons olive oil
½ cup crushed tomatoes
½ cup water
1 teaspoon granulated sugar
¼ teaspoon celery salt

> **Serves 2–4**
>
> If desired, this recipe can easily be halved to make dinner for one. Serve with cooked brown rice for a nutritious meal.
>
> ∽

1. Cut the beef across the grain into thin strips about 2 inches long (see "How to Cut Beef Across the Grain," page 99). Place the beef in a bowl. Add 1 tablespoon of the soy sauce and the cornstarch to the beef, mixing the cornstarch into the meat with your fingers. Let marinate for 20 to 30 minutes.

2. While the beef is marinating, prepare the vegetables. Wash the pepper, remove the seeds, and cut into cubes. Peel and chop the onion. Smash, peel, and chop the garlic clove.

3. Heat 1 tablespoon olive oil in a frying pan. Add the meat. Cook until browned on both sides. Remove and set aside.

4. Clean out the pan and add 1 tablespoon olive oil. Add the chopped onion and garlic clove. Cook on medium heat until the onion is tender. Add the crushed tomatoes, water, sugar, celery salt, and the remaining 1 tablespoon soy sauce. Bring to a boil, reduce heat to medium-low, and cook for 5 minutes.

5. Return the meat to the pan. Cover and simmer for 45 minutes or until the meat is tender. Serve hot with brown rice.

Beef and Onion Rings: A Classic Combination

When making Budget Beef, Liver, and Onions (page 106) you can make onion rings instead of chopped onion. To make the onion rings, peel the onion, slice, and separate the rings. Instead of cooking the onions in bacon fat, clean out the frying pan and add 2 tablespoons butter or margarine. Fry the rings as you would chopped onion, remove from the pan, and clean out the pan before adding the liver. Follow the recipe directions from that point.

Simple Beef Stir-Fry

2 bok choy stalks with leaves	1 tablespoon soy sauce
1 garlic clove	4 teaspoons prepared stir-fry
8 ounces round beef steak	sauce
1 tablespoon vegetable oil	½ teaspoon granulated sugar

1. Wash the bok choy and drain. Shred the leaves and cut the stalks into thin slices on the diagonal. Smash and peel the garlic clove. Cut the beef into thin strips about 2 inches long.
2. Heat 1 teaspoon of the oil in a frying pan. Add the garlic. Cook briefly and add the bok choy. Splash the soy sauce over the bok choy. Cook until the stalks are tender.
3. Push the bok choy off to the sides of the pan or remove. Add the remaining oil. When the oil is hot, add the beef and cook until browned. Mix in the stir-fry sauce and sugar. Mix the bok choy in with the beef and heat through. Serve hot.

Hot Plate Noodles with Pork

8 ounces egg noodles	1 (10¾-ounce) can condensed
4 boneless pork chops	mushroom soup
½ small white onion	5 ounces water
½ cup baby carrots	

1. Cook the noodles according to the package instructions. Drain thoroughly.
2. Rinse the pork chops, pat dry, and trim off any fat. Peel the onion and chop. Wash and drain the baby carrots.
3. Lay the pork chops flat in a large nonstick frying pan. Cook for a total of 15 minutes on medium heat, turning over once, until both sides are browned. Drain excess fat from the pan.
4. Add the soup, water, onion, and carrots. Cook for 30 minutes or until the pork chops are tender. Mix in the noodles. Serve hot.

Chicken Creole

8 (7- to 8-ounce) bone-in
   chicken thighs
2 garlic cloves
1 small white onion
4 celery stalks
1 green bell pepper
4 teaspoons olive oil, divided
1¾ cups crushed tomatoes
¼ teaspoon (or to taste)
   cayenne pepper

½ teaspoon dried thyme
½ teaspoon (or to taste) dried
   parsley
1 bay leaf, optional
Salt and pepper, to taste
1 package Lipton's Chicken
   Risotto or 2 recipes Chicken-
   Flavored Risotto Side Dish
   (page 95)

Serves 4

This recipe is designed
to provide lots of sauce
to mix in with the risotto.

∽

1. Remove the skin from the chicken thighs. Rinse the chicken thighs and pat dry.
2. Smash, peel, and chop the garlic cloves. Peel and chop the onion. Wash the celery and green pepper. Cut the green pepper in half, remove the seeds, and cut into bite-sized chunks. Cut the celery on the diagonal into 1-inch pieces.
3. Heat 1 teaspoon of the oil on medium-high in a deep-sided frying pan. Add the chicken thighs and cook until browned on both sides. Transfer to a plate.
4. Clean out the frying pan. Heat the remaining olive oil. Add the garlic and onion. Cook over medium heat until the onion is tender. Add the celery and bell pepper. Add the crushed tomatoes, cayenne pepper, thyme, dried parsley, bay leaf if using, and salt and pepper.
5. Return the chicken to the pan and reduce heat to medium-low. Cover and simmer for 25 minutes or until the chicken juices run clear when pierced with a fork.
6. While the chicken is simmering, prepare the risotto. When the chicken is done, remove the bay leaf. Serve over the risotto.

Basic Hamburgers

½ teaspoon salt
½ teaspoon black pepper
1 pound ground beef
¼ cup finely chopped onion
1 cup bread crumbs
¼ cup Worcestershire sauce
2 tablespoons butter or
   margarine
6–8 hamburger buns, as
   needed

1. Mix the salt and pepper with the ground beef. Mix in the chopped onion, bread crumbs, and Worcestershire sauce. Form the ground beef into 6 to 8 patties.
2. Melt the butter or margarine in a frying pan. Add the hamburger patties and cook for a total of 6 to 8 minutes or until browned on each side and cooked through, turning the burgers only once. Toast the hamburger buns before assembling the burgers if desired.

Budget Beef, Liver, and Onions

1 pound beef liver
¼ teaspoon dried parsley
⅛ teaspoon (or to taste) salt
⅛ teaspoon (or to taste) black
   pepper
2 tablespoons all-purpose flour
2 slices bacon
Vegetable oil, as needed
1 cup chopped white onion
½ cup tomato sauce
½ cup water

1. Rinse off the liver. In a shallow dish, stir the dried parsley, salt, and pepper into the flour. Dredge the liver in the flour and set aside.
2. Cook the bacon and remove from the pan. Do not clean out the pan. Add vegetable oil if there is not enough fat from the bacon to cook the onion.
3. Add the chopped onion and cook until tender and shiny. Remove from the frying pan. Clean out the pan.
4. Heat 1 tablespoon vegetable oil. Add the liver. Cook on medium heat until browned.
5. Return the onion and bacon to the frying pan with the liver. Add the tomato sauce and water. Cover and simmer on low heat for 30 to 35 minutes or until the liver is tender.

Curried Shrimp with Coconut Risotto

*2 cups Coconut Risotto
   (page 94) (about 1 recipe)*
*1 pound peeled and deveined
   medium shrimp*
2 tablespoons olive oil
*2 small garlic cloves, chopped
   (about 1 tablespoon)*

½ cup chopped white onion
⅓ cup tomato sauce
⅓ cup coconut milk
1 teaspoon curry powder
¼ teaspoon ground ginger
¼ teaspoon salt
Black pepper, to taste

Serves 2–4

Don't feel like rich risotto? This dish can also be served with long-grain rice. If using long-grain rice, you may want to increase the amount of sauce to serve over the rice. Just add equal amounts tomato sauce and coconut milk as needed.

∾

1. Prepare the Coconut Risotto.
2. If using frozen shrimp, rinse under cold running water for 3 minutes or until thawed. If using fresh shrimp, let stand in warm salted water for 5 minutes. Pat the shrimp dry with paper towels.
3. Heat the olive oil in a frying pan. Add the chopped garlic and onion. Cook on medium-low heat until the onion is tender. Add the shrimp. Cook on medium heat until the shrimp turns pink.
4. Stir in the tomato sauce, coconut milk, curry powder, ginger, salt, and pepper. Cook over medium-low heat for 5 minutes, until heated through. Serve over the risotto.

Rinsing Fresh Shrimp

Rinsing shrimp in warm salted water firms them up and brings out their flavor. When preparing the salted water, the idea is to reproduce the salty flavor of the ocean. For every cup of warm water, add at least ½ teaspoon of salt. Let the shrimp stand in the water for between 5 to 15 minutes, and pat dry with paper towels.

Quick and Easy Shrimp Creole

Serves 2

Made with fresh tomatoes and paprika instead of crushed tomatoes and cayenne, this dish has a more subtle flavor than Chicken Creole (page 105).

2 cups fresh shrimp
1 garlic clove
1 large tomato
1 celery stalk
3 teaspoons olive oil, divided

¼ cup chopped red onion
¼ cup water
¼ teaspoon paprika
½ teaspoon dried thyme

1. Rinse the shrimp by letting them stand in warm salted water for 5 minutes. Pat dry with paper towels.
2. Smash, peel, and chop the garlic clove. Wash and dry the tomato and celery. Slice the tomato, being careful not to lose any of the juice. Cut the celery stalk on the diagonal into 1-inch slices.
3. Heat 1 teaspoon of the olive oil in a frying pan. Add the shrimp and cook until they turn pink.
4. Push the shrimp off to the side of the frying pan and add the remaining 2 teaspoons olive oil in the middle. Add the chopped garlic and onion. Cook until the onion is tender.
5. Add the tomato, celery, water, paprika, and thyme. Gently push down on the tomato slices to break them up and squeeze out the juice. Cover and simmer on low heat for about 15 minutes, until the tomatoes are tender and the juice from the tomatoes is thoroughly mixed with the water. Serve with rice.

Flavorful Cooked Rice

Want to add extra flavor the next time you're preparing boiled rice? Try replacing the water with another liquid. Coconut milk, chicken or vegetable broth, and even fruit juices work well. The only limit is your imagination!

Sautéed Mushrooms

*3 ounces fresh button
    mushrooms*
1½ tablespoons olive oil

*1½ tablespoons butter or
    margarine*
*⅛ teaspoon (or to taste) chili
    powder*

1. Clean the mushrooms with a damp cloth. Slice thinly and cut off the stems if desired.
2. Heat the olive oil in the frying pan. Lay the mushrooms flat in the pan. Cook on medium heat until most of the oil is absorbed, about 3 to 5 minutes.
3. Add the butter or margarine. Stir in the chili powder. Cook the mushrooms on medium-high heat, stirring frequently, for 2 to 3 minutes or until browned. Serve hot.

> **Serves 1–2**
>
> Cooking mushrooms releases their water content, giving them extra flavor. Feel free to adapt this basic recipe to use with stronger-tasting mushrooms, such as portobello.
>
> ∾

Steamed Broccoli

4 ounces broccoli   *Water, as needed*

1. Wash the broccoli and drain. Chop the broccoli into bite-sized pieces.
2. Fill a medium-sized saucepan with 1 inch of water. Place a metal steamer inside the pan. Make sure the water is not touching the bottom of the steamer. Heat the water to boiling.
3. When the water is boiling, add the broccoli pieces to the steamer. Cover and steam until the broccoli is tender, about 10 minutes. Drain and serve.

> **Serves 1–2**
>
> Next to enjoying them raw in a salad, steaming is the healthiest method of preparing vegetables, as it seals in their nutrients. You can use this same method to steam a variety of vegetables, from asparagus to snap peas.
>
> ∾

Buying Cheaper Beef

Don't feel that your only options for beef are ground beef, steak, or stewing meat. Cheaper cuts of beef, such as beef liver and oxtails, taste fine when braised or cooked in a sauce, as in Budget Beef, Liver, and Onions (page 106).

French Fries from Scratch

5 cups vegetable oil for frying,   *4 large baking potatoes*
*   or more as needed*

1. Add the oil to a deep-sided heavy saucepan or a wok. Heat the oil until it is at least 350°.
2. While the oil is heating, wash and peel the potatoes. Cut lengthwise into pieces about ¼ to ½ inch thick. Place in a bowl of cold water for 5 minutes. Drain thoroughly and dry with paper towels.
3. Make sure paper towels are handy near the stove before you begin deep-frying. To cook, carefully slide the sliced potatoes into the hot oil, a handful at a time. Deep-fry for 4 to 5 minutes, until golden brown and crispy. Carefully remove with a slotted spoon and drain on paper towels. Fry the next batch.
4. When all the potatoes have been fried once, raise the oil temperature to 375°. Deep-fry the French fries a second time for about 2 minutes, until crispy. Remove with a slotted spoon and drain. Serve with salt, ketchup, or vinegar as desired.

Chapter 7

Nuke It! Microwave Meals

Easy Omelet

2 eggs
2 tablespoons milk
Salt and pepper, to taste

1 tablespoon butter or
   margarine
2 slices American cheese or ¼
   cup grated cheese

1. In a small bowl, lightly beat the eggs with the milk. Stir in the salt and pepper.
2. Place the butter or margarine in a microwave-safe shallow bowl. Microwave on high heat for 15 seconds or until the butter melts.
3. Pour the egg mixture into the butter and stir to mix. Microwave on high heat for 1 to 2 minutes, until the egg mixture is nearly cooked. Add the American cheese slices or grated cheese on top. Microwave for another 30 seconds or until the cheese melts.

Soy Cheese Breakfast

2 slices rye bread
1 cup soy cheese
4 teaspoons granola

1 teaspoon toasted wheat germ
8 tablespoons cranberry juice

1. Toast the bread, cut into cubes, and set aside.
2. Combine the remaining ingredients in a microwave-safe bowl. Microwave on medium-high heat for 2 minutes. Stir, and then microwave in 1-minute intervals for another 1 to 3 minutes, stirring regularly, until the cheese melts. Use a dipping fork to dip the bread cubes.

Your Microwave Knows Best

Always follow the owner's manual when it comes to choosing the correct temperature and power for defrosting meat, reheating food, and preparing specialty items such as popcorn. This will give the best results with your specific size and model of microwave.

Microwave Borscht

1 tablespoon butter or
margarine
¼ cup chopped white onion
2 cups water

2 beef bouillon cubes
1 cup canned beets
1 teaspoon granulated sugar
1 teaspoon lemon juice

1. Combine the butter or margarine and the onion in a microwave-safe casserole dish. Microwave on high heat for 1 minute. Stir and microwave for another 1 to 2 minutes, until the onion is tender.
2. Add the water, beef bouillon, beets, sugar, and lemon juice. Microwave on high heat for 3 minutes. Stir and microwave for another 2 to 3 minutes. Serve hot or cold.

> **Serves 1**
>
> For a thicker soup, increase the amount of canned beets to 1½ cups. Like all borscht recipes, this can be served hot or cold, plain or garnished with a bit of sour cream.
>
> ∾

Easy Onion Soup au Gratin for One

1½ cups water
2 tablespoons instant onion
soup mix (about ½
package)

1 slice crusty bread or toast
⅓ cup grated Cheddar cheese

1. Place the water in a microwave-safe casserole dish. Stir in the onion soup mix.
2. Microwave on high heat for 2 minutes until the soup is heated through.
3. Cut the crusty bread or toast into several cubes. Add the cubes and sprinkle the grated cheese on top. Microwave on high heat for 3 more minutes or until the cheese melts.

> **Serves 1**
>
> Don't have a hot plate? This quick and easy recipe shows you how to prepare instant soup mixes in the microwave.
>
> ∾

Microwave Green Beans

Serves 1–2

The trick to this recipe is making sure the green beans are covered with the broth. This recipe also works well with fresh snow peas—be sure to trim the ends before cooking.

3½ ounces fresh green beans   *⅓ cup chicken broth*

1. Rinse the green beans under cold, running water. Drain and pat dry.
2. Place the green beans in a microwave-safe bowl and cover with the chicken broth. Cook on high heat for 1½ to 2 minutes, or until they are crisp and bright green. Serve with butter, margarine, or soy sauce if desired.

Wrapping Food

When covering food in plastic or wax paper to be cooked, be sure to leave a corner opened. This allows steam to vent through the opening.

Fruity Snow Peas

Serves 2–3

Canned fruit cocktail juice adds a sweet flavor to delicate snow peas. It would make a nice side dish to accompany tart Lemony Chicken (page 167).

6 ounces fresh snow peas   *½ cup canned fruit cocktail juice*

1. Rinse the snow peas under cold, running water. Drain and pat dry. Trim the ends.
2. Place the snow peas in a shallow, microwave-safe bowl and add the fruit cocktail juice. Cook on high heat for 1½ to 2 minutes or until the snow peas are crisp and bright green.

Are Your Dishes Microwave Safe?

There is an easy way to find out. Fill the dish with water and microwave on high heat. If the water heats up and the dish remains room temperature, it is safe to use.

Corn on the Cob

1 ear corn

Remove the husk from the corn. Wrap the corn in wax paper and place on a paper towel or microwave-safe dish. Microwave on high heat for 2 to 3 minutes. Let stand in microwave for a few minutes. Serve with salt and butter if desired.

Setting the Microwave Temperature

Many microwaves are automatically set to cook everything at high power. Check the instruction manual to find out how to cook food at lower temperatures.

> **Serves 1**
>
> The microwave gives a quick and easy alternative to boiling corn in a large pot of water. If cooking 2 ears of corn at once, increase the cooking time to 4 to 5 minutes.
>
> ∾

Baked Potato

1 baking potato

1. Wash the potato, scrubbing off any dirt. Pierce the potato in several spots with a fork.
2. Place the potato on a paper plate or microwave-safe plate and cook on high heat for 3 to 7 minutes, until cooked through (the internal temperature should be 210°). Slice the potato open and add whatever the toppings of choice.

Defrosted Meat Warning

Meat defrosted in the microwave should always be cooked immediately afterward. Otherwise, there is a danger of bacteria developing on the partially cooked meat.

> **Serves 1**
>
> Want a bit of melted butter with your baked potato? Slice it open, add 1 tablespoon of butter, and place the potato back into the microwave for about 30 seconds.
>
> ∾

Stuffed Potato

Serves 1

Potato cooking times can vary quite a bit, depending on the exact size of the potato and the power output of your microwave. Feel free to add your own favorite ingredients to the potato stuffing.

∾

1 large (about 8 ounces) baking potato
2 tablespoons sour cream
1 tablespoon butter or margarine

¼ teaspoon paprika
¼ teaspoon salt
Pepper, to taste
2 teaspoons shredded Cheddar cheese

1. Wash the potato, scrubbing off any dirt. Pierce the potato in several spots with a fork.
2. Place the potato on a paper plate or microwave-safe plate and cook on high heat for 3 to 7 minutes, until cooked through. Let the potato sit for about 1 minute before removing from the microwave.
3. Slice the potato open. Carefully scoop out most of the potato, leaving about ¼ inch pulp around the skin.
4. Mash the potato pulp with the sour cream, butter, paprika, salt, and pepper. Sprinkle the shredded cheese on top.
5. Spoon the mixture into the potato shell and microwave for 3 to 5 minutes, until the cheese melts.

How Does a Microwave Work?

Microwaves, which operate within the same frequency as radio waves, bounce off the metal walls of the oven. When the microwaves hit the food, they cause the water molecules in the food to vibrate. This in turn produces the heat that cooks the food. All microwave ovens have duo safety systems to ensure that the microwaves stop moving the moment the oven door is opened so that no radiation escapes into the room.

Easy Egg Noodles

3 cups water   *8 ounces egg noodles*

1. Place the water in a microwave-safe casserole dish. Cook on high heat for 3 to 4 minutes, until the water is hot.
2. Add the noodles, stirring to cover completely with the water. Cook on high heat for 4 to 5 minutes, until the noodles are tender. Drain the water.

Choosing Cooking Times

Cooking times can vary depending on the size and age of your microwave. When following a recipe for the microwave, always cook the food for the minimum time indicated, and then check to see if further cooking is required.

> **Serves 1–2**
>
> The microwave is a quick and easy way to cook noodles without waiting for boiling water. After cooking, use as called for in whatever recipe you are preparing.
>
> ∾

Pocketless Pita Shrimp Creole

⅓ cup leftover Quick and Easy   *1 pocketless pita*
  Shrimp Creole (page 108)

Spread the Shrimp Creole over the middle of the pocketless pita. Roll it up and microwave on medium-high heat for 1 to 2 minutes, until heated through.

Microwaves and Metal Don't Mix!

While microwaves pass right through plastic and glass, they bounce off metal. This can cause sparks or even a fire in the oven. Always use microwave dishes that don't contain metal or lead.

> **Serves 1**
>
> Thicker than regular pita bread and not meant to be filled, pocketless pitas make a flavorful alternative to sliced bread in a sandwich.
>
> ∾

Chicken Creole Sandwich

Serves 1

For a healthier lunch, try using one of the low-fat versions of pita bread.

ᴏᵛ

1 leftover thigh and ¼ cup sauce and vegetables from Chicken Creole (page 105)

1 pita pocket

1. Remove the cooked chicken from the thigh bone and cut into bite-sized pieces.
2. Lay the pita pocket flat. Spread the sauce and vegetables over it. Lay the chicken thigh slices on top.
3. Microwave on medium-high heat for 1 to 2 minutes or until the chicken is heated through. Cut the pita into 6 equal wedges.

Teriyaki Chicken

Serves 1

White wine vinegar makes a convenient substitute for Japanese mirin in this recipe. You can use mirin, saké, or any other type of rice wine in this recipe.

ᴏᵛ

1 (6-ounce) boneless, skinless chicken breast
¼ cup soy sauce

¼ cup white wine vinegar
1 tablespoon granulated sugar

1. Rinse the chicken breast under running water and pat dry. Cut into bite-sized pieces.
2. In a small bowl, mix together the soy sauce, white wine vinegar, and sugar.
3. Place the chicken breast in a microwave-safe glass baking dish. Pour the sauce over the chicken. Cover with plastic wrap.
4. Microwave the chicken on high heat for 3 minutes. Turn the chicken over and microwave for 2 to 3 more minutes, checking every 30 seconds during the last minute of cooking to see if it is done.

Classic Tuna Melt

1 recipe Easy Egg Noodles (page 117)
1 cup frozen peas
1 tablespoon butter or margarine, optional
¼ cup chopped onion, optional

1 (10¾-ounce) can condensed cream of mushroom soup
¾ cup milk
6 ounces Velveeta processed cheese, sliced
8 ounces canned tuna
⅛ teaspoon (or to taste) salt

1. Prepare the Easy Egg Noodles.
2. Place the frozen peas in a microwave-safe bowl. Cover with plastic wrap and microwave on high heat for 2 to 3 minutes, until cooked.
3. Add the butter or margarine and chopped onion to the casserole dish if using. Microwave on high heat for 1½ to 2 minutes or until the onion is tender.
4. Add the cooked peas, soup, milk, Velveeta, tuna, and salt. Cover with plastic wrap. Microwave on medium heat for 2 minutes. Stir and microwave on high heat for 3 to 4 minutes, until the Velveeta melts. Stir in the noodles and cook for 1 to 2 minutes, until the mixture is heated through.

What Can You Microwave?

Because microwaves work by causing water molecules to vibrate, food with a high liquid content cooks best. Casseroles such as Classic Tuna Melt are a good choice. Raw meat should always be combined with a liquid, as in Easy "Tandoori" Chicken (page 121). Without the added liquid, a piece of microwaved chicken might blacken on the outside before being thoroughly cooked through on the inside.

Garlic Chicken

Serves 1

If your microwave is large enough, feel free to microwave the garlic butter with the chicken during the last 30 seconds of cooking.

❧

2 garlic cloves
1 (6-ounce) boneless, skinless chicken breast
1½ teaspoons olive oil

1 teaspoon dried oregano
¼ cup chopped onion
3 tablespoons butter or margarine, divided

1. Smash, peel, and chop the garlic cloves. Rinse the chicken breast under cold, running water and pat dry. Use a pastry brush to brush the olive oil over the chicken. Rub the dried oregano on both sides of the breast.
2. Place the chicken breast in a microwave-safe bowl and cover with plastic wrap. Microwave on high heat for 3 minutes. Turn the chicken over and microwave on high heat for 3 more minutes, or until the chicken is cooked through.
3. Place the onion and 2 tablespoons of the butter or margarine in a microwave-safe bowl. Microwave on high heat for 1 minute. Stir and microwave for 30 seconds. Stir in the garlic and the remaining 1 tablespoon butter or margarine. Microwave for 1 to 1½ minutes, until the onion is tender and the garlic aromatic. Pour the garlic butter over the chicken.

Speedy Reheating in the Microwave

A microwave provides a quick alternative to reheating food on the stovetop. To reheat, spread out the food on a microwave-safe dish, arranging it so that the thicker or meatier sections are on the outside. For meat or other dry foods, add a bit of liquid to speed up cooking. Use the reheat setting if your microwave has one. If not, cook at 70 percent power for 2 to 3 minutes.

Easy "Tandoori" Chicken

2 (7-ounce) boneless, skinless
   chicken breasts
1 teaspoon or to taste curry
   powder

2 teaspoons lemon juice
¼ cup plain yogurt
½ cup coconut milk

1. Rinse the chicken breasts under cold, running water and pat dry with paper towels. Cut 4 diagonal slits on the top side of each chicken breast, being careful not to cut completely through the meat. Turn the breasts over and make 2 to 3 diagonal cuts, again being careful not to cut completely through the meat.
2. Mix the curry powder and lemon juice into the yogurt. Rub the yogurt mixture thoroughly over the chicken breasts so that the yogurt fills the cut areas. Place the breasts in a bowl or plastic container, seal or cover with plastic wrap, and refrigerate overnight.
3. Remove the marinated chicken from the refrigerator and cut into cubes. Place the chicken cubes in a microwave-safe casserole dish. Add the coconut milk. Cover the dish with plastic wrap. Microwave on high heat for 5 minutes.
4. Uncover the chicken and microwave for 1 to 3 more minutes, until the chicken breasts are cooked but still tender.

Potato Cooking Times

The time it takes to cook a potato in the microwave can vary quite a bit, depending on the size of the potato and the strength of your microwave. To be safe, cook the potato on high heat for 3 minutes, check it with a fork, and then continue cooking in 2-minute segments as required. The potato is cooked when it is tender and can easily be pierced with a fork. The skin may also be slightly wrinkled.

Chili

1 tablespoon olive oil or
   margarine
¼ onion, chopped
½ green bell pepper, chopped
½ pound ground beef
½ tablespoon (or to taste) chili
   powder

½ tablespoon brown sugar
1 cup canned chickpeas, with
   liquid
½ cup canned green beans,
   with liquid
1½ cups tomato sauce

1. Place the olive oil and chopped onion in a shallow 2-quart microwave-safe casserole dish. Microwave on high heat for 1 minute. Add the chopped green pepper and microwave on high heat for 1 more minute or until the onion is tender.
2. Stir in the ground beef. Microwave on high heat for 5 minutes. Stir, and cook for 3 to 4 minutes, until the meat is thoroughly browned. Remove from the microwave and drain the fat from the ground beef.
3. Stir in the chili powder and brown sugar. Microwave on high heat for 1 minute.
4. Stir in the chickpeas, green beans, and tomato sauce. Microwave on high heat for 10 to 15 minutes, until the chili has thickened. Make sure the ground beef is cooked through. Enjoy hot.

Blanching Vegetables in the Microwave

The microwave makes a handy alternative to the stovetop for blanching vegetables. To blanch, place a small amount of vegetables in a microwave-safe dish and cover with water. Cook the vegetables on high heat. Depending on the quantity of vegetables used, microwave times for blanching vegetables may be higher than what is shown in Appendix A (page 254) for stovetop blanching.

Garlicky Shrimp

½ pound large shrimp (about
    8 shrimp), shells removed
2 garlic cloves

2 tablespoons butter or
    margarine
½ teaspoon lemon juice
Pinch cayenne pepper

Serves 1

This recipe calls for the larger shrimp, which are also called prawns. Enjoy with French bread for soaking up the buttery sauce!

∾

1. Rinse the shrimp by letting them stand in warm, running water for 5 minutes. Pat dry with paper towels.
2. Smash, peel, and chop the garlic cloves. Place the chopped garlic, butter or margarine, lemon juice, and cayenne pepper in a microwave-safe bowl. Microwave on high heat for 30 seconds. Stir, and microwave for another 30 seconds. Stir again, and microwave for 15 to 30 seconds.
3. Add the shrimp to the garlic-butter mixture and cover with plastic wrap. Microwave on high heat for 3 minutes. Stir, and microwave in 30-second intervals for another 1 to 3 minutes, until the shrimp turns pink.

Pork with Italian Seasonings

½ pound pork tenderloin
¼ teaspoon (or to taste) dried
    basil
¼ teaspoon (or to taste) dried
    parsley

¼ cup chopped onion, optional
1 tablespoon butter or
    margarine, optional
1 cup condensed cream of
    mushroom soup

Serves 1

For a quick and easy dinner, serve the pork with canned chickpeas or leftover hummus dip. The flavor of the chickpeas goes nicely with pork.

∾

1. Rinse the pork and pat dry. Rub the dried basil and dried parsley over the pork. Cut into cubes.
2. If using the onion and butter or margarine, combine in a microwave-safe casserole dish. Microwave on high heat for 1 minute. Stir and microwave for another 1 to 2 minutes, until the onion is tender.
3. Add the pork cubes and soup. Cover with plastic wrap and microwave on 70 percent power for 4 minutes. Rotate the dish. Microwave on 70 percent power for 2 to 3 more minutes, until the pork is cooked. (The pork is done when it feels firm when pressed and the juices run clear when poked with a fork.)

Pesto Pizza

Serves 2–4

Pesto sauce is readily available in the sauce or international cuisine section of most supermarkets.

4 mushrooms
3 tablespoons jarred basil and
    tomato pesto sauce

1 pita pocket
⅓ cup grated mozzarella
    cheese

1. Wipe the mushrooms clean with a damp cloth and slice.
2. Spread the pesto sauce on the pita pocket. Lay the mushroom slices on the sauce. Sprinkle the cheese on top.
3. Place the pita pocket on a microwave-safe plate or a paper towel. Microwave on high heat for 3 to 5 minutes, until the cheese melts.

Cheese Fondue

Serves 6

The trick to this recipe is to stir the cheese frequently so that it doesn't burn. If the fondue is too thick, add a bit more apple juice. If it is too thin, stir in extra cornstarch.

4 cups grated Swiss cheese
1 garlic clove
2 teaspoons cornstarch

¼ teaspoon (or to taste)
    nutmeg
1 cup apple juice
About 20 breadsticks

1. Cut the garlic clove in half. Rub it over the insides of a 2-quart microwave-safe casserole dish.
2. Add the cheese to the casserole dish and stir in the cornstarch and nutmeg. Add the apple juice and mix thoroughly.
3. Place the casserole dish in the microwave and microwave on high heat for 3 minutes. Stir, and microwave for 3 more minutes in 30-second intervals, stirring each time. Serve in a warmed fondue pot or in the casserole dish. (Serving in the casserole dish will make it easier to reheat if necessary.) Serve with the breadsticks for dipping.

Chocolate Toblerone Fondue

½ pound strawberries
2 (3.5-ounce) Toblerone bars

6 tablespoons light cream or
    half-and-half

1. Wash the strawberries and remove the hulls (the green leaves and "core" on top). Dry with paper towels.
2. Break the Toblerone bars into pieces. Place the Toblerone and the cream in a microwave-safe bowl. Microwave the chocolate and milk on high heat for 1 minute. Stir, and microwave for another 30 seconds. Stir, and cook for 2 more minutes in 15-second intervals, stirring each time, until the chocolate is completely melted.
3. Pour the chocolate fondue into a ceramic dessert fondue pot with a candle as the heat source. Serve with the strawberries for dipping. (Use a dipping fork to spear the strawberries and dip them in the chocolate.)

> **Serves 2–4**
>
> The trick to preparing microwave chocolate fondue is to stir frequently and be careful not to overcook the chocolate.
>
> ∾

Fast Mocha Fudge

2¼ cups granulated sugar
¾ cup semisweet chocolate
    chips
½ cup butter or margarine
½ cup sweetened condensed
    milk

¼ cup brewed coffee
¼ cup instant hot chocolate
    mix
½ cup walnut pieces

1. Grease an 8" × 8" baking pan.
2. Combine the sugar, chocolate chips, butter, milk, coffee, and instant hot chocolate mix in a microwave-safe bowl. Microwave on high heat for 3 minutes. Stir, and microwave at high heat for 1-minute intervals, stirring each time, until the butter and chocolate are melted.
3. Pour the mixture into the prepared baking pan. Stir in the walnuts. Cover and refrigerate until it has set. Slice into 2-inch squares.

> **Yields about 24 bars**
>
> Don't slice the bars too thickly. This recipe makes a very sweet fudge with a strong mocha flavor—a little goes a long way.
>
> ∾

S'mores!

2–3 whole graham crackers
8 mini-marshmallows

½ cup semisweet chocolate chips

1. Break each of the graham crackers in half and set aside.
2. Combine the mini-marshmallows and chocolate chips in a shallow microwave-safe bowl. Microwave on high heat for 1½ minutes. Stir, and microwave for about 1½ more minutes in 30-second intervals, stirring each time, until the chocolate and marshmallows are melted. (Reduce the cooking time to 15-second intervals the last 30 seconds if worried about the chocolate burning.)
3. Let the chocolate and marshmallows cool briefly, give a final stir, and spread 1 to 2 tablespoons on top of each of the 4 to 6 graham cracker halves, depending on how thick of a layer you prefer.

Vegetarian Lasagna

½ cup crushed tomatoes
⅓ cup ricotta cheese
⅓ cup grated mozzarella cheese
1 tablespoon grated Parmesan cheese

⅛ teaspoon dried oregano
⅛ teaspoon dried basil
6 "oven-ready" lasagna noodles

1. Place the crushed tomatoes in a bowl. Stir in the ricotta, then the mozzarella, and then the Parmesan. Make sure each cheese is thoroughly mixed in before adding the next. Stir in the oregano and basil.
2. Lay out 2 lasagna noodles in a large bowl or small (½-quart) microwave-safe casserole dish. Break the noodles in half or as needed to fit the shape of the dish. Spoon approximately ⅓ of the tomato sauce and cheese mixture evenly over the top. Repeat the layering 2 more times.
3. Cover the dish with wax paper. Microwave on high heat for 3 minutes. Turn the bowl, and microwave on high heat for another 3 to 5 minutes, until the cheese is cooked. Let stand for 10 minutes before serving.

Chapter 8

Cold Call: Frozen Food Fixers

Basic Peas

Serves 1

Cooked frozen peas make a quick and easy vegetable dish on busy weeknights. Serve alone, or add to cooked noodles or rice just before serving.

½ cup water   1 cup frozen peas

Bring the water to a boil. Add the peas and cook until they turn a bright color and are tender (3 to 5 minutes). Drain and serve.

Cheesy Hash Browns

Serves 2

This dish makes either a nutritious side dish or a hearty breakfast. For extra protein, add 3 to 4 slices of cooked ham before sprinkling on the final ½ cup of grated cheese.

¼ cup milk   1¾ cups frozen hash browns
¼ cup chicken broth   1 cup grated cheese, such as
¼ teaspoon garlic powder   Cheddar or Monterey jack

1. Preheat oven to 350°.
2. Mix together the milk, chicken broth, and garlic powder.
3. Lay the frozen hash browns on the bottom of a deep-sided 9" × 4" casserole dish. Pour the milk mixture over the top. Sprinkle with ½ cup of the grated cheese.
4. Bake for 50 minutes. Sprinkle the remaining cheese over and bake for another 5 minutes.

Homemade Creamed Corn

1 tablespoon low-fat margarine   *1 teaspoon granulated sugar*
1 cup frozen corn niblets   *Salt and pepper, to taste*
¼ cup skim milk   *1 teaspoon cornstarch*

1. Melt the margarine over low heat in a medium-sized saucepan.
2. Add the corn, milk, sugar, and salt and pepper. Increase heat to medium and bring to a boil, stirring constantly. Reduce heat to low and simmer for 5 more minutes, stirring throughout.
3. Push the corn off to the sides of the pan. Increase heat to medium-high and add the cornstarch to the liquid in the middle of the pan, stirring constantly until thickened. Make sure there are no lumps. Stir the corn and milk a few times. Serve hot.

> **Serves 1–2**
>
> Don't have cornstarch on hand? Reduce the milk to 2 tablespoons and serve hot after simmering. Don't substitute flour, as this will impart a floury taste to the corn.
>
> ॐ

Baked Sausages

1 pound frozen beef sausages   *2 tablespoons soy sauce*

1. Thaw the sausages and pat dry with paper towels.
2. Preheat oven to 350°.
3. Lay the sausages on a roasting pan (so that the juices will drain). Cook the sausages for 35 to 45 minutes, until cooked through. Halfway through cooking, turn the sausages over. Baste with the soy sauce once or twice during cooking. Serve with mustard, ketchup, or soy sauce as desired.

> **Serves 4**
>
> Baked sausages have less fat and calories than pan-fried sausages. However, they can dry out during baking, so be sure to add back lost flavor by basting frequently.
>
> ॐ

One-Pot Frozen Meatballs

Serves 2

Two good meatball and vegetable combinations for this dish are Italian-style frozen meatballs with frozen green beans, and frozen sweet-and-sour meatballs with a stir-fry mix. Serve over rice or egg noodles for a complete meal.

∾

½ pound (about 12) frozen meatballs
1½ cups beef broth
1 cup frozen mixed vegetables

½ cup crushed tomatoes
1 teaspoon dried basil or parsley
Salt and pepper, to taste

1. Combine the frozen meatballs, beef broth, frozen vegetables, and crushed tomatoes in a medium-sized saucepan. Bring to a boil.
2. Stir in the dried basil or parsley, and salt and pepper. Reduce heat, cover, and simmer for 15 minutes or until the meatballs are cooked through.

Teriyaki Shrimp

Serves 1

For a quick dinner on busy weeknights, prepare this with Simple Vegetarian Stir-Fry (page 138), substituting 1 tablespoon teriyaki sauce (reserve it from the marinade) for the stir-fry sauce.

∾

1 cup peeled and deveined frozen small shrimp
¼ cup soy sauce

1 tablespoon, plus 1 teaspoon cooking sherry
1½ teaspoons granulated sugar
1 tablespoon vegetable oil

1. Place the shrimp under cold, running water for at least 5 minutes until thawed. Drain and pat dry on paper towels.
2. Combine the soy sauce, cooking sherry, and sugar in a small bowl. Pour the marinade into a large resealable plastic bag, or split equally into 2 smaller resealable plastic bags. Place the shrimp in the marinade and move the bag around to make sure all the shrimp are covered in the marinade. Refrigerate for 30 minutes.
3. Heat the oil in a frying pan. Sauté the shrimp until they turn pink. Serve hot.

Spaghetti with Meatballs

3 ounces dried spaghetti
1 garlic clove
¼ cup chopped onion
6 fresh mushrooms
2 teaspoons olive oil
1 cup prepared tomato sauce

¾ cup water
¼ teaspoon dried oregano
¼ teaspoon dried basil
6 frozen Italian meatballs,
   thawed

Serves 2

Feel free to load up this basic spaghetti sauce recipe with your favorite vegetables and pasta seasonings. Green and red bell peppers, dried parsley, and even spicy chili powder are all good choices.

෨

1. Cook the spaghetti in boiling water until tender but still firm (al dente), and drain thoroughly. Smash, peel, and chop the garlic. Peel and chop the onion. Wipe the mushrooms clean with a damp cloth and slice.

2. Heat the olive oil on medium-low in a frying pan. Add the garlic and onion. Cook for 1 minute, then add the mushrooms. Cook until the onion is tender.

3. Add the tomato sauce and water. Stir in the dried oregano and dried basil.

4. Add the spaghetti and meatballs and bring to a boil. Reduce heat to medium-low and simmer for 15 minutes, until the mixture is thickened and cooked through. Serve hot.

Safe Thawing

Never leave food out on the counter to thaw. Food thawed at room temperature can pick up bacteria. Instead, thaw the food in cold water, in the refrigerator, or in the microwave.

Easy Quiche with Spinach

Serves 2–4

To cut down on preparation time, take the frozen spinach out to thaw earlier in the day. Swiss, Monterey Jack, or mozzarella cheese can be used in place of Cheddar.

∾

1½ cups frozen spinach
1 tablespoon butter or
    margarine
½ cup Bisquick
1 cup milk
2 eggs

Salt, to taste
Black pepper, to taste
¼ teaspoon (or to taste)
    paprika
⅔ cup grated Cheddar cheese

1. Thaw the spinach. Preheat oven to 350°. Grease a 9- or 10-inch pie plate or spray with nonstick cooking spray.
2. Heat the butter or margarine in a frying pan. Cook the thawed spinach over medium-low heat, just enough to cook through. Don't overcook.
3. Whisk together the Bisquick and milk. Whisk in the eggs. Stir in the salt, pepper, and paprika.
4. Lay the thawed spinach on the bottom of the pie plate. Sprinkle the grated cheese on top. Pour the Bisquick, milk, and egg mixture over the top.
5. Bake for 35 to 45 minutes or until a toothpick inserted into the center comes out clean.

Build Up Your Quiche

The recipe for Easy Quiche with Spinach is a basic recipe that can be adjusted according to whatever food you have on hand. For example, try reducing the frozen spinach to ¾ cup and adding 2 slices bacon, ¼ cup onion, 1 tomato, and 3 sliced mushrooms, all sautéed. Just be sure to keep the filling ingredients (minus the grated cheese) to approximately 1½ cups.

Souped-Up Ramen Noodles

1 package ramen noodles
1 (10¾-ounce can) condensed
    mushroom soup, plus 1 can
    water
1 (6-ounce) can tuna, drained
1 cup frozen peas

¼ teaspoon (or to taste) salt
¼ teaspoon (or to taste) black
    pepper
2 tablespoons grated Parmesan
    cheese

> **Serves 2–4**
>
> Canned tuna, ramen noodles, and frozen peas make a quick and easy one-dish meal on busy weeknights.
>
> ❧

1. Combine the ramen noodles, soup, water, tuna, and frozen peas in a frying pan. Use the back of a spoon to break up the ramen noodles. Stir in the salt and pepper.
2. Cook on medium-low heat until the noodles have softened and all the ingredients are heated through. Stir in the Parmesan cheese. Taste and add more salt or pepper if desired.

Snow Peas à la Ramen

4 ounces frozen snow peas
1 cup chopped cooked ham
1 package chicken-flavored
    ramen noodles

2 cups water
2 tablespoons soy sauce

> **Serves 2**
>
> Don't have time to cook during the week? This recipe makes enough for 2 dinners. Try a different flavor of ramen noodles if desired.
>
> ❧

1. Rinse the snow peas in warm running water for 2 minutes. Drain thoroughly.
2. Bring the water to a boil in a frying pan. Add the ramen noodles, breaking up the noodles with a spatula. Bring back to a boil over medium heat.
3. Add the flavor packet from the noodles and stir to mix. Stir in the snow peas, cooked ham, and soy sauce. Cook until the noodles are tender and all the ingredients are heated through, about 3 to 5 minutes.

Fish Fajita

Serves 1

You can transform this dish from a taco into an enchilada or quesadilla by varying the type of wrap used. Dieters can replace the tartar sauce with low-fat mayonnaise if desired.

2 frozen fish sticks
2½ tablespoons tartar sauce
1 teaspoon lime juice
¼ teaspoon (or to taste) paprika

1 soft tortilla wrap
1 lettuce leaf
1 tablespoon chopped red onion
4 fresh capers, optional

1. Cook the frozen fish sticks according to the package directions.
2. In a small bowl, mix together the tartar sauce, lime juice, and paprika.
3. Lay out the tortilla wrap flat on a plate. Place the lettuce leaf on the wrap, add the cooked fish sticks, and spread the dressing on top. Sprinkle the onion on top, along with the capers, if desired. Fold the wrap in half and serve.

Fruit with Yogurt

Serves 1–2

Need to get rid of some containers of leftover fruit or cheese cluttering up the refrigerator? This recipe is perfect, as it's very flexible. Ricotta cheese, cream cheese, or even whipping cream can replace the yogurt, and any type of canned fruit can be used.

½ cup (about 16) maraschino cherries
⅔ cup fruit cocktail, drained
¾ cup plain yogurt

½ cup walnuts
¼ teaspoon ground cinnamon
1 teaspoon granulated sugar

Mix all the ingredients together in a large bowl. Cover the bowl with aluminum foil and freeze until solid.

Braised Fish

2 frozen fish fillets, such as cod or halibut
2 tablespoons cornstarch
½ cup chicken broth
2 teaspoons brown sugar
1 tablespoon soy sauce
2 tablespoons butter or margarine, divided

2 slices fresh peeled ginger
1 cup canned straw mushrooms, drained and sliced
1 tomato, sliced
2 green onions, thinly sliced

> **Serves 1**
>
> Braising is a great way to tenderize tougher cuts of meat and firm-fleshed fish. For a different flavor, try replacing the chicken broth with clam juice or vegetable broth.
>
> ∾

1. The night before, thaw the frozen fish by moving it from the freezer to the refrigerator.
2. When the fish is nearly thawed, remove it from its packaging and pat dry. Cut into bite-sized pieces. Dredge the fish in the cornstarch. In a small bowl, combine the chicken broth, brown sugar, and soy sauce. Set aside.
3. Heat 1 tablespoon of the butter or margarine in a frying pan over medium-low heat. Add the ginger. Cook for 1 minute, stirring, then add the fish. Cook, turning over once, until lightly browned on both sides. Remove the fish cubes from the pan.
4. Add the remaining 1 tablespoon butter or margarine. Add the mushrooms and sliced tomato. Cook for 1 minute, stirring. Add the chicken broth mixture. Bring to a boil.
5. Return the fish to the pan. Cover tightly and simmer for 15 minutes or until the fish is tender. Stir in the green onions and serve.

How Long Can You Freeze Meat and Seafood?

Most meat can be frozen for up to 3 to 4 months, including ground beef, stewing beef, pork, and veal. Fish and seafood can be frozen for a maximum of 4 to 6 months. Always throw out frozen meat if it looks strange, smells funny, or is moldy.

Chicken Lo Mein

Serves 2

This recipe can easily be halved to make an easy dish for 1 person. Or, cook as is and refrigerate the leftovers for busy weeknights when you don't have time to cook.

∽

2 (6-ounce) skinless, boneless chicken breasts
1 tablespoon soy sauce
2 packages ramen noodles
½ cup chicken broth
2 tablespoons oyster sauce

1 teaspoon granulated sugar
2 green onions, optional
1 tablespoon vegetable oil
2 cups frozen broccoli
1 cup frozen carrots

1. Rinse the chicken breasts under cold, running water and pat dry. Cut into cubes. Toss with the soy sauce and let marinate for 30 minutes. Cook the ramen according to package directions and drain.
2. In a small bowl, combine the chicken broth, oyster sauce, and sugar. Set aside. Wash the green onions in hot water and drain. Cut into 1-inch pieces and set aside.
3. Heat the vegetable oil in a frying pan over medium heat. Add the chicken breasts. Increase heat to medium-high and stir-fry the chicken cubes until white and nearly cooked.
4. Add the frozen broccoli and carrots. Cook briefly, then add the chicken broth mixture. Bring to a boil, reduce heat to medium-low, and simmer for about 5 minutes. Stir in the noodles and green onion. Cook until heated through.

Cool Down Quickly

For safety's sake, cooked food must be frozen within 2 hours after cooking. Cool the food in a cold water or ice-water bath, or in a container in the refrigerator. Never allow poultry, meat, fish, eggs, or dairy products to cool down to room temperature before freezing—they can pick up airborne bacteria.

Green Tea Ice Cream Sandwich

1 (12-inch) sub roll
½ cup semisweet chocolate
  chips

2 tablespoons cream or milk
⅛ teaspoon ground cinnamon
½ cup green tea ice cream

1. Cut the sub roll in half. Chill briefly in the freezer.
2. Place the chocolate chips and cream in a metal bowl on top of a saucepan filled with nearly boiling water. (You can also use a double boiler if you have one.) Melt the chocolate on low heat, stirring continuously. Be sure not to let the chocolate burn.
3. Remove the chocolate from the heat. Cool briefly and stir in the ground cinnamon.
4. Place a piece of aluminum foil on a plate, and place the chilled bread on the foil. Use a knife to spread the cooling chocolate on the inside of both halves of the bread. Place the plate with the foil and bread in the freezer, and chill briefly until the chocolate hardens.
5. Spread the ice cream over the chocolate. Quickly close the sandwich, wrap up in the foil, and freeze for at least 2 hours. Cut into slices if desired.

> **Serves 2**
>
> Bread takes the place of angel food cake or pound cake in this simplified variation on a standard ice cream sandwich recipe.
>
> ❧

Can You Freeze Dairy Products?

It all depends on how you plan to use the frozen food. The texture of many dairy products, such as milk and cheese, changes during freezing. And some products—such as eggs—require so much extra preparation before freezing that it's not worth the trouble. Eggs can't be frozen whole or cooked, but instead need to be lightly beaten before freezing. Emulsified dressings made from eggs—such as mayonnaise—don't freeze well alone, but are usually alright when mixed with other food (as in a casserole).

Simple Vegetarian Stir-Fry

2 teaspoons vegetable oil
1 cup frozen stir-fry vegetable
  mix

2 tablespoons prepared stir-fry
  sauce

Heat the vegetable oil in a frying pan. Add the frozen vegetables. Cook, stirring continually, over medium to medium-high heat for at least 5 minutes or until the vegetables are brightly colored and tender. Stir in the stir-fry sauce. Mix through and serve hot.

Cooking with Frozen Vegetables

Frozen vegetables are processed at the peak of freshness, and they have the same nutrients as fresh ones. They can generally be stored for up to eight months. Unless the instructions specifically state otherwise, don't thaw frozen vegetables before cooking.

Chapter 9

Leave It to Me:
Ideas for Leftovers

French Toast Sandwich

*Italian-Style French Toast
(page 18)*

2 tablespoons peanut butter
½ small banana, or as needed

Spread 1 tablespoon peanut butter on the inside of each slice of French toast. Peel and slice the banana. Lay the banana slices on top of the peanut butter and close up the sandwich. If desired, microwave before eating, for the amount of time indicated on your brand of microwave.

Broiled Potato Skins

½ slice leftover cooked bacon
1 leftover baked potato
*1 tablespoon butter or
    margarine*

*2 tablespoons grated Cheddar
    cheese*

1. Position oven rack about 4 to 5 inches from heat source. Preheat broiler. Chop the bacon into tiny pieces.
2. Cut the potato in half lengthwise. Scoop out the insides of the potato, leaving ¼ to ½ inch of potato pulp around the skin. Cut the skin in half, from top to bottom to yield 4 potato skins.
3. Spread the butter on the inside of the potato skins. Place the potato skins on a baking sheet, skin-side down. Sprinkle the grated cheese and the chopped bacon on top. Broil until the cheese melts, about 2 minutes.

Pan-Fried Coleslaw

1 teaspoon vegetable oil
1 cup Coleslaw for a Crowd
   (page 188)

1 tablespoon soy sauce,
   optional

Heat the vegetable oil in a frying pan over medium heat. Add the coleslaw. Cook for 1 to 2 minutes, stirring until the coleslaw is heated through. Stir in the soy sauce if using, and serve.

Make-Ahead White Sauce

While white sauce takes mere minutes to make, after a long day of classes the thought of standing over a hot stove stirring and whisking can seem overwhelming. Fortunately, white sauce can be prepared ahead of time. Refrigerate in a sealed container for 2 to 3 days, or freeze for up to 3 months.

Meatball Sandwich

1 (12-inch) sub roll
3 tablespoons marinara sauce

2 tablespoons shredded
   mozzarella cheese
5–6 leftover Stovetop Italian
   Meatballs (page 183)

1. Cut the sub roll in half. Spread the sauce on both halves.
2. Sprinkle the mozzarella cheese on one half. Place the meatballs on the other half and close the sandwich.
3. Heat the sandwich briefly in the oven, toaster oven, or microwave. To microwave, place the sandwich on a paper towel and cook for 1½ to 2½ minutes, until the meatballs and sauce are heated through and the cheese is melted.

Meatball Soup

2 teaspoons olive oil, divided
¼ cup chopped onion
6–8 leftover uncooked Caribbean-Meatballs (page 182)

4 cups beef broth or 2 bouillon cubes and 4 cups water
1 tomato, sliced
1 cup drained canned green beans

1. Heat 1 teaspoon of the olive oil in a medium-sized saucepan on medium to medium-low heat. Add the onion and cook until tender.
2. Heat the remaining 1 teaspoon of olive oil and add the meatballs. Cook on medium-low heat for 6 to 8 minutes, turning occasionally, until the meatballs are cooked. Use a slotted spoon to remove the meatballs. Clean out the saucepan.
3. Add the beef broth and sliced tomato to the saucepan and bring to a boil. Return the onion and meatballs to the pan. Add the green beans and stir to mix. Simmer for 2 to 3 minutes, and serve hot.

Serves 1–2

Feel free to add your favorite beans or green vegetables to this soup, such as red kidney beans or canned spinach. Blanched fresh snow peas make a nice substitute for canned green beans.

∾

Easy Borscht

2 teaspoons olive oil
¼ cup chopped yellow onion
½ cup baby carrots, cut in half
½ green bell pepper, chopped
1 cup leftover canned beets, cooked

2 cups beef broth
Salt, to taste
Freshly ground black pepper, to taste
2 tablespoons sour cream or plain yogurt

1. Heat the olive oil in a medium-sized saucepan on medium-low. Add the chopped onion. Cook until tender, then add the carrots and green pepper.
2. Add the canned beets, beef broth, salt, and pepper. Bring to a boil. Reduce heat. Cover and simmer on low heat for 45 minutes or until the vegetables are tender, stirring occasionally.
3. Remove from heat. Stir in the sour cream or yogurt and serve.

Yields about 2½ cups

This soup can be enjoyed hot or cold. For a heartier version, increase the broth to 3 cups and add 2 boiled potatoes.

∾

Split English Muffins with Mornay Sauce

4 English muffins
1½ tablespoons butter or
margarine
1½ tablespoons all-purpose
flour
¾ cup milk

¼ cup shredded Parmesan or
Swiss cheese
1 teaspoon prepared mustard
¼ teaspoon ground nutmeg
Salt and pepper, to taste
4 slices cooked ham

1. Split the English muffins in half and toast.
2. Melt the butter in a small saucepan over low heat. Stir in the flour. Cook on low heat for 3 minutes, stirring continually. Gradually whisk in the milk. Whisk in the cheese. Stir in the prepared mustard, nutmeg, and salt and pepper.
3. Place 1 piece of ham on one half of an English muffin. Spoon ¼ of the sauce on the other half and close up the muffin. Repeat with the remaining muffins.

> **Serves 2–4**
>
> For fuller flavor, substitute Swiss cheese such as Gruyère or Emmental for the Parmesan. Cooked chicken, turkey, or other cooked meat can be substituted for the ham.
>
>

No-Work Ham and Bean Soup

¾ cup chopped leftover cooked
ham
¾ cup refried beans

2 cups chicken broth
1 cup water
2 tablespoons sour cream,
optional

Combine the ham, refried beans, chicken broth, and water in a medium-sized saucepan. Bring to a boil over medium heat. Simmer briefly. Remove from heat and stir in the sour cream, if using. Serve hot.

> **Serves 2**
>
> Refried beans and cooked ham provide the flavor in this easy-to-make dish—all you need to do is chop the ham. Feel free to thin or thicken the soup by increasing or decreasing the amount of ham and refried beans as desired.

Fried Slaw with Bacon

Traditionally, pan-fried coleslaw is combined with chopped bacon. To add bacon to fried coleslaw in Pan-Fried Coleslaw (page 141), cook the bacon first and remove it from the pan, but don't clean out the pan. Cook the coleslaw in the bacon fat instead of vegetable oil. Chop the bacon and mix with the fried coleslaw before serving.

Cabbage Rolls with Spanish Rice

Yields 6–8 cabbage rolls

Boiling the cabbage before removing the leaves makes it much easier to keep them whole. This recipe can easily be adapted to make more or fewer cabbage rolls, depending on how much Spanish Rice you have left over.

1 head green cabbage
1 tablespoon olive or vegetable oil

2 cups Spanish Rice (page 96)
1 tablespoon water

1. Preheat oven to 350°. Grease a casserole dish.
2. Bring a large pot of salted water to a boil. Remove the core from the middle of the cabbage and discard. Place the cabbage in the boiling water. Cook for 5 minutes or until the leaves have softened. Use a wooden spoon to gently remove the outer leaves from the cabbage. Continue until you have removed all the leaves or as many as you need (depending on how much Spanish Rice you have left over). Drain the leaves and dry on paper towels.
3. Heat the oil in a frying pan. Add the Spanish Rice and heat through.
4. Lay out a cabbage leaf flat. Place ¼ to ⅓ cup of Spanish Rice in the center of the leaf. Fold over the right side of the leaf, then the bottom, then the left side, and roll up the cabbage leaf. Fasten with a toothpick if desired.
5. Place the rolls in the prepared casserole dish and cover with aluminum foil. Bake for 45 minutes or until heated through.

Preparing Cabbage Leaves for Cabbage Rolls

Want an easier alternative to softening cabbage leaves in boiling water? The day before you plan to make the cabbage rolls, place the head of cabbage in the freezer. The next morning, take the cabbage out of the freezer to thaw. By the time you return home from classes that afternoon, the leaves will be easy to peel off the thawed cabbage. Pat dry with paper towels to remove excess water before using.

Simple Ham and Cheese Strata

4 slices bread
2 large slices leftover cooked
   ham
1 tomato
3 large eggs

½ cup milk, divided
1 tablespoon honey mustard
Salt and pepper, to taste
1 cup grated Cheddar cheese,
   divided

Serves 2–4

Got family in town for the weekend? Impress them by baking a ham for dinner, then using the leftovers to prepare strata to serve for breakfast the next morning.

1. Preheat oven to 350°.
2. Cut the bread into cubes. Finely chop the ham to yield 1 cup. Wash the tomato and cut into small pieces.
3. In a small bowl, lightly beat the eggs with ¼ cup milk. Stir in the honey mustard, salt, and pepper.
4. Lay half the bread cubes in a deep-sided 1½- to 2-quart casserole dish. Add the ham, ½ cup grated cheese, and the chopped tomato. Lay the remaining bread cubes on top. Sprinkle the remaining ½ cup cheese on top. Pour the beaten egg mixture over the top. Add as much of the remaining ¼ cup milk as necessary to make sure all the bread cubes are entirely covered. Refrigerate overnight.
5. Bake for 35 to 45 minutes or until the strata is cooked through.

Storing Leftovers FAQs

Leftover food should be refrigerated within 2 hours. Always store the leftover food in a sealed container. With a few exceptions, most leftovers will last up to 5 days. Leftover food with meat should be used within 3 days.

Shrimp with Easy Cocktail Sauce

Serves 1

Tomato sauce and a dollop of horseradish are all that's needed to spice up leftover cooked shrimp. Serve with rice, a salad, or steamed vegetables for a nutritious meal. Store leftover sauce in a sealed container in the refrigerator and use within 7 days.

∾

½ cup tomato sauce or ketchup
1½ teaspoons prepared
  horseradish
1½ teaspoons lemon juice

A few drops Worcestershire
  sauce, optional
6 ounces leftover cooked
  shrimp

Combine the tomato sauce, horseradish, lemon juice, and Worcestershire sauce in a bowl. Chill. Toss the cooked shrimp with the cocktail sauce.

Salmon Substitute

Scrambled Eggs with Tuna Patties (page 148) can be made with canned salmon instead of tuna. Just be sure to go through the salmon and remove any bones before using.

Teriyaki Shrimp with Noodles

Serves 1

Adding noodles to a dish is an easy way to stretch your leftovers.

∾

2 ounces vermicelli noodles
½ cup baby carrots
2 tablespoons pineapple juice

1 cup shrimp and 2
  tablespoons sauce from
  Teriyaki Shrimp (page 130)
1 teaspoon brown sugar
2 teaspoons vegetable oil

1. Soak the vermicelli noodles in hot water for 5 minutes or until softened. Drain thoroughly and cut in half. Wash the baby carrots, drain, and cut in half. Mix together the pineapple juice, teriyaki sauce, and brown sugar, and set aside.
2. Heat the oil on medium heat. Add the noodles. Cook briefly over medium-high heat, stirring to separate the strands. Push the noodles off to the sides of the frying pan and add the carrots. Cook for 1 to 2 minutes, then add the shrimp. Cook for another 1 to 2 minutes and add the sauce. Heat through and serve hot.

Versatile Tuna Casserole

1 can tuna
1 can condensed cream of
  mushroom soup, plus 1 cup
  milk

1½ teaspoons brown sugar
1 cup peas, canned or frozen
2 cups leftover cooked rice

1. Preheat oven to 350°.
2. Drain the liquid from the canned tuna and cut tuna into chunks.
3. Combine all the ingredients in a 1- to 2-quart casserole dish. Bake for 30 to 45 minutes, until heated through. Serve hot.

Serves 2–3

Don't have cooked rice on hand? Spoon the heated tuna and soup mixture onto toast or crusty bread. For stovetop cooking, melt 1 tablespoon butter or margarine in a frying pan, add all the ingredients, and cook on medium heat until cooked through.

Curried Shrimp Salad

1 tomato
1 cup cooked pasta
2 cups Curried Shrimp (from
  Curried Shrimp with
  Coconut Risotto, page 107)

2 tablespoons (or to taste)
  grated Parmesan cheese

1. Wash the tomato and cut into thin slices.
2. Place the pasta on a plate. Spoon the shrimp over the pasta. Arrange the tomato slices in a ring around the shrimp. Sprinkle the slices with the Parmesan cheese.

Serves 2–4

Savory tomatoes combine nicely with curried shrimp in this simple salad dish.

❧

Creamy Pasta with Béchamel Sauce

Serves 2–3

This recipe is designed to make extra sauce for leftovers that can be used to make Scrambled Eggs with Tuna Patties.

☙

3 tablespoons butter or
   margarine
2 tablespoons all-purpose flour
¾ cup milk
⅓ cup chopped white, yellow,
   or red onion
1 garlic clove

⅛ teaspoon (or to taste) salt
⅛ teaspoon (or to taste) black
   pepper
½ teaspoon dried parsley
1 cup canned tuna, drained
3 cups cooked fusilli vegetable
   pasta

1. Melt the butter in a small saucepan over low heat. Stir in the flour. Cook for 3 minutes, stirring continually to remove any lumps.
2. Increase heat to medium-low and gradually whisk in the milk. Continue whisking while adding the onion, garlic, salt, pepper, and dried parsley. Stir in the tuna.
3. Arrange the cooked pasta on a plate. Spoon approximately 1 cup of the sauce over the pasta, or as much as desired.

Scrambled Eggs with Tuna Patties

Serves 4

Don't feel like scrambled eggs? Basic Peas (page 128) or steamed vegetables also make a good accompaniment to the tuna patties.

☙

¾ cup leftover tuna sauce
   from Creamy Pasta with
   Béchamel Sauce
¼ cup crushed soda crackers
½ teaspoon prepared
   horseradish

2 teaspoons vegetable oil
1 recipe Perfect Scrambled Eggs
   (page 15), optional
1 tablespoon (or to taste) tartar
   sauce

1. Using your hands, mix together the tuna sauce, crushed crackers, and horseradish. Form the mixture into patties roughly the size of large golf balls, and flatten with the palm of your hand.
2. Heat the oil in a frying pan. Cook the tuna patties over medium heat until browned on the bottom, about 3 to 4 minutes. Turn over and cook the other side for another 3 to 4 minutes. Remove the patties from the frying pan and set aside.
3. Clean out the frying pan and prepare the Perfect Scrambled Eggs. Serve the eggs and tuna patties together, with the tartar sauce on the side for the tuna patties.

Chicken Lettuce Wraps

⅓ cup sesame seeds
1 leftover (5-ounce) cooked
   skinless, boneless chicken
   breast

1 cucumber
4 large iceberg lettuce leaves
¼ cup plain yogurt
2 teaspoons honey

Serves 4

You can also used canned chicken meat in this recipe. For extra flavor, try the canned chicken made with dark meat.

∾

1. Toast the sesame seeds by heating them in a frying pan over medium heat, shaking continually, until golden brown. Remove from the heat and let cool, making sure you have ¼ cup. (You will lose a few seeds in toasting.)
2. Cut the cooked chicken into thin slices. Wash the cucumber, peel, and cut into thin slices. Rinse the lettuce leaves and drain.
3. Combine the yogurt and honey in a small bowl. Toss the sliced chicken with the yogurt mixture.
4. Lay out a lettuce leaf flat in front of you. Place ¼ of the cucumber slices in the middle. Spoon ¼ of the chicken and yogurt mixture on top of the cucumber slices. Sprinkle with ¼ of the sesame seeds. Repeat with the remaining lettuce leaves.

Fried Rice—the Perfect Use for Leftovers!

Fried rice is the perfect dish to make on days when you're cleaning out the refrigerator and need to use up leftovers. Cooked peas, broccoli, carrots, mushrooms, and mung bean sprouts all lend flavor to fried-rice dishes. When it comes to meat, cooked turkey, chicken, and ham are all good choices.

Roasted Chicken Soup

Serves 1–2

This is a great recipe for those nights when you're cleaning out the vegetable crisper in the refrigerator. Feel free to substitute other vegetables as desired.

༈

1 garlic clove
½ zucchini
1 carrot
6 fresh mushrooms
2 green onions, optional
2 teaspoons olive oil
¼ cup chopped yellow onion

4 cups chicken broth
1 cup leftover chopped roasted
    chicken meat
1 teaspoon dried oregano
¼ teaspoon Tabasco, chili
    sauce, or other hot sauce
Salt, to taste

1. Smash, peel, and chop the garlic clove. Wash the zucchini, peel if desired, and cut into thin slices, about ¼ inch thick. Wash and peel the carrot. Cut into thin slices. Wipe the mushrooms clean with a damp cloth and slice. If using the green onions, wash under hot, running water, drain, and cut into thin slices.

2. Heat the olive oil in a medium-sized saucepan. Add the garlic and yellow onion. Cook over medium-low heat until the onion is tender. Add the zucchini and carrot. Cook for 1 to 2 minutes, stirring. Add the mushrooms and cook for 1 more minute.

3. Add the chicken broth and bring to a boil. Add the chicken. Stir in the dried oregano, Tabasco sauce, and salt. Add the green onions, if using. Reduce heat and simmer for 15 minutes or until the carrots are tender. Taste and adjust the seasoning if desired.

Easy Fried Rice

1 large egg
Salt and pepper, to taste
1 green onion

1 tablespoon vegetable oil
1 cup cooked white rice
½ cup frozen peas

Serves 1–2

Fried rice always tastes best made with cold, cooked rice. Classic Chinese fried rice is made without soy sauce, but you can stir in 1 to 2 tablespoons with the frozen peas if desired.

1. Lightly beat the egg with a fork. Stir in the salt and pepper and set aside. Wash the green onion and dice.
2. Heat the vegetable oil in a frying pan over medium-high heat. Add the rice and cook, stirring frequently.
3. Push the rice to the edges of the frying pan. Add the beaten egg in the middle. Use a spatula to scramble the egg. Mix the scrambled egg with the rice.
4. Stir in the frozen peas. Stir in the green onion, and cook for another 2 to 3 minutes, until heated through. Add more salt, pepper, or other seasonings if desired.

Turkey Sandwich

4 teaspoons mayonnaise
2 slices white bread
Sliced cooked turkey
1 tablespoon cranberry sauce

2 tablespoons leftover stuffing
4 teaspoons, plus 1 tablespoon
* butter or margarine,*
* optional*

Serves 1

Many people enjoy turkey leftovers more than the turkey dinner itself! This sandwich tastes great served cold or heated in a frying pan or the microwave.

1. Spread 2 teaspoons mayonnaise on the inside of each slice of bread. Place the turkey on one bread slice and spread the cranberry sauce over the top. Spread the stuffing on the other slice of bread. Close up the sandwich.
2. If you want to toast the sandwich, spread 2 teaspoons of butter or margarine on the outside of each slice of bread. Heat 1 tablespoon of butter or margarine in a frying pan, and brown the sandwich on both sides.

Terrific Turkey Tetrazzini

Serves 1

Examples of pastas that would work well in this recipe include corkscrew fusilli, bow tie pasta, and tube-shaped penne.

❧

1 tablespoon butter or margarine
1 cup leftover cooked Turkey au Vin (page 224)
1 cup cooked vegetable pasta
½ cup, plus 1 tablespoon condensed cream of mushroom soup
¼ cup water
⅛ teaspoon (or to taste) salt
⅛ teaspoon (or to taste) pepper
2 tablespoons grated Parmesan cheese, optional

1. Heat the butter or margarine in a frying pan over medium-low heat. Add the turkey. Cook for 2 to 3 minutes.
2. Stir in the pasta, soup, water, salt, and pepper. Heat through. Sprinkle the Parmesan cheese on top, if desired.

One-Step Chicken Casserole

Serves 1

Want a more filling meal? Bake 1 to 2 sausages ahead of time and place them in the casserole.

❧

1 leftover cooked chicken breast
1 leftover cup cooked white rice
1 cup Warming Herbed Tomato Soup (page 45)

1. Preheat oven to 250°.
2. Cut the chicken breast into bite-sized pieces. Line the bottom of a casserole dish with the rice. Add the chicken and stir in the soup. Bake for 15 to 20 minutes or until heated through.

Poached Leftover Meatballs

2 cups beef broth

6 leftover uncooked Caribbean Meatballs (page 182)

Bring the beef broth to boil in a medium-sized saucepan. Add the meatballs and simmer for 8 to 10 minutes until cooked through. Drain and serve.

Serves 1

Don't feel like getting out the roasting pan? Poaching meatballs in beef broth is easy and takes mere minutes. Just make sure to use enough broth to cover the meatballs.

Basic Béchamel Sauce

Don't let the fancy name throw you. Béchamel Sauce—also known as white sauce—is easy to make. The trick is to cook the butter and flour on low heat for at least 3 minutes, stirring constantly. This prevents the flour from imparting a starchy taste into the sauce.

Leftover Pesto Salad

½ cup water
1 cup frozen broccoli
1 tomato
¼ cup leftover Basil and Tomato Pesto (page 75)

2½ to 3 cups cold, cooked pasta
½ cup canned tuna, drained

Serves 1

The pesto for this dish can be found in Whole-Wheat Pasta with Basil and Tomato Pesto (page 75). For an even more nutritious dish, steam the broccoli instead of cooking it in boiling water.

1. Bring the water to a boil. Cook the frozen broccoli in the boiling water for 5 to 8 minutes, until the broccoli is tender. Drain. Wash and slice the tomato.
2. Add the pesto to the pasta and toss. Arrange the pasta on a plate. Mix in the tuna. Top with the tomatoes and the broccoli.

Instant Shepherd's Pie for One

Serves 1

This is a simple dish that is great for busy weeknights. To use uncooked leftover ground beef, heat the ground beef in a frying pan, season as desired, and drain thoroughly before mixing with the other ingredients.

~

1 (4-ounce) package instant
   mashed potatoes
½ pound leftover cooked
   ground beef

½ cup canned corn
3 tablespoons tomato sauce or
   ketchup
Salt and pepper, to taste

1. Preheat oven to 350°.
2. Prepare the mashed potatoes according to package instructions.
3. Place the ground beef in a small (about 1-quart) casserole dish. Stir in the corn, tomato sauce or ketchup, and salt and pepper. Spread 1 cup of the mashed potatoes on top in an even layer, completely covering the beef mixture. (Store the leftover potatoes in a sealed container in the refrigerator to use at another time.)
4. Bake for 15 minutes or until heated through.

Noodles with Spinach

Serves 2

Spinach and noodles make a protein-packed lunch or dinner that takes minutes to put together. The time is reduced even more if you use leftover cooked noodles.

~

1½ cups egg noodles
2 garlic cloves
1 tomato
1 tablespoon olive oil, butter, or
   margarine

1 cup leftover thawed frozen
   spinach
2 tablespoons (or more to taste)
   grated Parmesan cheese
¼ teaspoon (or to taste) salt

1. Cook the noodles according to the package instructions. Drain thoroughly. Smash, peel, and chop the garlic cloves. Slice the tomato.
2. Heat the oil or butter in a frying pan over medium heat. Add the garlic and tomato. Cook briefly, turn the heat up to high, and add the noodles.
3. Stir in the spinach. Cook very briefly, mixing the spinach with the noodles, and remove from the heat. Stir in the Parmesan cheese. Season with salt as desired.

Vegetarian Chili Casserole

*1 cup leftover cooked brown
    rice*
*2 cups leftover Vegetarian Chili
    (page 197)*

*2 tablespoons tomato sauce or
    water*

Serves 1–2

A combination of brown rice and beans provides a protein-packed dish to fortify you through long hours of studying.

∾

1. Preheat oven to 350°.
2. In a deep-sided casserole dish (about 8" × 4" × 3"), mix together the rice with the chili. Stir in the tomato sauce or water.
3. Bake for 15 minutes or until heated through.

Flavor-Packed Instant Mashed Potatoes

"Dehydrated potato flakes"—more commonly known as instant mashed potatoes—have come a long way since Edward A. Asselbergs first invented them in 1962. Simply stir the flakes into boiled water, and you have an easy dish that comes close to the taste and texture of homemade, without the work of boiling and peeling potatoes. (Instant mashed potatoes can also be prepared in the microwave, following package instructions.) One note: sodium levels in instant mashed potatoes can be rather high, so it's best not to incorporate them into your daily diet. However, they provide a quick and satisfying alternative on nights you don't have time to prepare the homemade version.

Chapter 10

Double Take: Got a Date?

Crab Rangoon

Serves 2

Sweet-and-sour sauce, hot chili sauce, or soy sauce are all good dipping sauce choices for Crab Rangoon.

∽

About 4½ cups oil
¼ cup canned or fresh
* crabmeat, drained*
½ green onion
¼ cup cream cheese
½ teaspoon Worcestershire
* sauce or steak sauce*

¼ teaspoon (or to taste) garlic
* powder*
12 wonton wrappers, or as
* needed*
1 egg, lightly beaten

1. Heat the oil for deep-frying in a deep-fat fryer, electric fondue pot, or wok, following the manufacturer's instructions. Lightly flake the crabmeat with a fork. Wash the green onion and dice.
2. Combine the crabmeat, green onion, cream cheese, Worcestershire sauce, and garlic powder.
3. Lay out a wonton wrapper in front of you so that it forms a diamond shape. Use your finger to wet the edges with the beaten egg. Place up to 1 teaspoon of the crabmeat mixture in the middle of the wrapper. Spread the mixture out toward the ends so that the middle isn't too bulky. Pinch the edges closed to seal.
4. Carefully slide the filled wonton into the hot oil. Repeat with the remaining wrappers and filling. Deep-fry the wontons in batches (to avoid overcrowding the fryer) until golden brown, about 2 to 3 minutes). Drain on paper towels. Serve the Crab Rangoon alone or with a dipping sauce such as Chinese hot mustard or sweet-and-sour sauce.

Baked Crab Rangoon

Not comfortable with deep-frying? Crab Rangoon can also be baked. Bake the Rangoon in a 425° oven for 10 minutes or until crisp. Brush the tops of the Rangoon with sesame oil or vegetable oil before baking. Alternately, you can leave out the wontons altogether and use the crab filling as a dip with crackers.

Cheesy Broccoli

8 ounces fresh broccoli
Water, as needed
2 tablespoons butter or
*   margarine*
1 tablespoon all-purpose flour
6 tablespoons milk

⅛ teaspoon (or to taste) garlic
*   powder*
Salt and pepper, to taste
⅓ cup grated Cheddar cheese
2 tablespoons sour cream

Serves 2

Sour cream adds rich flavor to this simple sauce. Steamed cauliflower or asparagus can be used in place of the broccoli.

1. Wash the broccoli and drain. Chop the broccoli into bite-sized pieces, separating the stalks from the florets.
2. Fill a medium-sized saucepan with 1 inch of water. Place a metal steamer inside the pan. Make sure the water is not touching the bottom of the steamer. Heat the water to boiling. When the water is boiling, add the broccoli to the steamer. Cover and steam until the broccoli is tender, about 10 minutes. Drain and set aside.
3. In a medium-sized saucepan, melt the butter over low heat. Stir in the flour. Cook for 2 minutes, stirring continually. Whisk in the milk, garlic powder, and salt and pepper. Bring to a boil over medium heat, whisking continually.
4. Reduce heat slightly and whisk in the cheese, and then the sour cream. Return to a boil and heat through. Arrange the broccoli on a plate and pour the cheese sauce over the top.

Lobster Butter

Making authentic lobster butter is a complex process. Lobster shells are finely crushed, blended with butter, and heated. The mixture is then strained to remove the shell fragments. If the butter is going to be used as a spread (instead of served with lobster tails for dipping), it is hardened in ice water. In Lobster Tails with Butter (page 160), clam juice makes a handy substitute for crushed lobster shells.

Classic Waldorf Salad

1 celery stalk
1½ cups chopped red apple
½ cup walnut pieces

1 tablespoon honey
3 tablespoons mayonnaise
1½ teaspoons lemon juice

1. Wash the celery and cut diagonally into 1-inch slices. In a serving dish, mix the celery with the apples and the walnuts.
2. Mix the honey into the mayonnaise to form a creamy dressing. Stir in the lemon juice.
3. Toss the celery mixture with the dressing. Chill until ready to serve.

Lobster Tails with Butter

2 (5-ounce) rock lobster tails,
    fresh or frozen
⅓ cup butter

1 tablespoon, plus 1 teaspoon
    clam juice

1. Preheat broiler. If using frozen lobster tails, thaw and pat dry with paper towels.
2. Melt the butter in a small saucepan over medium-low heat. Add the clam juice. Simmer for 5 minutes and remove from the heat.
3. Use scissors to cut lengthwise through the top of the lobster shell. Cut through the meat almost to the bottom, but do not cut right through the soft bottom shell. Use your hands to gently push apart the meat on both sides of the cut.
4. Lightly brush the lobster with a small amount of the butter mixture. Broil for 10 to 15 minutes, until cooked but still tender. Halfway through cooking, brush again with the butter. Serve the lobster tails with the remaining butter mixture.

Simple Shrimp Tempura

*¾ pound large shrimp (about
  16 shrimp)
1 egg, refrigerated
1 cup ice-cold water*

*1¼ cups all-purpose flour
About 4 cups vegetable oil, for
  frying*

Serves 2

Want to serve a romantic fondue dish other than cheese or chocolate? Try cooking this recipe in a fondue pot. It can also be prepared in a deep-fat fryer or a wok.

∾

1. Peel and devein the shrimp, leaving the tails on. Rinse the shrimp in cold water and pat dry with paper towels.
2. To prepare the batter, combine the egg with ¾ cup of the ice-cold water. Slowly stir in 1 cup of the flour, adding as much of the remaining ¼ cup of water as is necessary, until the batter has the thin, runny consistency of pancake batter. Do not worry about lumps of flour in the batter.
3. Heat the oil in an electric fondue pot, deep-fat fryer, or other appliance that is safe for deep-frying. Lightly dust the shrimp in the remaining ¼ cup of flour. Dip the shrimp in the batter and deep-fry until golden brown. Drain the shrimp on paper towels.

Aloha Grilled Shrimp

*1 pound shrimp, peeled and
  deveined, to make 1½ cups
½ red bell pepper
⅓ cup soy sauce*

*1 tablespoon cooking sherry
2 teaspoons brown sugar
1 cup pineapple chunks,
  drained*

Serves 2

Serve with Raspberry "Parfait" (page 170) for a summery meal that will take your mind off the cold weather outdoors. For best results, cover the shrimp and chill for 2 hours before cooking.

∾

1. Rinse the shrimp by letting them stand in warm salted water for 5 minutes. Pat dry with paper towels.
2. Wash the red pepper, remove the seeds, and cut into small chunks. Combine the soy sauce, cooking sherry, and brown sugar in a small bowl.
3. Preheat grill or oven broiler. Place 3 or 4 shrimp apiece on 2 metal skewers, alternating them with a piece of red pepper and a few slices of pineapple. Brush the sauce over the kebabs. Grill or broil for 5 to 8 minutes, turning occasionally and brushing with more sauce until the shrimp are opaque throughout.

Teriyaki Shrimp

Serves 2

For a different flavor, replace the pineapple juice with juice from a can of lychees. Lychees are an appropriate fruit to serve on a romantic evening, since they are a symbol of love in Chinese culture.

∽

1½ pounds frozen shrimp, peeled and deveined
½ cup soy sauce
2 tablespoons, plus 2 teaspoons pale, dry sherry
3 teaspoons granulated sugar
¼ cup pineapple juice
⅛ teaspoon ground ginger
1 tablespoon prepared mustard
1 tablespoon vegetable oil
1 cup steamed long-grain rice

1. Run the shrimp under cold, running water for at least 5 minutes until thawed. Drain and pat dry on paper towels.
2. Combine the soy sauce, pale sherry, and sugar in a small bowl. Pour the marinade into a large resealable plastic bag, or split equally into 2 smaller resealable plastic bags. Place the shrimp in the marinade and seal. Move the bag around to make sure all the shrimp are covered in the marinade. Refrigerate for 30 minutes.
3. Remove the shrimp from the bag(s), reserving ¼ cup of the marinade. Place the reserved marinade in a small saucepan over medium-high heat. Add the pineapple juice, ground ginger, and prepared mustard, and bring to a boil. Boil for 5 minutes. Keep warm on low heat while cooking the shrimp.
4. Heat the oil in a frying pan. Sauté the shrimp until they turn pink.
5. Add the sauce to the shrimp. Heat through, and serve over the steamed rice.

Careful Cutting

Contrary to popular belief, more people cut themselves with dull knives than with sharp ones. Always make sure to keep knives properly sharpened.

Simple Shrimp and Rice Skillet Dish

*1½ pounds peeled and
    deveined shrimp*
2 tablespoons olive oil
*2 small garlic cloves, smashed,
    peeled, and chopped*
½ cup chopped white onion
½ cup tomato sauce

*½ cup low-sodium chicken
    broth*
1 teaspoon curry powder
Salt and pepper, to taste
1 cup cooked long-grain rice

Serves 2

Curried shrimp and rice make a nice combination in this simple one-dish meal.

∾

1. If using frozen shrimp, rinse under cold running water for 3 minutes or until thawed. If using fresh shrimp, rinse by letting them stand in warm salted water for 5 minutes. Pat dry with paper towels.
2. Heat the olive oil in a frying pan. Add the garlic and onion. Cook over medium-low heat until the onion is tender. Add the shrimp. Cook over medium heat until the shrimp turn pink.
3. Stir in the tomato sauce, chicken broth, curry powder, and salt and pepper. Cook for 2 to 3 minutes, then stir in the cooked rice. Cook on medium-low heat for 5 minutes, until heated through.

Tempura Cooking Tips

Tempura batter is easy to make if you follow a few simple tips. Always use ice-cold water, a cold egg straight from the refrigerator, and don't overmix the batter. Tempura batter works best with fish, particularly shellfish, and crisp vegetables such as eggplant and broccoli.

Budget Romantic Pasta

Serves 2

While steak and seafood are nice, you don't need to splurge to cook a romantic meal for 2. Canned turkey combines nicely with spinach and pasta in this simple but flavorful dish.

❧

8 ounces shell or bow tie pasta
1 garlic clove
½ cup condensed cream of mushroom soup
½ cup water
1 roma tomato
2 teaspoons olive oil
¼ cup chopped onion
6½ ounces canned flaked turkey
¼ teaspoon (or to taste) dried parsley
⅛ teaspoon (or to taste) salt
½ cup frozen spinach, thawed

1. Cook the noodles in the microwave or in boiling water according to package directions. Drain and set aside. Smash, peel, and chop the garlic clove. Mix together the soup and water in a small bowl and set aside. Wash and slice the tomato.
2. Heat the olive oil in a frying pan over medium heat. Add the garlic and onion. Cook briefly, then add the tomato. Cook on medium-low heat until heated through.
3. Stir in the soup mixture. Stir in the flaked turkey, dried parsley, and salt. Stir in the spinach. Cover and simmer for 10 to 15 minutes. Serve over the noodles.

Lo Mein or Chow Mein?

Contrary to popular opinion, the main difference between lo mein and chow mein lies not in the type of noodles used, but in how the dishes are prepared. In chow mein dishes, food is stir-fried and poured over the chow mein noodles, which have been cooked separately. However, lo mein noodles are added directly to the food in the final stages of cooking, allowing them to soak up the sauce.

Romantic Picnic Dinner

*2 cups small round pasta, such
    as bow tie*
1 red bell pepper
¾ cup canned oysters
1 tablespoon olive oil
¼ cup chopped onion
¼ cup chicken broth

*2 teaspoons (or to taste)
    Worcestershire sauce*
Salt and pepper, to taste
1 cup canned peaches, drained
*1 cup canned pineapple,
    2 tablespoons juice reserved*
*2 tablespoons sweetened
    coconut flakes*

> **Serves 2**
>
> Crackers and hard cheese or a flavored cheese spread make a nice accompaniment to the pasta and fruit salad.
>
> ❧

1. Prepare the pasta according to package directions. While waiting for the pasta water to boil, prepare the other pasta ingredients. Wash and dry the red pepper. Cut in half, remove the seeds, and cut into bite-sized pieces. Remove the oysters from the can and rinse under cold water. Cut into small pieces.

2. Heat the olive oil on medium in a frying pan. Add the onion. Cook for 1 minute, then add the red pepper. Cook, stirring occasionally, until the onion is tender.

3. Add the chicken broth and bring to a boil. Add the chopped oysters and stir in the Worcestershire sauce. Simmer for 5 minutes. Add salt and pepper to taste.

4. Place the pasta in a large bowl. Add the oyster mixture to the pasta, and toss. Refrigerate in a sealed container until ready to use.

5. To prepare the fruit salad, cut the peaches into bite-sized pieces. Toss the pineapple and the peaches with the reserved pineapple juice. Stir in the sweetened coconut flakes.

Picnic Essentials

If your picnic destination for Romantic Picnic Dinner involves a long hike, be sure to pack other essentials such as water and granola bars or trail mix.

Quick and Easy Beef Medallions
with Fiddlehead Greens

2 teaspoons (or to taste) freshly ground black pepper
6 (3-ounce) beef medallions
2 garlic cloves

4 tablespoons olive oil, divided
1½ cups chicken broth
8 ounces frozen fiddlehead greens

1. Rub the freshly ground black pepper over the beef medallions. Set aside. Smash, peel, and chop the garlic cloves.
2. Heat 2 tablespoons of the olive oil in a frying pan on medium-low heat. Add the beef medallions. Cook for 3 to 4 minutes on each side, until both sides are thoroughly browned. Remove from the pan and clean out the frying pan.
3. Add the remaining 2 tablespoons olive oil. Add the garlic. Cook for 1 minute, then add the chicken broth.
4. Add the fiddlehead greens. Cook for 4 to 5 minutes or until the greens are heated through. Return the beef medallions to the pan. Heat through and serve hot.

Freezing Tip

Always be sure to label frozen food with the date that it is frozen. Although frozen food has a longer storage period than refrigerated food, it will eventually go bad. Labeling food with the freezing date means you're not relying on memory to know if it is still edible.

Lemony Chicken

2 (7-ounce) boneless, skinless chicken breasts
4 tablespoons lemon juice, divided
2 teaspoons vegetable oil
½ small white onion, chopped

1 zucchini, sliced
½ cup chicken broth
2 tablespoons tomato sauce
¼ teaspoon (or to taste) salt
¼ teaspoon (or to taste) pepper

Serves 2

Delicately flavored Steamed Jasmine Rice (see page 81) would make an excellent accompaniment to this dish. Prepare the rice while the chicken is simmering.

∾

1. Rinse the chicken breasts and pat dry. Place 2 tablespoons lemon juice in a resealable plastic bag. Add the chicken breasts. Seal the bag and refrigerate. Marinate the chicken for 1 hour, turning the bag occasionally so that all the chicken breast meat is covered in the juice. Remove the marinated chicken from the refrigerator and pat dry. Discard the marinade.
2. Heat the vegetable oil in a frying pan over medium heat. Add the onion and cook until tender. Add the chicken and cook until it turns white, about 5 minutes. Add the zucchini and cook for 1 minute.
3. Add the chicken broth, tomato sauce, remaining 2 tablespoons lemon juice, and salt and pepper. Cover and simmer for 20 minutes. Serve hot.

Adjusting Recipes

When adjusting the portions of a recipe, remember that the quantity of food affects the total cooking time. For example, the cooking time for 4 potatoes will be longer than the cooking time for 1.

Creamy Chicken with Noodles

Serves 2

To serve the basic sauce in this recipe with other foods, leave out the frozen spinach and experiment with a different combination of seasonings, such as cayenne pepper or a hot sauce for seafood.

ॐ

2 (7-ounce) boneless, skinless
    chicken breasts
8 ounces egg noodles
2 ounces frozen spinach
3 tablespoons all-purpose flour,
    divided
¼ teaspoon salt

¼ teaspoon pepper
½ teaspoon dried parsley
2½ tablespoons butter or
    margarine, divided
¾ cup milk
¼ cup grated Parmesan cheese
¼ teaspoon paprika

1. Rinse the chicken breasts under cold, running water. Pat dry and cut into bite-sized pieces. Cook the noodles according to the package directions. Drain. Defrost the frozen spinach in boiling water or in the microwave on high heat for 5 minutes. Squeeze out excess water with a paper towel.

2. In a small resealable plastic bag, combine 2 tablespoons of the flour, the salt, pepper, and dried parsley. Add the chicken, seal the bag, and shake.

3. Heat 1 tablespoon of the butter in a frying pan. Add the chicken and cook on medium-high heat until cooked through. Remove from the pan.

4. Melt the remaining 1½ tablespoons butter in a small saucepan over low heat. Stir in the remaining 1 tablespoon flour. Cook on low heat for 3 minutes, continually stirring. Gradually whisk in the milk. Whisk in the cheese, stirring until thickened. Stir in the paprika. Stir in the spinach. Taste and add salt and pepper if desired. Pour the sauce over the chicken and noodles.

Chocolate-Covered Strawberries

½ pound (about 16) fresh strawberries

8 ounces semisweet chocolate
2 teaspoons shortening

Serves 2

Feel free to experiment with using different flavors of chocolate chips and other types of fresh fruit, such as banana slices and pineapple chunks, for dipping in the warm chocolate.

1. Wash the strawberries and dry. Do not break off the hulls. Break the chocolate into pieces. Lay out a sheet of wax paper on a 9" x 13" baking sheet. Keep the baking sheet near where you will be cooking the chocolate.

2. To cook on the stove: Fill a heavy pot halfway with barely simmering water. Combine the chocolate and shortening in a metal bowl and place on top of the pot (or use the top of a double boiler if you have one). Melt at low heat, stirring regularly and making sure the chocolate doesn't burn.

3. To cook in the microwave: Place the chocolate and shortening in a microwave-safe bowl. Microwave on medium heat for 30 seconds, and stir. Microwave for another 30 seconds and stir again. Microwave for about 2 more minutes in 15-second intervals, stirring between each, until the chocolate is completely melted. Make sure that the chocolate does not overcook and burn.

4. Remove the chocolate from the stovetop or the microwave. Dip each strawberry into the chocolate and set on the wax paper. Cool briefly in the refrigerator, and serve when the chocolate has hardened.

Cheesy Parmigiana

For many people, parmigiana refers to a classic Italian dish made with breaded veal cutlets. Actually, the term simply means "with Parmesan cheese." Vegetables, meat, and even shellfish can all be cooked parmigiana-style.

Raspberry "Parfait"

1 cup soft tofu
3 teaspoons lime juice

2 teaspoons granulated sugar
1 cup frozen raspberries

In a blender, blend together the soft tofu, lime juice, and sugar. Add the frozen fruit and process again. Pour into 2 parfait or tall drinking glasses. Serve immediately or freeze.

Perfect Parfait

Did you know? The word parfait is French for "perfect." In the United States, November 25 has been designated as National Parfait Day.

Decadent Chocolate Fondue

3 bananas
6 ounces semisweet chocolate

½ cup, plus 2 tablespoons light cream or half-and-half
2 teaspoons liqueur, optional

1. Set up the fondue pot on the table. Peel the bananas and cut diagonally into slices approximately ¼ inch thick. Break the chocolate into pieces.
2. Melt the cream and chocolate in the top half of a double boiler if you have one, stirring and making sure the chocolate does not burn. If you don't have a double boiler, fill a medium-sized saucepan halfway with water, and heat until the water is nearly boiling. Turn the heat to low, and place the cream and chocolate in a metal bowl on top of the saucepan. (Make sure the bottom of the metal bowl does not touch the water. If it does, pour out some of the water.) Melt the chocolate on low heat, stirring with a rubber spatula and making sure the water doesn't boil.
3. Light the candle underneath the fondue pot. Pour the melted chocolate into the pot. Stir in the liqueur, if using. Use a fondue dipping fork to spear the banana slices and dip them into the warm chocolate.

Romantic Eggplant Parmigiana

1 medium eggplant
1 teaspoon dried basil
⅛ teaspoon (or to taste) garlic
  salt
1 cup tomato sauce

¼ cup pine nuts
½ cup shredded mozzarella
  cheese
¼ cup grated Parmesan cheese

1. Preheat oven to 350°. Spray an 8" × 8" baking sheet with nonstick cooking spray.
2. Wash the eggplant and cut into thin slices, about ¼ inch thick. Stir the dried basil and garlic salt into the tomato sauce.
3. Lay out the eggplant slices flat on the baking pan. Spoon the tomato sauce over the top. Sprinkle the pine nuts on top.
4. Cover the eggplant with foil and bake for 20 minutes or until the slices are tender when speared with a fork. Remove from oven.
5. Sprinkle the mozzarella and the Parmesan cheeses on top. Bake, uncovered, for 10 to 15 minutes, until the cheese has melted.

> **Serves 2**
>
> Eggplant Parmigiana is really just eggplant topped with an Italian pesto sauce. To jazz up this recipe, replace the tomato sauce and spices mixture with the sauce in Whole-Wheat Pasta with Basil and Tomato Pesto (page 75).
>
> ∾

What Type of Vegetarian Are You?

Once you've made the decision to become a vegetarian, there are a number of different diets you can follow. The most common is the ovo-lacto vegetarian diet. Ovo-lacto vegetarians steer clear of meat, but will eat eggs and dairy products. On the other hand, vegans eschew all animal products, including fish, egg, and dairy. In total, there are at least 5 types of vegetarian diets, with several variations.

Chapter 11

Party Hearty:
Easy Foods for a Group

∾

Popcorn Munchies

4 tablespoons butter
4 tablespoons condensed
    mushroom soup
¼ teaspoon dried parsley
    flakes

¼ teaspoon dried thyme
¼ teaspoon red pepper flakes
4 cups store-bought caramel
    popcorn
2 cups pretzel mix

1. In a frying pan, melt the butter over low heat. When it starts to melt, stir in the soup. Stir in the parsley, thyme, and red pepper flakes.
2. Place the popcorn in a medium-sized bowl. Pour the soup mixture over, stirring to make sure it is thoroughly mixed. Stir in the pretzel mix. Sprinkle extra red pepper flakes over, and serve.

Glazed Pecans

2 tablespoons margarine
¼ cup brown sugar
2 tablespoons corn syrup

1 teaspoon ground cinnamon
1 cup pecans

1. Melt the margarine over low heat in a small saucepan. Add the brown sugar, corn syrup, and ground cinnamon. Add the pecans, stirring to coat in the mixture.
2. Increase heat to medium and bring to a boil, stirring to dissolve the brown sugar. Let the mixture boil for several minutes.
3. Pour the pecan mixture onto a greased baking sheet and cool. Separate the mixture and store in an airtight container or plastic bag. (They will last for about 1 week.)

Easy Deviled Egg Appetizer

8 Hard-Boiled Eggs (page 14)
4 tablespoons mayonnaise

2 tablespoons Worcestershire sauce
½ teaspoon (or to taste) curry powder

Yields 8 eggs

The trick to this recipe is to carefully remove the egg yolks without damaging the whites, and mashing the yolk until it's fluffy.

❧

1. Peel the eggs. Cut each egg in half lengthwise. Carefully remove the yolks.
2. In a small bowl, use a fork to mash the yolks with the mayonnaise, Worcestershire sauce, and curry powder.
3. Carefully fill each egg half with a portion of the mashed yolk mixture. Store in the refrigerator until ready to serve. Serve cold or at room temperature.

How to Separate an Egg

Many recipes call for the egg white and yolk to be separated. This is easy to do. First, set two small bowls on the counter. Take the egg and lightly tap the middle against the edge of one of the bowls until cracks appear. Use both your hands to break the egg open so that you are holding ½ of the egg shell in each hand. Then, simply transfer the egg back and forth between the shell halves, allowing the egg white to slide into the bowl. (Pour the egg yolk into the other bowl.) Use both the egg white and egg yolk as called for in the recipe.

Spiced Nuts

2 cups walnut halves
6 tablespoons margarine

6 tablespoons granulated sugar
2 teaspoons five-spice powder

1. Preheat oven to 350°.
2. Place the walnuts on an ungreased baking sheet. Toast for 8 to 10 minutes, checking frequently near the end of the baking time to make sure they do not burn.
3. While the nuts are toasting (about 2 to 3 minutes before they are finished), begin melting the margarine on low heat in a frying pan. Add the sugar, stirring to dissolve. Stir in the five-spice powder.
4. Add the toasted nuts, and stir to coat. Cook briefly until the liquid is nearly absorbed. Pour the walnuts onto the ungreased baking sheet and separate. Let cool.

Caramel Walnuts

½ cup granulated sugar
2 tablespoons corn syrup

2 tablespoons unsweetened
condensed milk
1 cup walnut pieces

1. In a medium-sized saucepan, stir together the sugar, corn syrup, and milk over low heat. Add the walnut pieces, stirring to make sure they are entirely coated in the sugar mixture. Increase heat to medium and bring to a boil. Let boil for several minutes, stirring occasionally, as the sugar darkens. When it has browned on the edges, remove from the heat.
2. Pour the walnut mixture onto a greased baking sheet and cool. Separate the walnuts and store in an airtight container or plastic bag. (They will last for about 1 week.)

Stuffed Olive Appetizer

2 teaspoons white wine vinegar
¼ teaspoon garlic powder

¼ cup ricotta cheese
48 extra-large black pitted olives

1. Stir the white wine vinegar and garlic powder into the ricotta cheese.
2. Drain the olives and wipe dry. Use a butter knife to gently force a small amount of the cheese mixture into the olive (depending on the size, each olive will take between ⅛ and ¼ teaspoon). Serve immediately.

> **Yields 48 olives**
>
> This simple appetizer takes mere minutes to make and doesn't require any cooking. The exact amount of olives used will depend on their size—the recipe can easily be halved if desired.
>
> ❧

Stuffing Olives

Using soft cheese is a great way to add flavor to large olives that have had their pits removed. Besides ricotta cheese, olives can be filled with cream cheese, blue, or even crumbled feta cheese. To fill the olive, all you need is a butter knife; however, a piping bag can also be used. For a fancier appearance, cut a thin slice off the bottom of each olive before filling, so that it can stand upright.

Stuffed Mushroom Appetizer

24 mushrooms
1 tablespoon prepared
horseradish

4 ounces cream cheese, divided
2 teaspoons lemon juice
⅛ teaspoon chili powder

1. Preheat oven to 350°.
2. Wipe the mushrooms clean with a damp cloth. Remove the stems, carefully working the edge of each stem with a knife so that you can pull it right out.
3. In a small bowl, mix the prepared horseradish with half of the cream cheese. In another small bowl, mix the lemon juice and chili powder with the remaining cream cheese.
4. Spoon approximately 1 level teaspoon of cream cheese and horseradish filling into 12 of the mushroom caps (the exact amount of filling needed will depend on the size of the mushroom). Spoon the same amount of the cream cheese and lemon juice filling into the other 12 mushroom caps. Place the mushrooms on an ungreased baking sheet.
5. Bake for 10 to 12 minutes or until the cream cheese is heated through.

Fabulous Five-Spice Powder

Don't let the name fool you—five-spice powder may contain 6 or even 7 spices. Used in China since ancient times, this popular condiment is an intriguing mix of sweet, salty, bitter, and spicy. Five-spice powder is used to add flavor to everything from sauces to soups. In Spiced Nuts (page 176), five-spice powder helps turn plain walnuts into a tasty cocktail snack.

Buffalo Wings

2 pounds chicken wings (about 10–12 wings)
¼ teaspoon black pepper
About 4 cups oil, for deep-frying
5 tablespoons butter or margarine

2 teaspoons white vinegar
¼ cup hot sauce, such as Tabasco
1 cup blue cheese dressing

Serves 5–6

Buffalo wings are always a hit at parties! Just be sure to keep lots of napkins nearby.

~

1. Rinse the chicken wings under cold, running water and pat dry with paper towels. Sprinkle with the black pepper.
2. Set up the wok or deep-fryer that you are using according to the manufacturer's instructions and heat the oil to 360°.
3. While waiting for the oil to heat, bring the butter or margarine, vinegar, and hot sauce to a boil in a small saucepan. Keep warm on low heat until needed.
4. Deep-fry the chicken wings until browned and cooked through. Remove the wings and drain on paper towels.
5. Brush with the hot sauce. Serve with the blue cheese dressing for dipping.

No-Fry Buffalo Wings

Not comfortable with deep-frying? Buffalo wings can also be baked. Preheat the oven to 350° and bake for 1 hour, or until the wings are cooked. To make sure you have lots of sauce to brush on the baking wings, increase the amounts to 7 tablespoons butter, 3 teaspoons vinegar, and 6 tablespoons hot sauce.

Sweet-and-Sour Chicken Wings

Serves 6

These can be prepared a day or two in advance and refrigerated in a sealed container. Serve cold or reheat briefly before serving.

ॐ

*2½ pounds chicken wings
(about 12 wings)*
2 teaspoons cornstarch
4 teaspoons water

⅓ cup red wine vinegar
⅓ cup soy sauce
⅓ cup granulated sugar
3 tablespoons tomato sauce

1. Preheat the oven to 350°.
2. Rinse the chicken wings under cold, running water and pat dry with paper towels. Dissolve the cornstarch in the water and set aside.
3. In a small saucepan over medium-high heat, bring the red wine vinegar, soy sauce, sugar, and tomato sauce to a boil. Add the cornstarch mixture, stirring constantly until thickened. Keep the sauce warm on low heat.
4. Place the chicken wings on a baking sheet and brush with the sauce. Bake for 30 minutes, brushing with the sauce occasionally. Turn over, brush with sauce, and bake for another 30 minutes or until the wings are cooked.

Buffalo Wings

Nearly everyone knows that "buffalo wings" are actually made with chicken wings. However, fewer people realize that, until recently, chicken wings were usually relegated to the soup pot. It took a housewife from Buffalo, New York, to see the potential behind deep-frying chicken wings and serving them with a hot sauce. Today, numerous variations on the original recipe exist, and chicken wings are a staple on many restaurant appetizer menus.

Chicken Fingers

*4 (6-ounce) skinless, boneless
    chicken breasts
1¼ cups tortilla chips*

*¾ cup butter or margarine
¾ teaspoon dried basil
½ teaspoon dried oregano*

Serves 8–10

Serve as is, or with any of the traditional dipping sauce accompaniments for chicken wings, including blue cheese dressing, soy sauce, or plain ketchup.

∾

1. Preheat oven to 400°. Spray a large baking sheet with nonstick cooking spray.
2. Rinse the chicken breasts under cold, running water. Pat dry with paper towels. Cut into thin strips approximately 3 inches long and ½ inch thick (about the size of a finger).
3. Crush the tortilla chips into a shallow bowl. Melt the butter in a small saucepan over low heat. Stir the oregano and basil into the melted butter.
4. Place the chicken strips, crushed tortilla chips, melted butter, and prepared baking sheet within easy reach of one another. Dip the chicken pieces into the melted butter, then coat with the crushed tortilla chips. Lay out on the baking sheet.
5. Bake the chicken fingers for 40 to 45 minutes, until cooked through and golden brown. Turn over the chicken fingers halfway through cooking.

Raw Chicken—Handle with Care!

Despite the best efforts of poultry producers, raw chicken can carry salmonella and other bacteria. Always rinse raw chicken thoroughly under cold, running water. After cooking, wash your hands and any cooking equipment that came into contact with the chicken, including knives and the cutting board. Be sure the chicken is thoroughly cooked before serving.

Caribbean Meatballs

1 large egg
½ teaspoon ground ginger
¼ teaspoon ground cloves
¾ teaspoon granulated sugar
½ cup bread crumbs

*¼ cup finely chopped green
  bell pepper*
1 pound ground beef
1 tablespoon skim milk

1. Preheat oven broiler. In a small bowl, beat the egg well and set aside.
2. Mix the ginger, cloves, and sugar thoroughly with the bread crumbs. Mix the green pepper with the ground beef.
3. Add the beaten egg, the bread crumb mixture, and milk to the ground beef and pepper mixture. Add more milk if the mixture is a bit dry.
4. Roll the mixture into small balls about 1½ inches in diameter (slightly smaller than a golf ball).
5. Spray a rack with nonstick cooking spray and place the rack in a shallow roasting pan. (A baking sheet won't allow the fat to drain from the meatballs.) Place the meatballs on the rack and broil for 5 to 8 minutes, until cooked through.

Terrific Tex-Mex

As the name implies, Tex-Mex incorporates the best of Texan and Mexican cuisine. Burritos, nachos, tacos, and Chili con Carne (page 97) are all examples of Tex-Mex cooking. Tex-Mex dishes are characterized by a heavy reliance on beef, beans, onion, and shredded cheese. The food is also much more heavily spiced than authentic Mexican cuisine—both ground cumin and chili powder make a frequent appearance in Tex-Mex dishes.

Stovetop Italian Meatballs

1¾ pounds ground beef
¾ cup crushed soda crackers
½ teaspoon dried oregano
¼ teaspoon dried parsley
3 tablespoons grated Parmesan
    cheese

1 garlic clove, smashed, peeled,
    and finely chopped
About 5 teaspoons water,
    divided
About 4 teaspoons olive oil,
    divided

> **Yields 30–34 meatballs**
>
> Getting meatballs to cook through evenly in the frying pan can be a challenge. One trick is to shake the pan during cooking to help the meatballs retain their round shape. If that doesn't work, finish the meatballs off by simmering in beef broth.
>
> ❧

1. In a large bowl, use your hands to mix together the ground beef, crushed crackers, oregano, parsley, Parmesan cheese, and garlic. Mix in 3 teaspoons of the water. Continue adding water 1 teaspoon at a time as needed until the mixture is lightly moistened—not too dry or too wet.
2. Form the mixture into balls approximately 1½ inches in diameter.
3. Melt 2 teaspoons of the olive oil over medium heat in a frying pan. Add half the meatballs and cook for about 15 minutes, turning occasionally, until the meatballs are cooked through. Remove the meatballs with a slotted spoon and place on paper towels to drain. Clean out the frying pan, add the remaining olive oil, and cook the remaining meatballs.

Cooking Meat to Perfection

To keep hot fat from splattering when browning meat, sprinkle flour on the bottom of the skillet before adding the meat. You also can add water as the meat cooks.

Guacamole with Tortilla Chips

1 small red onion
2 garlic cloves
4 avocados

3 tablespoons (or to taste) lemon juice
¼ cup salsa
Corn tortilla chips

1. Peel and chop the red onion. Smash, peel, and finely chop the garlic cloves. Slice the avocados lengthwise, working around the pit. Remove the skin and pit, and mash the avocados in a medium-sized bowl.
2. Mix the onion, garlic, lemon juice, and salsa with the mashed avocado. Refrigerate briefly to give the flavors time to blend, and then serve with the tortilla chips.

No-Bake Tex-Mex Nachos

About 4½ ounces tortilla chips
1½ cups canned chili-style red kidney beans
2 teaspoons vegetable oil

2 tablespoons sour cream
½ cup grated Cheddar or Monterey jack cheese

1. Lay the tortilla chips on a baking sheet. Add more chips if necessary to cover the baking sheet.
2. Drain the kidney beans. Mash the beans by hand or purée in a food processor.
3. Heat the oil in a frying pan on medium. Add the mashed kidney beans and heat through, stirring. Stir in the sour cream.
4. Carefully spoon the kidney bean mixture onto the tortilla chips. Sprinkle with the grated cheese and serve.

Chicken Quesadillas for a Crowd

2 (6-ounce) skinless, boneless
    chicken breasts
⅓ cup soy sauce
1 large garlic clove, smashed,
    peeled, and chopped
2 thin slices fresh ginger
1½ tablespoons brown sugar
1 tablespoon vegetable oil
4 large fresh button mushrooms
    (about 3 ounces total)

2 green onions
2 tablespoons butter or
    margarine, divided
4 flour tortillas
2 cups shredded Monterey jack
    cheese
6 black olives, chopped
½ cup sour cream or salsa,
    optional

> **Yields 12 servings**
>
> Marinating the chicken before cooking gives this dish extra flavor. If you don't have time for marinating, try tossing the chicken with ½ teaspoon hot chili powder before frying.
>
> ❧

1. Rinse the chicken breasts and pat dry. Combine the soy sauce, garlic, ginger, and brown sugar. Pour the marinade into a large resealable plastic bag. Add the chicken breasts and seal the bag. Marinate the chicken in the refrigerator for at least 1 hour. Turn the bag occasionally to make sure the marinade covers all the chicken.

2. Heat the vegetable oil in a frying pan. Add the chicken and cook until it turns white and is nearly cooked through. Remove from the frying pan and cut the chicken into thin strips. Clean out the pan.

3. Wipe the mushrooms clean with a damp cloth and slice. Wash the green onions in hot water, drain, and dice.

4. Melt 1 tablespoon butter or margarine in the frying pan. Add 1 flour tortilla. Cook for 1 minute, then sprinkle ½ cup of the shredded cheese over the tortilla. Let the cheese melt, then add half the mushrooms, green onions, olives, and chicken.

5. Lay a second flour tortilla on top. Press down with a spatula so it adheres to the first tortilla. Cook until the first tortilla is browned on the bottom. Turn over and cook the other side. Sprinkle ½ cup of the shredded cheese over the top of the quesadilla during the last minute of cooking.

6. Clean out the frying pan, add the remaining 1 tablespoon of margarine, and repeat the process with the other 2 flour tortillas. To serve, cut each quesadilla into 6 equal wedges. Serve with sour cream or salsa for dipping.

Spicy Chicken Thighs

Serves 4–8

This easy dish lets you take care of last-minute party preparations while the thighs are cooking.

∾

8 chicken thighs, bone-in (about 2 pounds)
2 small garlic cloves
3 tablespoons ketchup
3 tablespoons molasses
3 teaspoons brown sugar
6 tablespoons water
1 teaspoon grated orange peel

1. Rinse the chicken thighs under cold, running water and pat dry.
2. Smash, peel, and chop the garlic cloves. Combine the garlic, ketchup, molasses, brown sugar, water, and orange peel. Place ¼ cup of the sauce in a large resealable plastic bag. Add the chicken thighs (separate the thighs and sauce in half and use 2 bags if necessary). Seal the bag(s) and place in the refrigerator. Marinate the chicken for at least 2 hours, turning the bag occasionally so that all the chicken is coated. Reserve the remaining sauce in a sealed container in the refrigerator.
3. Preheat oven to 350°. Spray a baking sheet with nonstick cooking spray.
4. Place the thighs on the prepared baking sheet. Brush part of the reserved sauce on the thighs with a pastry brush. Turn the thighs over to make sure both sides are covered with the sauce.
5. Bake the thighs for 50 minutes or until cooked through. Brush sauce on the thighs at least twice more while they are cooking.

Chili Accompaniments

The same accompaniments that give nachos their crowd-pleasing appeal also go well with chili. Try serving the chili with individual bowls of sour cream, green onions, and shredded cheese. For an added touch, sprinkle a bit of shredded cheese on top of the chili just prior to serving. Another idea is to turn the chili from a main dish into a dip by serving it with tortilla chips.

Middle Eastern Party Platter

1 large, ripe tomato
1 teaspoon dried basil
⅛ teaspoon salt
Freshly cracked black pepper,
   to taste
3 garlic cloves
2 pita pockets

1 (19-ounce) can chickpeas,
   4 tablespoons juice reserved
2 tablespoons, plus 1 teaspoon
   lemon juice
2 tablespoons tahini
¼ teaspoon (or to taste)
   ground cumin

> **Serves 12**
>
> If you want, toast the pita slices at 350° for 8 to 10 minutes before serving. For an extra touch, serve with cubes of feta cheese for guests to add to the pita along with the hummus spread and tomato.

1. Wash the tomato and finely chop. Toss with the basil, salt, and pepper. Set aside. Smash, peel, and chop the garlic.
2. Cut each pita into 6 or 8 equal wedges, as desired. Place the pita wedges on a serving platter and set aside.
3. Drain the chickpeas (reserving 4 tablespoons juice) and mash.
4. Blend the mashed chickpeas with the garlic, lemon juice, tahini, cumin, and reserved chickpea juice.
5. Serve the pita wedges with the tomato and hummus on the side.

Make Mine Medium-Rare!

Ever wonder what it means when someone orders their steak "rare" or "well done"? It all comes down to cooking temperature. Rare steak is cooked to an internal temperature of 140°, while the internal temperature of well-done steak is 170°. In between, medium and medium-rare steaks are cooked to internal temperatures of 145° and 160° respectively.

Picnic Potato Salad

2 pounds potatoes
3 Hard-Boiled Eggs (see page 14)
1 celery stalk
⅔ cup mayonnaise

¼ cup red wine vinegar
2 teaspoons granulated sugar
½ red onion, chopped
Salt and pepper, to taste

1. Peel the potatoes and cut into cubes. Fill a pot with enough salted water to cover the potatoes. Add the potatoes and bring the water to a boil over medium-high heat. Reduce heat to low, cover, and simmer the potatoes until tender and easily pierced with a fork.
2. Chop the eggs. Wash the celery and cut diagonally into 1-inch pieces. In a small bowl, combine the mayonnaise, vinegar, and sugar.
3. Place the potatoes, eggs, celery, and red onion in a large bowl and toss with the mayonnaise mixture. Add salt and pepper to taste. Cover and chill until ready to serve.

Coleslaw for a Crowd

1 head green cabbage (about 1½ pounds)
2 large carrots
2 red bell peppers

1 tablespoon Dijon mustard
1 teaspoon granulated sugar
½ cup apple cider vinegar

1. Wash the vegetables and dry. Shred the cabbage (should yield about 9 cups). Peel and shred the carrots. Cut the red peppers in half, remove the seeds, and dice. In a large bowl, combine the vegetables and toss to mix.
2. In a small bowl, whisk the Dijon mustard and sugar into the vinegar. Pour the dressing into a large bowl.
3. Add the vegetables to the dressing, tossing again to mix thoroughly. Refrigerate the coleslaw in a sealed container until ready to serve.

Stuffed Potatoes with Spinach

*8 large baking potatoes (about
   8 ounces each)*
4 cups fresh spinach leaves
2 teaspoons vegetable oil
1 cup sour cream
½ cup butter or margarine

2 teaspoons garlic powder
2 teaspoons salt
Pepper, to taste
*½ cup shredded Monterey jack
   cheese*

> **Serves 8**
>
> These can be prepared a few hours in advance. Cover tightly with plastic wrap and store in the refrigerator until ready to cook.
>
> ∾

1. Preheat oven to 400°.
2. Wash the potatoes, scrubbing off any dirt. Pierce the potatoes in several spots with a fork. Wash the spinach leaves, drain, and chop.
3. Bake the potatoes for 45 minutes or until done. To test for doneness, pierce the potatoes with a fork. It should go through easily. Remove from the oven.
4. While the potatoes are cooking, heat the oil in a frying pan. Briefly sauté the spinach leaves until bright green.
5. Slice the potatoes open lengthwise. Carefully scoop out most of the potato pulp, leaving about ¼ inch around the skin. Place the potato pulp in a large bowl and mash. Mash in the spinach, sour cream, butter, garlic powder, salt, and pepper.
6. Place the potato shells on a baking sheet. Spoon an even amount of the potato mixture into each shell. Sprinkle each potato with 1 tablespoon shredded cheese. Place in the oven and bake for another 15 minutes or until the cheese is melted.

Make-Ahead Chicken Wings

Want to make a batch of chicken wings ahead of time to serve to a crowd? Cook the chicken wings according to the recipe, place in freezer bags, and seal. Mark the date the wings were frozen. When ready to use, thaw the frozen chicken wings in the refrigerator. Cooked chicken wings (and left-over unused sauce) can be frozen for up to 1 month.

Five-Minute Nachos

2 tomatoes
2 teaspoons vegetable oil
½ cup chopped red onion
1½ pounds ground beef
1 package taco seasoning
1 (13.5-ounce) bag tortilla chips

2½ cups mix of shredded Monterey jack and Cheddar cheese
½ cup sliced black olives, optional

1. Preheat oven to 350°. Wash the tomatoes, dry, and chop.
2. Heat the oil in a frying pan. Add the onion and cook on medium-low heat until tender. Add the ground beef. Stir in the taco seasoning. Cook until the ground beef is browned. Drain off fat from pan.
3. Spread out approximately half of the tortilla chips in the bottom of a 9" × 13" × 2" glass baking dish. Spoon the cooked ground beef over the chips. Sprinkle 1 cup of the shredded cheese over the ground beef. Cover with the remaining chips (there will probably be a few chips left over), and 1 cup of the cheese. Sprinkle the tomatoes and olives (if using) on top. Sprinkle the remaining cheese on top.
4. Bake the nachos for 5 minutes or until the cheese is melted. Serve hot.

Crowd-Pleasing Sloppy Joes

Invented during the Depression as a means of stretching ground beef through several meals, Sloppy Joes (page 194) are simply hamburgers fortified with extra tomato sauce or ketchup. There are no hard and fast rules to making Sloppy Joes. The sauce can be soup-like, or only slightly more watery than chili. Instead of beans, extra vegetables can be added to the ground beef. Feel free to spice up the dish with chili powder or other seasonings, depending on your guest's preferences.

Grilled Honey and Garlic Spareribs

6 pounds pork spareribs
4 garlic cloves
¼ cup molasses
¼ cup ketchup
¼ cup liquid honey

1. Cut the ribs into 2 rib sections. Bring a large pot of water to a boil.
2. Add the ribs, cover, and simmer for 30 minutes or until the ribs are tender. (Cook the ribs in batches or use 2 large pots if necessary.) Drain.
3. Preheat grill to medium heat. Smash, peel, and chop the garlic cloves. Combine the chopped garlic with the molasses, ketchup, and honey.
4. Place the spareribs on the grill and cook for 20 to 25 minutes or until heated through, turning the ribs occasionally and brushing them with the honey and garlic marinade.

> **Serves 8–12**
>
> Don't have a grill? The ribs can also be baked at 350° for 1½ hours or until tender. Baste the spareribs frequently with the honey and garlic marinade during the final 30 minutes of cooking.
>
> ∾

Make-Ahead Beef Tenderloin Salad

2 pounds beef tenderloin
3 garlic cloves
2 tablespoons mayonnaise
2 tablespoons lime juice
2 tablespoons liquid honey
4 large tomatoes
1 head green lettuce

1. Preheat oven to 425°. To cook the beef medium-rare, roast for at least 45 minutes. Let cool and slice into thin strips.
2. Smash, peel, and chop the garlic cloves. Mix together the mayonnaise, lime juice, honey, and garlic. Toss the sliced beef with the mayonnaise mixture. Cover and refrigerate overnight.
3. Just before serving, prepare the salad: Wash the tomatoes and lettuce, and slice the tomatoes. Place 2 lettuce leaves and several tomato slices on each plate. Dish out an equal amount of the beef slices on top of each serving.

> **Serves 12**
>
> A popular party dish, beef tenderloin salad is very easy to make. Feel free to add extra garnishes, such as fresh parsley leaves or crushed peanuts.
>
> ∾

Barbecued Spareribs

Serves 6–8

To cook in the oven, bake at 350° for 30 minutes on each side, brushing regularly with the sauce.

‍‌❧

2 racks spareribs (about 4 pounds total)
1 tablespoon olive oil
¼ cup chopped white onion
2 garlic cloves, smashed, peeled, and chopped
½ cup ketchup

½ cup apple cider vinegar
½ cup water
3 tablespoons brown sugar
2 tablespoons Worcestershire sauce
1 teaspoon (or to taste) hot chili sauce

1. Cut the ribs apart into serving-sized pieces (no more than 2 spareribs per serving).
2. Bring a large pot of water to a boil. Add the ribs. Bring the water back to a boil, then reduce heat to low. Simmer the ribs, covered, for 30 minutes or until tender.
3. While the ribs are simmering, heat the oil in a medium-sized saucepan. Add the onion and garlic. Cook on medium-low heat until the onion is tender. Add the ketchup, vinegar, water, brown sugar, Worcestershire sauce, and hot chili sauce. Increase heat to medium-high and bring to a boil. Reduce heat to low and simmer, uncovered, for 20 minutes.
4. Preheat grill to medium. Place the spareribs on the grill and brush with the barbecue sauce. Cook for approximately 20 minutes, turning the ribs regularly and brushing with the barbecue sauce.

Making Fresh Bread Crumbs

Easy to make, homemade bread crumbs allow you to add your own combination of spices and herbs. Start with slightly stale bread and chop roughly into cubes. If you have a food processor, simply stick the cubes in the food processor with the seasonings and process until it forms crumbs. If not, bread crumbs can also be made by hand: Grate the bread using the rough side of a cheese grater. Stored in a sealed bag in the refrigerator, bread crumbs will last for up to 1 week. They can also be frozen for up to 6 months.

Texas Chili

2 green bell peppers
1 medium-sized yellow onion
4 garlic cloves
2 jalapeño chili peppers,
    optional
¼ cup vegetable oil
3 pounds boneless beef cubes
6 cups tomato sauce
1 cup tomato paste

3 tablespoons granulated sugar
¼ cup chili powder
1 tablespoon dried oregano
Salt, to taste
½ teaspoon (or to taste) freshly
    cracked black pepper
2 (13.5-ounce) bags tortilla
    chips

Serves 6–8

Want to serve guests something a little more economical? Ground beef can be substituted for the boneless beef cubes. If using ground beef, reduce the amount of vegetable oil to 2 tablespoons.

∾

1. Wash the vegetables and dry. Cut the green peppers in half, remove the seeds, and cut into bite-sized chunks. Peel and chop the onion. Smash, peel, and chop the garlic cloves. If using the jalapeños, slice lengthwise, remove the seeds, and coarsely chop.

2. Heat the vegetable oil on medium-high in a large, heavy saucepan. Add ½ of the beef cubes and brown. Remove the beef cubes from the saucepan and drain on paper towels. Repeat with the remaining beef.

3. Add the green peppers, onion, garlic, and chili peppers to the saucepan. Cook on medium heat until the onion is tender. Add the tomato sauce, tomato paste, and sugar. Stir in the chili powder, oregano, salt, and pepper.

4. Bring the chili to a boil. Reduce heat to medium-low, cover, and simmer for 90 minutes or until the beef is tender. Add about 1 cup water to the chili to adjust consistency if desired. Serve with the tortilla chips.

Chili Pepper Safety

The same oil that gives chili peppers their fiery heat can cause serious damage if it gets in the eyes. Always wear plastic gloves when handling chili peppers. Be sure to wash your hands in soapy water immediately afterward.

Lazy Slow-Cooked Chili

1 yellow onion
3 celery stalks
2 pounds ground chuck
4 cups canned crushed tomatoes
4 cups canned chickpeas, with liquid

2 tablespoons (or to taste) chili powder
1 teaspoon (or to taste) ground cumin
1 teaspoon (or to taste) garlic powder
2 tablespoons granulated sugar
Salt and pepper, to taste

1. Peel the onion and roughly chop. Roughly chop the celery.
2. Brown the ground chuck in a frying pan over medium heat. Drain.
3. Transfer the meat to a slow cooker. Add the onion, celery, tomatoes, and chickpeas. Stir in the chili powder, ground cumin, garlic powder, sugar, and salt and pepper. Cook on low setting for approximately 4 hours or until the vegetables are tender and the chili is cooked.

Sloppy Joes

2 teaspoons butter or margarine
1 yellow onion, chopped
2 red bell peppers, sliced
2 pounds ground beef
2 cups canned kidney beans

2 cups tomato sauce
4 tablespoons tomato paste
1 cup water
1 teaspoon ground cumin
2 teaspoons granulated sugar
6–8 hamburger buns

1. Heat the butter or margarine on medium in a large frying pan or saucepan. Add the onion. Cook for 1 minute, then add the bell peppers.
2. Add the ground beef. Cook over medium heat until browned. Drain off any excess fat.
3. Add the kidney beans, tomato sauce, tomato paste, and water. Mix thoroughly and stir in the ground cumin and sugar.
4. Bring to a boil. Cover and simmer for 20 to 25 minutes, until heated thoroughly. Spoon the meat mixture over the hamburger buns, or serve in a large pot and invite guests to prepare their own.

Swiss Cheese Fondue

*1 loaf crusty bread, such as
    French bread
1 large garlic clove
About 1½ cups milk
1 tablespoon lemon juice*

*1½ pounds grated Swiss cheese,
    such as Gruyère
¼ teaspoon ground nutmeg
¼ teaspoon dried parsley
    flakes*

Serves 6

Preparing fondue for a crowd of 10 or more? Instead of simply doubling this recipe, it's best to prepare 2 batches of cheese fondue and use 2 separate fondue pots.

1. Cut the French bread into cubes.
2. Cut the garlic in half and rub it around the insides of a medium-sized saucepan. Add 1¼ cups of the milk to the saucepan and warm on medium-low heat. (The garlic can be added to the milk or discarded.) Be sure not to allow the milk to boil.
3. When the milk is warm, stir in the lemon juice. Add a handful of the grated cheese to the milk and stir in a figure-8 pattern. When the cheese is completely melted, add another handful. Keep adding a handful of cheese at a time, stirring continuously and taking care not to allow the mixture to boil. If the fondue is too thick, add as much of the remaining ¼ cup milk as necessary.
4. Increase heat until the mixture is just bubbling. Stir in the nutmeg and dried parsley flakes. Transfer to a fondue pot and set on the burner. Use fondue forks to dip the bread cubes into the cheese.

Cheese Fondue Tips

Making cheese fondue can be a little tricky. That's because the age of the cheese will affect the amount of liquid it absorbs. The same amount of wine that works perfectly with older cheese may make a less aged cheese turn out runny. When making Cheese Fondue (page 124) you may want to start with only ¾ cup of apple juice, and add more as needed.

Tofu Burgers

Serves 8

Vegans may want to use vegetarian Worcestershire sauce, which contains no anchovies, and a liquid egg substitute instead of an egg. Feel free to sub-stitute rice vinegar in place of white vinegar if you have it.

6 ounces firm tofu

6 tablespoons quick-cooking oats

2 tablespoons finely chopped onion

3 tablespoons Worcestershire sauce

⅛ teaspoon (or to taste) chili powder

1 egg

2 teaspoons olive oil

1 cup crushed tomatoes

2 tablespoons (or to taste) white vinegar

2 teaspoons (or to taste) granulated sugar

8 English muffins

1. Drain the tofu and crumble. Stir in the oats, onion, Worcestershire sauce, and chili powder. Add the egg and mix together with your hands to make sure the tofu is thoroughly mixed with the other ingredients.

2. Heat the olive oil in a frying pan. Form the tofu mixture into balls approx-imately the size of large golf balls and flatten with the palm of your hand. Add the burgers to the frying pan, using a spatula to gently flatten them and push together any portions that are separating from the main burger. Cook the burgers for 3 to 4 minutes on each side, until browned.

3. Heat the crushed tomatoes, vinegar, and sugar in a small saucepan. Taste and adjust the seasoning if desired. Keep warm on low heat while toasting the muffins.

4. Split the muffins in half and toast. Serve open-faced, with a portion of the tomato mixture spooned onto one muffin half and the burger on the other.

Tofu Types

Tofu comes in a variety of textures. Designed to hold their shape in Asian stir-fries, firm and extra-firm tofus are fairly solid. On the other hand, soft tofu have a texture similar to Jell-O, while silken tofu are creamy. For best results, use soft or silken tofu in dessert recipes such as Creamy Tofu Shake (page 65).

Vegetarian Chili

4 medium potatoes
2 cups baby carrots
4 cups drained mixed beans,
    such as kidney or pinto
2 cups drained chickpeas
3 cups canned French green
    beans, drained
5 cups tomato sauce

1 cup vegetable broth
4 teaspoons dehydrated minced
    onion
5 teaspoons (or to taste) chili
    powder
2 teaspoons ground cumin
½ teaspoon (or to taste) salt

Serves 6–8

A bowl of chili wouldn't be complete without a dipper. Tortilla chips, sourdough bread, and crusty French or Italian bread are all good choices, Or, serve the chili on hamburger buns or rolls to create your own version of "Vegetarian Sloppy Joes."

1. Peel the potatoes, rinse, and chop into small chunks. Wash the carrots and pat dry.
2. Combine the potatoes, carrots, mixed beans, chickpeas, green beans, tomato sauce, and vegetable broth in a large saucepan. Stir in the minced onion, chili powder, ground cumin, and salt.
3. Bring to a boil over medium heat. Reduce heat to low and cover. Simmer for approximately 1 hour or until the vegetables are tender. Taste and adjust the seasoning if desired.

Make-Ahead Coleslaw

Want to prepare coleslaw earlier in the day? Wash and prepare the vegetables, toss, and store in a sealed container in the refrigerator. Toss the vegetables with the vinegar dressing just before serving.

Elegant Cocktail Wieners

Serves 12

For a sweeter flavor, add up to ¼ cup of a jelly such as cranberry or grape, or orange marmalade.

∽

1 (16-ounce) package cocktail wieners
¾ cup ketchup
2 tablespoons lemon juice

1 tablespoon prepared horseradish
¼ teaspoon hot chili sauce or Tabasco sauce

Separate the cocktail wieners. Heat the ketchup, lemon juice, and horseradish in a small saucepan on medium. Stir in the hot chili sauce or Tabasco sauce. Add the cocktail wieners and heat through. Serve hot.

Chapter 12

Home Sweet Home:
When the Folks Visit

Sunday Morning French Toast

4 eggs
¼ teaspoon salt
¼ teaspoon black pepper
½ cup milk
½ cup half-and-half
1 teaspoon vanilla extract

About 2 tablespoons butter or
  margarine
8–10 slices white bread
Brown sugar, to taste
Maple syrup, to taste

1. In a small bowl, lightly beat the eggs. Stir in the salt, pepper, milk, half-and-half, and vanilla extract.
2. Heat 2 tablespoons butter or margarine in a frying pan on medium-low heat.
3. Take a slice of bread and dip one side into the beaten egg, letting it sit for a few seconds so that it soaks up the egg mixture. Turn the bread over and repeat with the other side. Lay the bread flat in the frying pan. Repeat with the remaining slices of bread, but soak only as many slices of bread as you are cooking at a time. Add more butter or margarine to the frying pan as needed.
4. Cook until the bread is browned on the bottom, then turn over and repeat with the other side. Serve with the brown sugar and maple syrup.

Healthy Fat

Don't let a high fat content deter you from enjoying a plate of freshly grilled salmon or swordfish steaks. Fish classified as "oily" contain omega-3—a type of fatty acid that does not clog arteries. Better yet, omega-3 acids are essential for healthy brain functioning!

Basic Baked Potato

*4 baking (russet or Idaho)
  potatoes*

*2 tablespoons (or to taste)
  butter or margarine*

1. Preheat oven to 400°.
2. Wash the potatoes and scrub to remove any dirt. Poke a few holes in each potato with a fork. Place directly on the middle oven rack.
3. Bake the potatoes for 45 minutes or until done. To test for doneness, pierce the potatoes with a fork. It should go through easily. Remove from oven. Cut each potato in half lengthwise while still hot. Add the butter or margarine. Serve hot.

Serves 4

After cooking, you can load the potato with sour cream, bacon bits, chives, shredded cheese, or your own favorite toppings.

Lucky Mashed Potatoes

*4 large potatoes
4 tablespoons butter or
  margarine
About 2½ tablespoons cream*

*¼ teaspoon (or to taste)
  nutmeg
Salt and pepper, to taste
2 teaspoons dried or chopped
  fresh parsley, optional*

1. Wash and peel the potatoes, and cut into quarters.
2. Fill a medium-sized saucepan with enough salted water to cover the potatoes, and bring to a boil over medium-high heat. Cook the potatoes in the boiling water until tender and easily pierced with a fork. Drain.
3. Place the potatoes in a bowl and add the butter or margarine. Use a fork or potato masher to whip the potatoes until fluffy. Add the cream as you mix, being sure not to add more than is needed. Stir in the nutmeg, salt, and pepper. Garnish with the parsley.

Serves 4

An old tradition calls for sprinkling mashed potatoes with nutmeg for good luck.

Caramelized Onions

Serves 2

Trying to cut down on sugar? Use salt and pepper instead of sugar to fry the caramelized onions.

∾

8 pearl onions
2 tablespoons butter or margarine

4 teaspoons granulated sugar

1. Fill a deep-sided frying pan with 1 inch of water. Add the pearl onions and bring to a boil over high heat. Reduce heat to medium-low, cover, and cook for at least 15 minutes or until the onions are tender. Remove the onions from the pan. Drain. They should be shiny and translucent.
2. Melt the butter or margarine in the frying pan. Stir in the sugar. Return the onions back to the pan. Cook on medium heat for about 5 to 7 minutes, until the onions are nicely glazed with the sugar.

Basic Gravy

Yields about 1 cup

For best results, wait until the meat is cooked before making the gravy. Flour-thickened gravy is often served with turkey, as in Thanksgiving Turkey with Gravy (page 217).

∾

2½ tablespoons meat drippings
2 tablespoons all-purpose flour
1 cup milk

Salt and pepper, to taste
⅛ teaspoon (or to taste) celery salt

1. Heat the meat drippings in a frying pan on medium.
2. While the drippings are heating, whisk the flour into the milk, trying to remove all the lumps.
3. Reduce heat to low and use a whisk to slowly add the milk and flour mixture to the meat drippings. Whisk constantly until the mixture thickens into gravy (this will take several minutes).
4. Stir in the salt, pepper, and celery salt. Serve immediately.

Baked Onion Soup in a Bread Bowl

½ white onion
4 large sourdough bread
    rounds

2½ packages instant onion
    soup mix
1 cup grated Swiss or Cheddar
    cheese

Serves 4

The exact amount of
onion soup you need
will depend on the size
of the sourdough bread
bowl.

1. Preheat oven to 375°.
2. Peel and finely chop the onion. Fill a deep-sided frying pan with 1 inch of water. Add the onions and bring to a boil over high heat. Reduce heat to medium-low, cover, and cook for at least 15 minutes or until the onion is tender. (The chopped onion should be very shiny and translucent.) Remove from the frying pan.
3. Carefully cut around the sides of the sourdough bread to remove the top, leaving about ½ inch around the edges. Remove most of the filling, but leave enough on the inside base at the bottom so that the soup won't go right through (the process is very similar to preparing a Halloween jack-o'-lantern). Cut a small amount of the spongy interior into cubes to add back into the soup.
4. Prepare the instant onion soup according to the package directions.
5. Carefully ladle 2 cups of onion soup into each sourdough bowl. Add up to ¼ cup of the chopped onion and the spongy bread cubes. Sprinkle ¼ cup of grated cheese over each bowl of soup. Place the bowls on a large baking sheet without the tops on. Cook for 20 to 25 minutes or until the cheese is melted. Serve hot.

Peeling Pearl Onions

Roughly the size of a marble, pearl onions have a milder, sweeter flavor than larger onions. The easiest way to peel pearl onions is to boil them in enough water to cover for 2 minutes. Drain the pearl onions in cold water and push off the papery skins. Be sure to trim off the root end before boiling the onion.

Gourmet Steamed Vegetables

Serves 4

Steaming vegetables in chicken broth instead of water gives them extra flavor.

∾

2 zucchini
1 green bell pepper
2 carrots

About 1 cup chicken broth
1½ teaspoons dried parsley

1. Wash all the vegetables and drain. Cut the zucchini diagonally into thin slices, no less than ¼ inch thick. Cut the green pepper in half, remove the seeds, and cut into cubes. Peel the carrots and cut diagonally into ¼-inch slices.
2. Fill a medium-sized saucepan with 1 inch of chicken broth. Place a metal steamer inside the pan. Make sure the bottom of the steamer is not touching the broth. Add the dried parsley to the broth and heat to boiling.
3. When the broth is boiling, add the carrots to the steamer. Cover and cook for about 2 minutes, then add the green pepper. Cook for another 2 to 3 minutes, and add the zucchini. Continue steaming until the vegetables are tender. Drain and serve.

Electric Steamers

When choosing a steamer, look for one that is easy to clean, with a timer that shuts off automatically when the food is cooked. If your budget permits, consider a larger model that can cook rice and steam food at the same time. The convenience of having your entire meal cooked all at once is well worth the slightly higher price tag.

Classic Broccoli in Cheese Sauce

1 pound broccoli, fresh or frozen
Water, as needed
2 tablespoons butter or margarine

2 tablespoons all-purpose flour
1 cup milk
¼ teaspoon ground nutmeg
Black pepper, to taste
¾ cup grated cheese

Serves 2–4

This recipe works well with many different varieties of cheese, including Cheddar, Swiss, and even soy cheese.

1. Wash the broccoli and drain. Chop the broccoli into bite-sized pieces.
2. Fill a medium-sized saucepan with 1 inch of water. Place a metal steamer inside the pan. Make sure the water is not touching the bottom of the steamer. Heat the water to boiling.
3. When the water is boiling, add the broccoli pieces to the steamer. Cover and steam until the broccoli is tender, about 10 minutes. Drain and set aside.
4. In a medium-sized saucepan, melt the butter on low heat. Stir in the flour. Whisk in the milk, nutmeg, and pepper. Bring to a boil over medium heat, whisking continually.
5. Reduce heat slightly and whisk in the grated cheese. Bring to a boil again and stir in the broccoli. Heat through and serve hot.

Electric Steamer—A Dieter's Aid

An electric steamer is a great way to lower the fat and calorie count in food since the food isn't cooked in oil or butter.

Vegetables in Béchamel (White) Sauce

2 (14-ounce) cans French green beans
1½ tablespoons butter
1 tablespoon all-purpose flour
¼ cup milk
¼ teaspoon (or to taste) ground nutmeg
Salt and pepper, to taste

1. Heat the green beans on medium in a saucepan. Reserve ¼ cup of juice from the cooked beans to use in the sauce. Keep the green beans warm on low heat while preparing the sauce.
2. Melt the butter in a small saucepan over low heat. Stir in the flour. Cook on low heat for 3 minutes, continually stirring.
3. Gradually whisk in the milk and the reserved green bean juice. Bring to a boil, continually whisking until thickened. Stir in the nutmeg, salt, and pepper. Pour over the green beans and serve.

Tender Glazed Carrots

2 cups baby carrots
1 tablespoon olive oil
1 cup apple juice
2 tablespoons maple syrup

1. Wash the baby carrots and drain.
2. Heat the olive oil in a frying pan over medium heat. Add the carrots. Cook briefly until browned.
3. Add the apple juice. Cover and cook over medium heat until the liquid is absorbed, 20 to 30 minutes.
4. Increase heat to high and add the maple syrup. Cook for 2 to 3 minutes, stirring, until the carrots are nicely glazed.

Roasted Tomatoes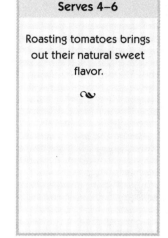

2 tablespoons olive oil
4 fresh tomatoes
4 garlic cloves
2 teaspoons dried basil or
    parsley flakes

Salt to taste
Freshly cracked black pepper,
    to taste

Serves 4–6

Roasting tomatoes brings out their natural sweet flavor.

◊

1. Preheat oven to 400°. Lay a piece of aluminum foil on a large baking sheet. Rub the olive oil over the foil.
2. Wash the tomatoes, dry, and cut in half crosswise. Smash, peel, and chop the garlic cloves.
3. Lay the tomato halves on the aluminum foil. Sprinkle the dried basil or parsley flakes over the tomato, followed by the salt, pepper, and chopped garlic. Roast the tomatoes for 30 minutes or until the outside edges are blackened. Let cool and serve.

Baked Ham with Soy Glaze

2 tablespoons soy sauce
1 teaspoon honey mustard
2 teaspoons brown sugar

1 teaspoon pineapple juice
3-pound precooked ham

Serves 4

This is a great recipe for those occasions when you want to entertain your parents instead of being stuck in the kitchen cooking. Serve with Basic Baked Potato (page 201) and Gourmet Steamed Vegetables (page 204) for a complete meal.

◊

1. Preheat oven to 325°.
2. In a small bowl, combine the soy sauce, honey mustard, brown sugar, and pineapple juice to make the glaze.
3. Place the ham in a shallow dish and baste with the glaze.
4. Bake for 45 minutes or until done, brushing with the glaze several times during the cooking process. The ham should be cooked to an internal temperature of at least 130°.

Shepherd's Pie

½ yellow onion
2 large carrots
4 medium or 6 small potatoes
1 beef bouillon cube
½ cup water
1 tablespoon Worcestershire
    sauce
1 teaspoon granulated sugar

¼ teaspoon garlic salt
2 teaspoons vegetable oil
1 pound ground beef
2 tablespoons margarine
3 tablespoons milk
¼ teaspoon paprika
1 cup canned corn

1. Preheat oven to 350°. Chop the onion and set aside. Wash, peel, and chop the carrots. Wash the potatoes and cut into chunks.
2. Bring the water to a boil. Dissolve the beef bouillon in the boiling water. Stir in the Worcestershire sauce, sugar, and garlic salt.
3. Heat the oil in a frying pan and add the ground beef. When the ground beef is nearly cooked, drain off excess fat from the pan. Add the onion and carrots. Cook until the onion is tender. Add the bouillon sauce, reduce heat, and simmer for about 30 minutes.
4. Meanwhile, prepare the potato topping. Place the potatoes in a large saucepan with water to cover. Boil the potatoes until tender. Remove from heat and drain. Add the margarine and milk, and mash the potatoes. Stir in the paprika.
5. Stir the canned corn into the ground beef mixture. Place the mixture in a deep casserole dish. Spread the mashed potatoes on top. Bake for 20 minutes or until the potatoes are browned and the meat mixture is bubbling.

Leftover Mashed Potatoes

Nothing beats food that just needs reheating for those nights you're in a rush to hit the books. The recipe for Basic Mashed Potatoes for One (page 93) can easily be doubled so that you have leftovers for another night. Simply cover the leftover mashed potatoes and refrigerate. To reheat, fry in a bit of oil, or heat in the microwave.

Sweet-and-Sour Country-Style Ribs

2½ pounds boneless, country-style pork ribs
1 cup long-grain rice
¼ cup pineapple juice
¼ cup water
2 teaspoons brown sugar

1 teaspoon soy sauce
2 teaspoons white vinegar
2 teaspoons cornstarch, dissolved in 3 teaspoons water

Serves 4

This recipe makes an interesting variation from traditional Sweet-and-Sour Pork (page 101).

1. Place the ribs in a large saucepan with enough water to cover. Place the lid on the saucepan and heat the water to boiling. Reduce heat to medium-low and simmer the ribs, covered, for about 45 minutes or until tender.

2. During the last 15 minutes of cooking, prepare the rice (see Basic Cooked Long-Grain Rice, page 95).

3. In a small saucepan, heat the pineapple juice, water, brown sugar, soy sauce, and vinegar over medium heat, stirring to dissolve the sugar. Bring to a boil and stir in the cornstarch and water mixture. Keep the sauce warm on low heat.

4. When the ribs are done, place them on the rack of a roasting pan. Brush part of the sauce over the ribs with a pastry brush. Broil for 15 to 20 minutes, brushing the ribs with the sauce occasionally. Make sure not to overcook the ribs. Serve with the cooked rice.

Deep-Fried Fish

About 5 cups oil, for deep-frying
1½ pounds fresh or frozen fish
*   fillets, thawed*

4 large egg yolks
3 cups bread crumbs
2 fresh lemons

1. Add the oil to a large, heavy saucepan, wok, electric fondue pot, or deep-fat fryer. Heat the oil to 350°. Be sure to follow the manufacturer's instructions for deep-frying with the specific appliance.
2. Rinse the fish fillets and pat dry with a paper towel. Cut the fillets into bite-sized cubes. Beat the egg yolks.
3. Place the fish cubes, beaten egg yolks, and the bread crumbs near the stove. Lay a paper towel on a plate and keep near the stove for draining the fish cubes.
4. Dip each fish cube into the beaten egg, and then coat with the bread crumbs. Deep-fry the fish according to instructions, making sure the fish is completely submerged. Drain the deep-fried fish on the paper towels.
5. Cut each lemon into wedges, and serve as garnish with the fish.

Fish Facts

Fish are commonly classified based on their fat content. Lean fish such as red snapper and halibut have a fat content under 3 percent. At the other end, oily fish like swordfish, salmon, and tuna have a fat content of over 10 percent. Lean fish are often sautéed or baked, while broiling is a good cooking method for fish with a higher fat content.

Red Snapper with Vegetables

4 red snapper fish fillets
3–4 pearl onions, as needed
¼ cup extra-virgin olive oil

1 tablespoon lemon juice
2 tomatoes

1. Rinse the fish fillets and pat dry. Place the fillets in a shallow glass baking dish.
2. Peel and chop the pearl onions. Combine the olive oil and the lemon juice. Pour the marinade over the fish. Add the pearl onions. Marinate the fish for 30 minutes in the refrigerator.
3. While the fish is marinating, preheat oven to 375°. Cut the tomatoes into wedges. Remove the fish from the refrigerator and add the tomatoes.
4. Bake the fish for 20 minutes or until opaque (a milky color) throughout.

> **Serves 4**
>
> Red snapper goes well with simple vegetable dishes, such as Gourmet Steamed Vegetables (page 204). Steamed rice also makes a nice accompaniment.
>
> ∾

Easy Baked Chicken

4 (7-ounce) boneless, skinless
    chicken breasts
3 cups cornflakes

½ cup, plus 2 tablespoons blue
    cheese dressing

1. Preheat oven to 350°. Grease a 9" × 13" glass baking sheet or spray with nonstick cooking spray. Rinse the chicken breasts under cold, running water and pat dry.
2. Place the cornflakes in a large plastic bag. Roll a rolling pin over the cornflakes until they are thoroughly crushed into crumbs.
3. In a small bowl, thoroughly mix together 1 cup of the crushed cornflakes with the blue cheese dressing (discard the remaining crushed cornflakes). Coat each breast with the cornflake mixture.
4. Lay the coated chicken breasts in the prepared baking dish. Bake for 35 to 45 minutes, until the chicken is cooked through.

> **Serves 4**
>
> This easy recipe pairs chicken with tangy blue cheese dressing and cornflakes. Serve with a simple salad or Gourmet Steamed Vegetables (page 204).
>
> ∾

Gourmet Chili

1½ pounds sirloin steak
½ small white onion
½ red bell pepper
2 tablespoons vegetable oil
1 tablespoon (or to taste) chili powder

½ teaspoon ground cumin
½ teaspoon garlic powder
2 cups canned kidney beans, with juice
2 cups crushed tomatoes

1. Cut the meat into bite-sized cubes, about 1 inch thick. Wash and dry the vegetables. Peel and chop the onion. Remove the seeds from the red pepper and chop into cubes.
2. Heat the oil on medium-low in a skillet. Add the onion and red pepper. Sauté until the onion is tender.
3. Add the meat and cook on low heat until browned. Do not drain. Stir in the chili powder, ground cumin, and garlic powder. Mix in the kidney beans and the crushed tomatoes.
4. Cover the chili and simmer on low heat for about 45 minutes. Serve hot with rice or bread.

Healthy Legumes

Beans and peas are a dieter's dream. Besides being low in fat and high in complex carbohydrates, starchy legumes like black-eyed peas, kidney beans, and lima beans are a good source of B vitamins and important minerals such as zinc. Use them in soups, salads, as a side dish or a protein-packed alternative to meat at a main meal.

Dinner Buttermilk Biscuits

1 teaspoon baking powder
½ teaspoon baking soda
1 teaspoon salt

2 cups all-purpose flour
¼ cup shortening
About 1¼ cups buttermilk

1. Preheat oven to 450°.
2. Stir the baking powder, baking soda, and salt into the flour, blending thoroughly.
3. Use a knife to cut the shortening into the flour.
4. Quickly stir 1 cup buttermilk into the flour mixture. If necessary, add as much of the remaining ¼ cup of buttermilk as needed. The dough should be just moist, and not too wet. Do not overmix the dough.
5. Drop a heaping tablespoon of dough onto an ungreased baking sheet. Continue with the remaining dough. Bake the biscuits for 9 to 12 minutes, until they are golden brown. Let cool briefly on a wire rack before serving.

> **Yields about 24 biscuits**
>
> There is no kneading or rolling dough in this easy-to-make biscuit recipe. For best results, stick with real buttermilk; biscuits made with milk that has been soured by adding lemon juice or cream of tartar won't have the same flavor.
>
> ❧

One-Step Meat Loaf

2 tablespoons instant tomato
   and basil soup mix
½ cup water
1 large egg

2 pounds ground beef
¾ cup crushed soda cracker
   crumbs

1. Preheat oven to 350°.
2. Bring the water to a boil in a small saucepan. Dissolve the soup mix in the boiling water. Lightly beat the egg.
3. In a deep casserole dish, combine the ground beef, beaten egg, cracker crumbs, and the soup. Mix thoroughly.
4. Bake for 60 minutes or until the meat loaf is cooked (the internal temperature of the meat loaf should be 160°). Let the meat loaf sit for 20 minutes before slicing and serving.

> **Serves 4**
>
> This simple recipe lets you visit with family or friends while dinner is cooking.
>
> ❧

Beef Stew

2 pounds stewing beef, cut into cubes
2 tablespoons all-purpose flour
½ white onion
About 2 tablespoons vegetable oil
¾ cup water
1 beef bouillon cube
2 cups tomato sauce
2 tablespoons soy sauce
2 tablespoons brown sugar
Salt and pepper, to taste
1 cup baby carrots
4 large potatoes

1. Toss the beef cubes with the flour to coat lightly. Peel the onion and chop into large chunks.
2. Heat the 2 tablespoons oil on medium in a large, heavy saucepan. Add the onion and cook until lightly browned. Add half the beef and cook in the oil until browned. Remove from the saucepan. Cook the remaining beef in the pan, adding more oil if necessary. Return the first batch of cooked meat to the pan.
3. In a small saucepan, bring the water to a boil. Dissolve the bouillon cube in the boiling water, stirring. Add the bouillon to the beef, along with enough extra water so that the beef is covered. Add the tomato sauce, soy sauce, brown sugar, salt, and pepper. Bring to a boil. Reduce heat to low, cover, and simmer.
4. While the stew is simmering, wash the carrots and potatoes. Peel the potatoes and cut into chunks.
5. After the stew has simmered for 1 hour, add the carrots and potatoes. Cook for another 30 minutes or until the potatoes are tender.

Garam Masala

The secret ingredient in Tandoori Chicken (page 219), this popular spice blend also lends flavor to Indian curries. Garam masala is available in the international section of many supermarkets. To make your own, try combining cloves and ground cinnamon with cumin, cardamom, and coriander seeds. (Feel free to experiment by varying the amounts of each spice.) Store in an airtight container.

Irish Stew

2 white onions
2 parsnips
4 red new potatoes
About 2 tablespoons vegetable
    oil
1½ pounds lean boneless lamb,
    cut into cubes for stewing

3 cups low-sodium chicken
    broth
2 sprigs chopped fresh parsley
¼ teaspoon (or to taste) celery
    salt
Salt and pepper, to taste

Serves 4

Lamb is traditionally used to make Irish stew, but you can substitute stewing beef if desired.

1. Peel and chop the onions. Wash and peel the parsnips and potatoes. Dice the parsnips and cut the potatoes into chunks.
2. Heat the 2 tablespoons oil in a large, heavy saucepan. Add half the chopped onion and cook until lightly browned. Add half the lamb and cook in the oil until browned. Remove from the saucepan. Cook the remaining batch of lamb in the pan, adding more oil if necessary. Return the first batch of cooked meat to the pan.
3. Add the chicken broth, parsley, celery salt, and salt and pepper. Bring to a boil. Reduce heat to low, cover, and simmer for 45 minutes.
4. Add the potatoes and parsnips. Simmer for 15 more minutes, then add the remaining onion. Simmer for another 15 minutes, or until the potatoes and parsnips are tender.

Cooking Stew Meat

Don't have time to cook the stew meat for Beef Stew (page 214) in 2 batches? Another option is to cook half the beef separately in a frying pan. Add back to the other half and continue adding ingredients according to the recipe directions.

Elegant Pot Roast

2 white onions
3 pounds beef roast, such as
 chuck or shoulder
1 teaspoon salt
1 teaspoon black pepper

2 tablespoons all-purpose flour
2 tablespoons vegetable oil
3 cups water
1 package instant onion soup
 mix

1. Preheat oven to 325°. Peel and chop the onions.
2. Pat the roast dry with paper towels. Rub the salt and pepper into the roast. Dust the meat with the flour.
3. Heat the oil in a heavy pan and brown the meat on all sides in the hot oil.
4. Bring the water to a boil in a medium-sized saucepan. Dissolve the instant soup mix in the boiling water. Add 2 cups of the soup mixture to the pan with the roast. Add the onions.
5. Reduce heat to medium-low, cover, and simmer for 1½ hours or until the meat is tender. Turn the meat occasionally while it is simmering, and add the remaining onion soup mixture if needed.

How Much Seasoning to Add?

It's a matter of personal taste. If you're uncertain how much seasoning to add to highly spiced dishes such as Chili con Carne (page 97), add less than the recipe calls for. Sample the sauce and adjust the seasoning if desired. Remember, it's always easier to add more seasoning than it is to take it away.

Thanksgiving Turkey with Gravy

1 (15-pound) turkey

2 tablespoons butter

Turkey Stuffing (page 218)

Basic Gravy (page 202)

> **Serves 4–6**
>
> This recipe provides plenty of leftovers for turkey sandwiches when serving 4 people.
>
> ❧

1. Begin thawing the turkey 3 days before you plan to serve it. Place the turkey in the refrigerator on a tray to catch drippings. Do not remove the turkey from its wrappings. Allow about 90 hours (6 hours per pound) of time to defrost the bird.

2. Preheat oven to 325°. Remove the giblet package from the turkey. Throw out if not using. Rinse the bird thoroughly and pat dry. Set it on a piece of aluminum foil in the roasting pan. Use a pastry brush to brush the skin with the butter.

3. Stuff both ends of the turkey with stuffing. Insert a meat thermometer into the thickest part of the thigh, facing the body of the turkey. Cover the turkey completely with foil, leaving a hole for the meat thermometer and seaming the ends of each sheet of foil together (it usually takes 3 or 4 sheets of foil). Place the roasting pan in the oven.

4. Cook the turkey for about 5 hours. The turkey is cooked when the temperature of the thigh reaches 170° and the temperature of the stuffing is 165°. Open the foil and cook the bird uncovered for the last 30 minutes to brown the skin. Baste often with juices.

5. Remove the turkey from the oven and serve with the gravy.

A Quicker Way to Thaw Turkey

Don't have 2 or 3 days to thaw a turkey before Thanksgiving? Instead of thawing the turkey in the refrigerator, try the cold-water method. Take the turkey in its original wrappings and immerse in a sink full of cold water. Change the water every 30 minutes. (This is necessary to remove risk of bacteria growth.) While this method is quicker than thawing the bird in the refrigerator (a 15-pound turkey can be thawed in under 8 hours) it is also more labor-intensive.

Turkey Stuffing

Stuffs a 14–16 pound turkey

Not sure how much stuffing to make? A general rule of thumb is to prepare ½ cup of stuffing per pound of turkey.

∾

1–1½ cups chicken broth
8 cups dried bread cubes
¾ pound bacon
1 cup chopped yellow onion
1 cup chopped celery

1 cup chopped mushrooms
1 tablespoon sage
1 teaspoon rosemary
1 teaspoon thyme
½ teaspoon salt

1. Warm the chicken broth in a small saucepan. Keep warm on low heat while preparing the other stuffing ingredients. Place the bread cubes in a large bowl.
2. Chop the bacon and cook in a large frying pan. Leave the cooked bacon and the fat in the pan and add the chopped onion and celery. Cook for 2 to 3 minutes, and add the mushrooms. Cook until the onion is tender.
3. Add the cooked ingredients to the bread cubes. Stir in the sage, rosemary, thyme, and salt. Slowly add 1 cup of the warmed chicken broth. Use your hands to shape the stuffing into firm balls roughly the size of snowballs (the stuffing should not be mushy). Add as much of the remaining ½ cup of warmed chicken broth as necessary.
4. To stuff the turkey, hold it so that the neck is facing upward, and begin spooning stuffing into the neck cavity. Use skewers to fasten the skin from the neck over the opening. Tuck the wing tips under the back of the bird. Stuff more stuffing into the body cavity of the bird. Tie the legs and tail of the bird together with string to seal the opening.

Classic Turkey Accompaniments

Simple is best when it comes to side dishes for turkey dinner. Potatoes, sweet potatoes (yams), and steamed green vegetables such as Brussels sprouts, broccoli, and asparagus are all good choices.

One-Step Roast Chicken

3½–5-pound fryer chicken   *2 teaspoons dried rosemary*
About 1½ tablespoons olive oil   *2 teaspoons dried thyme*

1. Preheat oven to 375°.
2. Rinse the chicken under cold, running water and pat dry. Rub the olive oil, dried rosemary, and dried thyme over the chicken. Place the chicken on a rack in a shallow roasting pan. Bake for 1 hour or until the juices run clear when the chicken is pricked with a fork. If checking doneness with a meat thermometer, the internal temperature of the chicken should be at least 175° at the thickest part of the thigh.

Serves 4

Once you've mastered the basic skill of roasting chicken, you may want to try a few creative variations, such as placing lemon slices underneath the skin.

∾

Tandoori Chicken

6 skinless chicken thighs   *2 tablespoons lemon juice*
1 garlic clove   *1 cup plain yogurt*
2½ tablespoons (or to taste)
  garam masala

1. Rinse the chicken thighs and pat dry. Cut 2 or 3 diagonal slits in each thigh. Smash, peel, and chop the garlic clove.
2. Mix the garam masala, lemon juice, and crushed garlic into the yogurt. Place the marinade in a resealable plastic bag and add the chicken thighs (use more than one bag if necessary).
3. Marinate the chicken in the refrigerator overnight. Turn the chicken several times so that all the thighs are completely covered in the marinade.
4. Preheat oven to 450°.
5. Place the chicken on the rack of a roasting pan. Bake for 30 minutes or until chicken is tender and no longer pink in the middle.

Serves 4

This popular Indian dish can also be broiled or cooked on the outdoor grill. Serve with Steamed Jasmine Rice (page 81) or baked potatoes for a complete meal.

∾

Chicken Risotto with Vegetables

4 (6-ounce) skinless, boneless
   chicken breasts
2 tomatoes
4 carrots
2 garlic cloves
½ small white onion
1 tablespoon olive oil

½ teaspoon salt
¼ teaspoon (or to taste) pepper
1½ cups arborio or short-grain
   rice
About 4½ cups chicken broth
2 teaspoons dried parsley or
   dried basil

1. Rinse the chicken breasts under cold, running water and pat dry. Cut the breasts into bite-sized pieces. Wash the vegetables. Chop the tomatoes. Peel and dice the carrots. Smash, peel, and chop the garlic cloves. Peel and chop the onion.

2. Heat the olive oil in a large, heavy saucepan. Add the garlic and onion and cook until the onion is tender. Add the chicken breasts and cook on medium heat, turning occasionally, until the chicken is browned on both sides and cooked about halfway.

3. Add the chopped tomatoes, carrots, and salt and pepper. Cook for about 1 minute. Stir in the rice and 1 cup of the chicken broth. Bring to a boil, then reduce heat slightly. Stir in the dried parsley or basil. Cook on medium heat, stirring constantly, until the broth is nearly absorbed. Add ½ cup of the broth and cook until nearly absorbed. Continue adding the broth ½ cup at a time and letting it absorb before adding more, until the rice is creamy (about 20 minutes). Make sure the chicken is cooked through before serving.

Chicken Risotto with Vegetables for One

Chicken Risotto with Vegetables can easily be adapted to make dinner for one person. Use 1 or 2 chicken breasts according to your preference, ½ cup rice with 1½ cups chicken broth, and add vegetables and seasonings as desired. Instead of a large saucepan, the dish can be prepared in a medium or large frying pan with deep sides.

Veal Medallions "aux Champignons"

12 veal medallions
3 shallots
3 garlic cloves
1¼ cups extra-virgin olive oil
⅓ cup all-purpose flour
2 ounces dried porcini
  mushrooms

3 ounces small fresh
  mushrooms
¼ cup Marsala wine
½ cup heavy whipping cream
½ teaspoon dried basil
1 fresh black truffle
3 tablespoons rinsed capers

> **Serves 4**
>
> Porcini mushrooms and truffles lend an elegant touch to this easy-to-prepare gourmet dish.
>
> ∾

1. Remove any extra fat from the veal medallions and place in a shallow glass dish. Peel and chop the shallots and garlic. Combine the shallots and garlic with 1 cup of the olive oil and pour over the veal. Cover and refrigerate the veal overnight.

2. Dredge the veal medallions in the flour. Soften the dried porcini by soaking them in hot water. Squeeze out excess water and slice thinly. Wipe the fresh mushrooms clean with a damp cloth and remove the stems.

3. Heat the remaining ¼ cup olive oil on medium in a frying pan. Sauté the medallions until lightly browned. Remove from the pan. Add all the mushrooms to the frying pan and sauté until browned.

4. Carefully add the Marsala wine to the mushrooms. Add the cream and dried basil. Cook on medium until the mixture is reduced by about half. Return the veal to the pan and briefly cook through.

5. Just before serving, clean the truffle and cut into thin shavings. Rinse the capers. Sprinkle the truffle shavings over the dish and garnish with the capers.

Forget the Foil!

Cookbooks used to routinely recommend wrapping potatoes in aluminum foil to shorten the baking time. However, today most experts recommend leaving off the foil. Covering the potato in foil means it is steamed instead of baked, which can lead to a moist potato with a soggy skin.

Simple Steak and Potatoes Dinner

Serves 4

If you don't have a microwave oven, replace the baked potato with Steamed Broccoli (page 109) or Basic Cooked Long-Grain Rice (page 95).

∾

8 ounces fresh brown mushrooms
1 garlic clove
4 (10-ounce) boneless rib-eye steaks, boneless

¼ cup barbecue sauce
4 large baking potatoes
2 tablespoons olive oil

1. Preheat oven broiler. Wipe the mushrooms clean with a damp cloth and slice.
2. Peel the garlic and cut in half. Rub the steaks with the garlic. Place the steaks on a broiling pan and brush the tops with half of the barbecue sauce. Broil for 8 to 10 minutes on the top side, then turn over and brush with the remaining barbecue sauce. Broil for 8 to 10 more minutes.
3. Begin preparing the potatoes and mushrooms after the steaks have finished cooking on the first side. Pierce the potatoes with a fork. Place on a microwave-safe plate or a paper towel and microwave on high heat for 10 minutes or until the potatoes are tender (the internal temperature should be 210°).
4. Melt the olive oil on low medium heat in a frying pan. Add the mushrooms and sauté on medium to medium-low heat until browned and tender. Serve all the food together.

Easy Defrosting in the Microwave

If you plan to use the microwave for defrosting meat on a regular basis, be sure to wrap all your meat in plastic wrap that is marked as microwave safe. That way, it can go straight from freezer to microwave.

Beef Stroganoff

16 ounces egg noodles
1 garlic clove
1 medium-sized white onion
2 cups fresh mushrooms
¼ teaspoon (or to taste) salt
¼ teaspoon (or to taste) black
  pepper

½ teaspoon (or to taste) dried
  basil
2 tablespoons all-purpose flour
2 pounds cubed stewing beef
4 tablespoons oil
1 cup beef broth
½ cup (or to taste) sour cream

> **Serves 4**
>
> For more sauce to coat the noodles, increase the beef bouillon to 1½ cups. The sour cream can be increased up to 1 cup.
>
> ∾

1. Cook the egg noodles according to package directions. Drain and set aside.
2. Smash, peel, and chop the garlic. Peel and chop the onion. Wipe the mushrooms clean with a damp cloth and slice.
3. Stir the salt, black pepper, and dried basil into the flour. Toss the beef chunks with the flour.
4. Heat 2 tablespoons of the oil in a frying pan on medium heat. Add the beef and brown on both sides. Remove the beef from the pan and clean out the pan. Add the remaining 2 tablespoons oil and heat on medium heat. Add the garlic, onion, and mushrooms. Sauté until the onion is tender.
5. Return the beef to the pan. Add the beef broth. Heat through, and stir in the sour cream. Heat for a few more minutes until warmed through. Serve over the noodles.

Demystifying Deglazing

Deglazing is a fancy chef's term for a very simple process. After browning, meat is removed from the pan but the pan is not cleaned (excess fat can be drained off). A liquid flavoring agent such as wine or chicken broth is added to the pan and heated. The flavorful brown bits of hardened meat juices at the bottom of the pan are scraped up and mixed with the liquid to make a sauce.

Turkey au Vin

1½ pounds boneless, skinless turkey breast
¾ teaspoon dried basil
4 tablespoons butter or margarine, divided
10 pearl onions, peeled
2 garlic cloves, peeled and chopped
2 carrots, peeled and sliced
1½ cups nonalcoholic red wine
½ cup chicken broth
Salt and pepper, to taste
4 recipes Basic Mashed Potatoes for One (page 93)
1 cup sliced fresh mushrooms

1. Rinse the turkey breast under cold, running water and pat dry with paper towels. Cut the turkey breast into pieces. If necessary, cut each piece in half through the middle so that it is not too thick. Rub the dried basil over the turkey breast pieces.
2. Heat 3 tablespoons of the butter or margarine in a frying pan on medium-low heat. Add the pearl onions. Cook for about 5 to 6 minutes, until they begin to brown. Add the garlic and carrots. Add the remaining 1 tablespoon butter and the turkey. Brown the turkey breast pieces.
3. Remove the turkey breast and vegetables from the pan. Add the wine and chicken broth and bring to a boil, scraping up the brown bits at the bottom of the pan. Return the turkey and vegetables to the pan. Bring to a boil over medium heat. Season with the salt and pepper. Reduce heat to medium-low and simmer for 1 hour.
4. Prepare the mashed potatoes after the turkey has cooked for about 30 minutes.
5. Add the sliced mushrooms to the turkey and vegetables and cook for 5 more minutes. Serve with the mashed potatoes.

Vegetarian Stew

2 potatoes

2 carrots

1 garlic clove

½ onion

2 teaspoons olive oil

1 cup red kidney beans, drained

½ cup drained Romano beans
(also called Italian green
beans)

½ cup drained chickpeas

6 cups vegetable broth

1 teaspoon ground cumin

½ teaspoon lemon juice

½ teaspoon brown sugar

1 teaspoon (or to taste) paprika

Salt, to taste

> **Serves 4**
>
> A great dish for cold winter days when you want to put together a hot meal for 4 in a hurry. Feel free to substitute your own favorite combination of beans.
>
> ❧

1. Wash and peel the potatoes and carrots. Cut the potatoes into bite-sized pieces, and slice the carrots. Smash, peel, and chop the garlic. Peel and chop the onion.
2. Heat the olive oil in a large saucepan on medium-low heat. Add the chopped garlic and onion. Cook for about 2 minutes, until the onion is tender.
3. Add the potatoes, carrots, kidney beans, Romano beans, chickpeas, and vegetable broth. Stir in the ground cumin, lemon juice, brown sugar, paprika, and salt. Bring to a boil.
4. Cover the stew and simmer for 30 minutes or until all the vegetables are tender.

Preparing a Dish "aux Champignons"

While it sounds quite elegant, aux Champignons is simply the French for "with mushrooms." In Veal Medallions "aux Champignons" (page 221), truffles, dried porcini, and fresh mushrooms lend extra flavor to a basic cream sauce.

Chapter 13

Last Resort: Desserts

Basic Rice Krispies Squares

⅓ cup butter or margarine
4½ cups mini marshmallows

6 cups Kellogg's Rice Krispies
Cereal

1. In a heavy skillet, melt the butter and marshmallows over low heat (otherwise the melted marshmallow will stick to the pan). When the marshmallows have completely melted, remove from heat.
2. Stir in the cereal and mix thoroughly. Spread out the mixture evenly in a 9" × 13" pan. Serve warm, or cool in the refrigerator for 1 hour first. Cut into squares before serving.

Simple Fruit Parfait

1 cup sliced banana
1 cup fresh blueberries
1 cup plain or vanilla-flavored
    yogurt

1 tablespoon lime juice
¼ cup sweetened coconut
    flakes

Divide the sliced banana among 4 wine or parfait glasses, then the blueberries, and finally the yogurt. Drizzle with the lime juice and sprinkle the coconut flakes over the top. Chill in the refrigerator, and serve.

Peanut Butter Rice Krispies

1 cup peanut butter
½ cup granulated sugar
½ cup brown sugar
¾ cup corn syrup
4 cups Kellogg's Rice Krispies Cereal

1 tablespoon butter or margarine
1½ cups semisweet chocolate chips

1. Melt the peanut butter, sugars, and corn syrup in a skillet over low heat, stirring continually. When the mixture is melted, gradually stir in the cereal.
2. Spread out the mixture evenly in a 9" × 9" baking pan.
3. Place the butter and chocolate chips in a metal bowl and place it on top of a saucepan filled halfway with nearly boiling water. Melt the butter and chocolate on low heat, stirring constantly to make sure the chocolate doesn't boil.
4. Spread the melted chocolate over the Rice Krispies mixture. Let cool and cut into squares.

Almond Fruit Cocktail Float

Serves 6–8

For a fancier presentation, cut the chilled gelatin into diamond shapes. Pour the fruit cocktail and juice into a large serving bowl and carefully add the gelatin.

∾

2 tablespoons unflavored
    gelatin, such as Knox
1½ cups water
½ cup boiling water

2 cups evaporated milk
½ cup granulated sugar
1 tablespoon almond extract
1 (15-ounce) can fruit cocktail

1. In a medium-sized bowl, add the gelatin to ½ cup of the water and let it sit for 2 to 3 minutes to soften. Pour the ½ cup boiling water over the soaked gelatin and stir until dissolved.
2. Stir in the remaining 1 cup of water, the milk, sugar, and almond extract. Pour into a 9" × 9" pan. Chill in the refrigerator until firm.
3. To serve, cut the chilled gelatin into 1-inch squares and serve in individual serving bowls with the fruit cocktail over the top.

Baked Pears

Serves 4

Bartlett, Bosc, and Anjou pears all work well in this recipe.

∾

4 firm ripe pears
½ cup brown sugar
4 tablespoons (or more to taste)
    red wine vinegar

4 tablespoons honey
¼ cup chopped walnuts
¼ cup unsweetened coconut
    flakes

1. Preheat oven to 350°.
2. Cut the pears in half, remove the cores and stems, and cut into chunks. Sprinkle the brown sugar over a nonstick baking pan. Lay the pear slices on top of the brown sugar.
3. Mix together the red wine vinegar and honey. Drizzle the mixture over the pear slices. Sprinkle half the pear slices with the chopped walnuts and the other half with the coconut flakes.
4. Bake the pears for 25 minutes or until tender. Let cool briefly, and serve while still warm.

Summer Fruit Compote

2 medium bananas
⅓ cup granulated sugar
1 cup water
1 teaspoon peeled and grated
   fresh ginger

¼ cup lemon juice
4 (5-inch) cinnamon sticks
3 cups dried tropical fruit

Yields 2 cups

On a cold winter's day, nothing beats a warming compote filled with summer fruit to take your mind off the freezing temperatures outdoors.

❧

1. Peel and slice the bananas.
2. Cook the sugar and water in a saucepan over low heat, stirring to dissolve the sugar. Add the ginger, lemon juice, and cinnamon sticks. Increase heat to medium and bring to a boil. Reduce heat to low and simmer for 5 minutes.
3. Add the dried fruit and bananas. Return to a boil. Reduce heat to low, cover, and cook at a low simmer until the dried fruit is tender. Remove the cinnamon sticks.
4. Let cool briefly and serve warm, or refrigerate overnight and serve cold.

Lemon Cranberry Sorbet

1 cup (about 48) cranberries,
   washed and drained
½ teaspoon grated fresh ginger,
   optional

¾ cup water, divided
4 tablespoons granulated sugar
2 tablespoons lemon juice

Serves 1

This easy sorbet makes a refreshing midafternoon or evening snack. Feel free to skip the final freezing if you're in a hurry. It just means the fruit won't have the firm, grainy texture of a sorbet.

❧

1. Place the cranberries, ginger (if using), and ½ cup of the water in a small saucepan. Cook on medium heat until the cranberries pop, about 5 to 6 minutes. Gently mash the cranberries.
2. Stir in the sugar, lemon juice, and remaining water. Bring to a boil, stirring. Remove from the heat and let cool. Pour into a serving bowl and place in the freezer until the sorbet is just starting to freeze, about 30 minutes.
3. Place in a blender or food processor and process until smooth. Freeze again.

Easy Brown Betty for Late-Night Snacking

Serves 4–6

Substituting applesauce and graham cracker crumbs for peeled apples and homemade bread crumbs takes most of the work out of this popular dessert.

1 cup applesauce
2 tablespoons granulated sugar
4 tablespoons brown sugar
2 teaspoons lemon juice

⅜ teaspoon ground cinnamon, divided
⅛ teaspoon ground ginger
⅓ cup butter
2 cups graham cracker crumbs

1. Preheat oven to 350°. Grease an 8" × 8" baking pan.
2. Combine the applesauce, granulated sugar, brown sugar, lemon juice, ⅛ teaspoon of the cinnamon, and the ground ginger. Set aside.
3. Melt the butter. Toss the graham cracker crumbs with the melted butter.
4. Press the graham cracker crumbs on the bottom of the prepared pan. Spread the applesauce mixture along the top. Sprinkle with the remaining cinnamon.
5. Cover with aluminum foil and bake for 30 minutes. Uncover and bake for another 5 minutes, to lightly brown the applesauce. Let cool on a rack. Cut into squares. Serve warm as is, or topped with ice cream or whipping cream.

Classic Brown Betty Dessert

½ cup brown sugar
1 tablespoon lemon juice
½ teaspoon ground cinnamon
¼ teaspoon ground nutmeg
3 cups peeled, sliced apples
   (about 3 to 4 apples)

½ cup butter or margarine
3½ cups bread crumbs or
   graham cracker crumbs
¼ cup water

Serves 6–8

This simple dessert originated in American colo-
nial times. Feel free to
substitute other fresh
fruit in season and to
replace the bread
crumbs with graham
cracker crumbs.

1. Preheat oven to 350°. Grease an 8" × 8" baking pan.
2. In a small bowl, combine the brown sugar, lemon juice, cinnamon, and nutmeg. Place the apples in a large bowl. Add the brown sugar mixture and use your hands to combine. Set aside.
3. Melt the butter in a small saucepan. Toss the crumbs with the melted butter.
4. Press 1½ cups of the crumbs on the bottom of the prepared pan. Carefully place half of the apple slices on top. Cover the slices with 1 cup of the crumbs. Place the remaining apple slices on top and cover with 1 cup of crumbs.
5. Add the water, cover with aluminum foil, and bake for 30 minutes. Uncover and check to see if the apples on the top layer are tender. If not, bake covered for a few more minutes. When the apples are tender, uncover and bake for another 15 minutes. Let cool on a rack. Cut into squares. Serve warm as is, or topped with ice cream or whipping cream.

Easy Apple Crisp

Yields 12 crisps

Serve warm, topped with a dollop of vanilla ice cream.

∾

¾ cup all-purpose flour
¾ cup quick-cooking oats
¾ cup brown sugar
¼ cup granulated sugar
¾ teaspoon ground cinnamon
½ teaspoon ground nutmeg

½ teaspoon ground allspice
½ cup butter or margarine, softened
2 (20-ounce) cans apple pie filling

1. Preheat oven to 375°. Grease a 9" × 9" baking pan.
2. Combine the flour, oatmeal, brown sugar, granulated sugar, cinnamon, nutmeg, and allspice. Cut the softened butter or margarine into the dry ingredients with a knife. The mixture should be crumblike and slightly moist.
3. Spread 1 can of the apple pie filling on the prepared baking pan. Sprinkle a portion of the crumb mixture over the top until the pie filling is completely covered. Spread the second can of apple pie filling on top. Top with as much of the remaining crumb mixture as necessary to cover (a bit of crumb mixture may be left over).
4. Bake for 30 minutes or until browned. Let stand on a wire rack to cool for at least 15 minutes. Spoon into bowls and serve warm with ice cream.

Quick-Cooking Oatmeal Confusion

Although it can be tempting, don't replace quick-cooking oats with instant oats in a recipe. While both are thinner than regular oats (making them cook more quickly), quick-cooking oats are merely steamed, while instant oats are actually precooked. Combining instant oats with a liquid can result in soggy muffins, cookies, and other baked goods.

Perfect Peanut Butter Cookies

1 cup chunky peanut butter
¾ cup butter or margarine,
*   room temperature*
⅔ cup packed brown sugar
⅓ cup granulated sugar
½ cup chopped pecans

1 large egg
½ teaspoon vanilla extract
½ teaspoon baking soda
½ teaspoon salt
1½ cups all-purpose flour

1. Preheat oven to 350°. Grease a 9" × 13" baking sheet.
2. In a large bowl, cream the peanut butter, butter or margarine, and the sugars. Stir in the pecans. Add the egg and vanilla extract.
3. In another bowl, sift the baking soda and salt into the flour. Gradually add it to the peanut butter mixture, stirring to mix. Roll the dough into balls about 1 to 1½ inches in diameter. Place on the prepared baking sheet, approximately 2 inches apart, and press down in the middle with a fork.
4. Bake for 12 minutes or until a toothpick inserted into the middle comes out clean. Let cool and store in a sealed container.

Yields about 40 cookies

These taste delicious served warm from the oven.

Did You Know?

Most cookie recipes are fairly adaptable—feel free to experiment by adding more fruit, nuts, or chocolate chips as desired. Just be sure to stick to the amount of flour called for in the recipe. Excess flour can make the cookies turn out hard and tough.

Double Chocolate Chip Peppermint Drop Cookies

Yields about 4 dozen cookies

Be sure to use real cocoa powder and not instant cocoa mix in this recipe.

½ cup, plus 2 tablespoons butter or margarine, room temperature
⅔ cup brown sugar
⅓ cup granulated sugar
2 tablespoons cocoa powder
1 egg

1 teaspoon vanilla extract
1 teaspoon peppermint extract
½ teaspoon baking soda
½ teaspoon salt
1½ cups all-purpose flour
1 cup semisweet chocolate chips

1. Preheat oven to 350°.
2. In a large bowl, cream the butter or margarine with the sugars and cocoa powder. Add the egg, vanilla extract, and peppermint extract.
3. In another bowl, sift the baking soda and salt into the flour. Gradually mix it into the butter and sugar. Stir in the chocolate chips.
4. Drop the cookies by teaspoonful onto an ungreased baking sheet, placed well apart (about 15 cookies per baking sheet). Bake for 10 to 12 minutes, depending on how crispy you like them.

Test Your Cookie IQ

Drops, bars, icebox cookies—it can all get a little confusing. Drop cookies have a wetter batter than traditional cookies. They are "dropped" from a teaspoon onto a baking sheet. Icebox or refrigerator cookies consist of cookie dough that can be refrigerated before cooking—a great idea if you want to prepare cookie dough ahead of time for quick baking later. To make bar cookies, simply spread cookie dough batter into a shallow pan, and then cut into bars after the dough is baked.

Oatmeal Cranberry Chews

1 cup butter or margarine
½ cup granulated sugar
½ cup brown sugar
1–2 eggs, as needed
½ teaspoon baking soda
½ teaspoon baking powder

¾ teaspoon ground cinnamon
½ teaspoon ground nutmeg
1 cup all-purpose flour
1½ cups quick-cooking oatmeal
½ cup dried cranberries

1. Preheat oven to 350°. Grease a 9" × 13" baking sheet.
2. In a large bowl, cream together the butter and sugars. Beat in 1 egg. In another bowl, sift the baking soda, baking powder, cinnamon, and nutmeg into the flour.
3. Add the flour to the butter mixture, blending thoroughly. Stir in the oatmeal and dried cranberries. If the cookie dough is too dry, beat in the remaining egg.
4. Drop a heaping teaspoon of dough onto the prepared baking sheet. Continue with the rest of the dough, placing the cookies about 2 inches apart. Bake for 10 to 12 minutes or until done.

**Yields about
4 dozen cookies**

Dried cranberries add a
tart flavor to these
chewy, crisp cookies.

∾

Quick and Easy Brownies

**Yields about
20 brownies**

This easy recipe takes
the work out of making
brownies. For a moister,
less "cakey" brownie,
use a 9" x 13" pan.

3 tablespoons unsweetened
cocoa powder
1 cup granulated sugar
1 stick unsalted butter
¾ teaspoon vanilla extract

¼ cup egg substitute
½ teaspoon baking powder
¼ teaspoon salt
½ cup all-purpose flour
1 cup chopped walnuts

1. Preheat oven to 350°. Grease a 9" x 9" pan.
2. In a large bowl, cream the cocoa and sugar into the butter until well blended. In a small bowl, stir the vanilla extract into the egg substitute. Beat the egg substitute into the cocoa mixture.
3. In another bowl, stir the baking powder and salt into the flour until well blended. Stir into the cocoa mixture, blending thoroughly. Stir in the chopped walnuts.
4. Spread the brownie batter evenly in the prepared pan. Bake for 20 to 25 minutes, until done. Let cool and cut into bars.

Versatile Vanilla Extract

The modern-day substitute for the vanilla bean, vanilla extract's delicate flavor is used to heighten the taste of everything from ice cream to chocolate. Desserts such as Easy Italian Panna Cotta (page 246) wouldn't be the same without it. Although pure vanilla extract is best, it is quite expensive. Synthetic vanilla extract—sold as vanilla flavoring or imitation vanilla—can be used instead.

Chocolatey Brownies

¼ teaspoon salt
½ teaspoon baking powder
½ teaspoon ground cinnamon
½ cup all-purpose flour
4 squares (4 ounces) semisweet
    chocolate

1 stick unsalted butter
2 large eggs
1 teaspoon vanilla extract
¾ cup granulated sugar
1 cup chopped pecans

1. Preheat oven to 325°. Grease a 9" × 9" baking pan.
2. In a bowl, stir the salt, baking powder, and cinnamon into the flour until well blended.
3. Break up the chocolate into pieces. Fill a heavy metal saucepan with water and heat on medium-low until barely simmering. Place the butter in a metal bowl on top of the saucepan. Turn the heat down to low and add the chocolate to the butter. Melt the chocolate, stirring constantly and being careful not to let the chocolate boil.
4. Remove from the heat and beat in the eggs. Add the vanilla extract. Stir in the sugar. Blend in the flour mixture. Stir in the pecans.
5. Spread the batter evenly in the prepared pan. Bake on the middle rack of the oven for 30 minutes or until a toothpick inserted in the middle comes out nearly clean. Let cool and cut into 16 bars.

Yields 16 brownies

Remove the brownies from the oven when a toothpick inserted in the middle still has a few moist crumbs on it. Cooking any longer will cause the brownies to dry out.

❧

Unsalted Butter Benefits

The name says it all—unsalted butter has no added salt. Cooks prefer it for baking, as salt can overpower butter's natural sweet flavor. The only drawback is that unsalted butter is more perishable—the salt in regular butter acts as a preservative. For long-term storage, keep it in the freezer section of the refrigerator.

Lemon Crisp Cookies

**Yields about
4 dozen cookies**

Serve these light, delicately flavored cookies with tea for a late-afternoon snack.

1 cup granulated sugar
2 sticks unsalted butter, softened
3 teaspoons lemon juice
4–5 drops yellow food coloring, optional

1 large egg
¾ teaspoon baking soda
¼ teaspoon salt
2 cups all-purpose flour
⅓ cup (or more to taste) powdered sugar

1. Preheat oven to 350°. Grease a 9" × 13" baking sheet.
2. In a large bowl, cream the granulated sugar into the butter until thoroughly blended. Blend in the lemon juice and the yellow food coloring, if using. Beat in the egg.
3. In a separate bowl, add the baking soda and salt to the flour and stir until well blended.
4. Using an electric mixture set at low speed, gradually add the flour to the butter and sugar mixture until it is just blended into a soft dough. Drop a heaping teaspoon of dough onto the baking sheet. Continue with the remaining dough, placing the cookies about 1½ inches apart (about 15 cookies to a baking sheet).
5. Bake on the middle rack of the oven for 9 to 10 minutes or until a toothpick inserted into the center comes out clean. Be careful not to overcook. Dust the cookies with powdered sugar while still warm. Let cool for 2 minutes and then remove from the baking sheet.

Crisp or Cobbler?

It is often hard to tell the difference from a crisp or a cobbler. Both consist of a fruit filling topped with flour and spices such as cinnamon, served bubbling hot with whipping cream or ice cream. The main difference lies in the topping. Crisp toppings consist mainly of flour and sugar, while cobblers are topped with biscuit dough.

Blender Chocolate Mousse for One

½ cup heavy whipping cream
2 tablespoons powdered sugar

2 tablespoons unsweetened
   cocoa powder
½ teaspoon vanilla extract

Combine all the ingredients, and blend with an electric blender until the mixture thickens. Chill before serving.

Serves 1

It's easy to indulge your sweet tooth with this simple but rich dessert. For best results, thicken further by chilling briefly in the freezer section of the refrigerator for 10 to 15 minutes before eating.

Speedy Mocha "Mousse" Pudding

2 cups heavy whipping cream
½ cup brewed instant coffee
½ cup powdered sugar
½ cup unsweetened cocoa
   powder
1 teaspoon vanilla extract

1 package instant vanilla
   pudding
½ cup (or to taste) prepared
   whipped cream
4–6 maraschino cherries

Combine the first 6 ingredients in a blender. Blend on low speed (prepare in 2 batches if necessary). Dish into parfait glasses and let sit for 5 minutes to allow the pudding to set. Just before serving, spray the whipped cream on top and add 1 maraschino cherry to the top of each.

Serves 4–6

Instant pudding takes the work out of making this tasty mousse.

Almond Biscotti

1 cup almonds
2 cups all-purpose flour
1 teaspoon baking powder
⅛ teaspoon salt
1 cup granulated sugar

4 eggs
1 teaspoon vanilla extract
½ teaspoon almond extract
3 ounces semisweet chocolate
1½ teaspoons shortening

1. Preheat oven to 325°. Grease 1 baking sheet.
2. Place the almonds on a baking sheet and bake for 8 to 10 minutes, until lightly browned. Remove, let cool, and chop coarsely.
3. Combine the flour, baking powder, salt, and sugar in a large bowl. Stir in the toasted almonds.
4. In a small bowl, lightly beat the eggs with the vanilla and almond extract. Add to the dry ingredients and blend thoroughly to form a sticky dough. Cut the dough in half. Flour your hands and shape each dough into a log about 14 inches long. Place the logs on the prepared baking sheet and bake for 30 minutes or until a toothpick inserted in the center comes out clean. Let cool for 10 minutes.
5. Cut the logs diagonally into slices about ½ inch thick. Place cut-side down on 2 ungreased baking sheets. Bake for a total of 15 minutes, removing the baking sheets from the oven at the halfway point and turning the cookies over. Return to the oven, moving the baking sheet that was on the top rack to the bottom rack and vice versa (this ensures the cookies cook evenly). Finish baking. Let cool.
6. Break the chocolate into pieces. Melt the shortening and chocolate in a metal bowl placed on top of a heavy pot filled halfway with barely simmering water (or use the top of a double boiler if you have one). Melt over low heat, stirring regularly and making sure the chocolate doesn't burn. Use the back of a metal spatula or wooden spoon to spread the melted chocolate over half of one side of each biscotti. Let dry. Store the biscotti in a cookie tin or other airtight container.

Chocolate Biscotti

5 eggs
1 teaspoon vanilla extract
2 cups all-purpose flour
1 teaspoon baking powder
⅛ teaspoon salt
1 cup granulated sugar

½ cup, plus 1¾ tablespoons
   unsweetened cocoa powder
¾ cup semisweet chocolate
   chips
6 ounces white chocolate
1½ teaspoons shortening

Yields about 40 cookies

These taste great served
with vanilla ice cream or
dipped in a decadent
chocolate fondue!

∾

1. Preheat oven to 325°. Grease a large baking sheet.
2. In a small bowl, lightly beat the eggs with the vanilla extract. In a large bowl, combine the flour, baking powder, salt, sugar, and cocoa powder. Blend thoroughly. Add the beaten egg and blend to form a sticky dough. Stir in the chocolate chips.
3. Cut the dough in half. Flour your hands and shape each half of dough into a 14-inch log. Place the logs on the prepared baking sheet and bake for 30 minutes or until a toothpick inserted in the center comes out clean. Let cool for 10 minutes.
4. Cut the dough diagonally into slices about ½ inch thick. Place cut-side down on 2 ungreased baking sheets. Bake for a total of 15 minutes, removing the baking sheets from the oven at the halfway point and turning the cookies over. Return to the oven, moving the cookie sheet that was on the top rack to the bottom rack and vice versa (this ensures the cookies cook evenly). Let cool.
5. Break the white chocolate into pieces. Melt the shortening and chocolate in a metal bowl placed on top of a heavy pot filled halfway with barely simmering water (or use the top of a double boiler if you have one). Melt over low heat, stirring regularly and making sure the chocolate doesn't burn. Use the back of a metal spatula or wooden spoon to spread the melted chocolate over one side of each biscotti. Let dry. Store the biscotti in a cookie tin or other airtight container.

Biscotti-Cutting Tip

When cutting biscotti dough after the first baking, push down hard on the knife instead of making a sawing motion. "Sawing" the dough can cause it to break into pieces.

Nanaimo Bars

*2 ounces liquid egg substitute
(equivalent of 1 egg)*
½ teaspoon vanilla extract
2 sticks (1 cup) unsalted butter
*3 teaspoons unsweetened
cocoa powder*
¼ cup granulated sugar
½ cup finely chopped pecans
*½ cup sweetened coconut
flakes*

1 cup graham cracker crumbs
2 tablespoons custard powder
*2 tablespoons, plus 1 teaspoon
half-and-half*
2 cups powdered sugar
2 tablespoons butter
*4 squares (4 ounces) semisweet
chocolate*

1. Grease an 8" × 8" pan. In a small bowl, stir together the egg substitute and vanilla extract. Set aside.
2. For the bottom layer, melt 1 stick (½ cup) of the butter in a metal bowl placed over a saucepan filled halfway with barely simmering water. (You can also melt the butter in the top half of a double boiler.) Stir in the cocoa powder and granulated sugar. Remove from the heat. Stir in the egg substitute and vanilla extract mixture.
3. Stir in the chopped pecans, coconut, and graham cracker crumbs, mixing thoroughly. Press the mixture into the prepared pan, spreading it out evenly. Refrigerate until the next layer is completed.
4. For the middle layer, use a wooden spoon to cream the custard powder into the butter in a large bowl. Gradually add the half-and-half while creaming in the powdered sugar. Spread the icing evenly over the lower layer. Freeze for at least 2 hours.
5. To make the top layer, melt the remaining 1 stick butter and the chocolate in a metal bowl placed over a saucepan filled halfway with barely simmering water. Remove from the heat and allow to cool briefly. When the chocolate is just beginning to solidify, use a plastic spatula to spread it evenly over the middle layer. Return to the freezer and freeze for at least 2 hours. Cut into bars and serve.

Maraschino Cherry Bars

2 ounces liquid egg substitute (equivalent of 1 egg)
½ teaspoon vanilla extract
2 sticks (1 cup), plus 3 tablespoons unsalted butter
3 tablespoons unsweetened cocoa powder
¼ cup granulated sugar
½ cup finely chopped walnuts
½ cup sweetened coconut flakes
1 cup graham cracker crumbs

2 tablespoons Instant Vanilla Jell-O Pudding
2 tablespoons, plus 1 teaspoon maraschino cherry juice
2 cups powdered sugar
5 maraschino cherries, finely chopped
Few drops red food coloring, optional
2 ounces semisweet chocolate
2 ounces white chocolate

> **Yields 20 bars**
>
> Vanilla pudding makes a handy substitute for custard powder in this variation on traditional Nanaimo Bars.
>
> ∾

1. Grease an 8" × 8" pan. In a small bowl, stir together the egg substitute and vanilla extract. Set aside.

2. For the bottom layer: Melt 1 stick of the butter in a metal bowl placed over a saucepan filled halfway with barely simmering water. (You can also melt the butter in the top half of a double boiler.) Stir in the cocoa powder and granulated sugar. Remove from the heat. Stir in the egg substitute and vanilla extract mixture.

3. Stir in the chopped walnuts, coconut, and graham cracker crumbs, mixing thoroughly. Press into the prepared pan, spreading it out evenly. Refrigerate until the next layer is completed.

4. For the middle layer: Use a wooden spoon to cream the instant vanilla pudding into 1 stick of the butter. Gradually add the maraschino cherry juice while creaming in the powdered sugar. Stir in the chopped cherries. Add the red food coloring for a darker pink color, if desired. Spread the icing evenly over the lower layer. Freeze for at least 2 hours.

5. For the top layer: Melt the remaining 3 tablespoons butter and the white and dark chocolate in a metal bowl placed over a saucepan filled halfway with barely simmering water. Remove from the heat and allow to cool briefly. When the chocolate is just beginning to solidify, use a plastic spatula to spread it evenly over the middle layer. Return to the freezer and freeze for at least 2 hours. Cut into bars and serve.

Easy Italian Panna Cotta

Serves 5–6

For best results, use cream with a fat content of at least 35 percent in panna cotta recipes.

∾

¼ cup warm water
1 envelope unflavored gelatin,
   such as Knox
1½ cups whipping cream or
   heavy cream

¼ cup granulated sugar
2 teaspoons vanilla extract
¾ cup milk

1. Pour the warm water into a small bowl. Pour the gelatin over the water and let it stand 5 minutes to soften.
2. In a medium-sized saucepan, bring the cream, sugar, and vanilla extract to a boil over medium heat. Reduce heat to low and simmer for 2 to 3 minutes, stirring occasionally to make sure all the sugar is dissolved. Add the milk and simmer for another 2 to 3 minutes.
3. Remove the saucepan from the heat and stir in the softened gelatin (check to make sure the cream and milk mixture is not boiling when you add the gelatin). Stir until the gelatin is completely dissolved.
4. Pour the mixture into a bowl. Set the bowl inside another bowl filled with ice water. Cool for 15 minutes, stirring regularly. Pour the liquid into 4-ounce ramekins or custard cups and refrigerate overnight.
5. To serve, dip the bottom of each ramekin briefly in a bowl of hot water, and use a knife to cut around the bottom of the panna cotta, loosening the edges. Dry the bottom of the ramekin and invert the panna cotta onto a plate. Enjoy as is, or top with seasonal fresh fruit.

Perfect Panna Cotta

Reputed to have originated in the Piedmont district of Northern Italy, panna cotta is Italian for "cooked cream." Traditionally, panna cotta is made with a vanilla bean, but vanilla extract makes a convenient substitute. If you want to use a vanilla bean instead, cut the bean in half lengthwise and scrape out the seeds. Add both the bean and the seeds in the saucepan with the heavy whipping cream, stirring to make sure the seeds are evenly distributed.

Italian Panna Cotta with Blueberry Glaze

*1½ cups frozen unsweetened
    blueberries, washed and
    drained*
*4½ tablespoons granulated
    sugar*
1½ teaspoons lime juice

*⅓ cup, plus 2 tablespoons
    water*
2 teaspoons cornstarch
*1 recipe Easy Italian Panna
    Cotta (page 246)*

Serves 5–6

Feel free to lower the serving portions to 3 ounces of panna cotta instead of 4, if desired.

∾

1. Bring the blueberries, sugar, lime juice, and ⅓ cup of the water to boil in a medium-sized saucepan. Reduce heat to low and simmer for 10 minutes, stirring occasionally. As the blueberries soften, gently press down on them with the back of a plastic spatula or wooden spoon.

2. When the blueberries are starting to lose their shape and the mixture is thickening, turn the heat up to boiling. Combine the cornstarch and remaining 2 tablespoons of water in a small bowl. Add the cornstarch and water mixture to the cooked blueberries, stirring constantly until thickened. Pour the mixture into a bowl and chill for at least 2 hours.

3. To serve, dip the bottom of each ramekin briefly in a bowl of hot water, and use a knife to cut around the bottom of the panna cotta, loosening the edges. Dry the bottom of the ramekin and invert the panna cotta onto a plate. Spoon a heaping tablespoon of the blueberry glaze over each.

Banana Mousse

3 large bananas, mashed
2 cups whipping cream
3 tablespoons powdered sugar
2 tablespoons lemon juice

¼ teaspoon (or to taste) ground nutmeg
1 tablespoon rum, optional

1. Purée the bananas in a blender. Whip the cream at medium-high speed until it forms high peaks. Add the powdered sugar and whip briefly until it forms soft peaks (the mixture should be light and fluffy).
2. Fold the whipped cream into the mashed banana. Carefully stir in the lemon juice, nutmeg, and rum, if using. Spoon into parfait glasses.

Mocha Shake

2 cups vanilla ice cream
½ cup cold brewed coffee

2 teaspoons unsweetened cocoa powder
2 crushed ice cubes

Blend the ice cream, coffee, and cocoa powder in a blender. Add the ice cubes and process again. Chill until ready to serve.

Frozen Cappuccino Dessert

1 cup cold brewed coffee
2 tablespoons plain cream
*   cheese*

1 tablespoon granulated sugar
2 teaspoons unsweetened
*   cocoa powder*

Combine all the ingredients in a blender and blend until smooth. Freeze for 2 hours, stirring occasionally. Serve chilled.

> **Serves 1**
>
> This tastes delicious served with whipped cream on top.
>
> ∿

Mascarpone Pudding

1½ cups milk
1 cup long grain rice
½ teaspoon ground cinnamon
1 teaspoon vanilla extract
¾ cup heavy cream

3 tablespoons granulated sugar
1 cup mascarpone
16–20 whole, unblanched
*   almonds*

1. In a medium-sized saucepan, add the milk to the rice. Stir in the cinnamon. Bring to a boil, uncovered, over medium heat. Cover, reduce heat to low, and simmer until cooked through, stirring occasionally.
2. Stir the vanilla extract into the heavy cream. Add to the rice, stirring. Continue cooking on low heat until the rice is tender. Remove from the heat.
3. Stir in the sugar and mascarpone. Spoon into dessert dishes and chill. Garnish with almonds.

> **Serves 6–8**
>
> The secret to this dessert lies in slowly cooking the rice until the grains are tender. Ricotta cheese can be substituted for the mascarpone.
>
> ∿

Chocolate Fudge Mousse
with Coffee Whipped Cream

Serves 4

You can use instant coffee crystals to make the coffee. Use parfait glasses or wineglasses with a wide bowl for a formal presentation.

1 package Jello sugar-free and fat-free instant chocolate fudge pudding mix
2 cups cold skim milk
¾ cup heavy cream, chilled

2–3 tablespoons granulated sugar
1 tablespoon prepared, very strong coffee, chilled
Fresh strawberry slices, for garnish (optional)

1. Combine the pudding mix and milk in a medium-sized mixing bowl. Use an electric mixer to beat for about 1½ minutes, until smooth. Equally divide the mixture between 4 parfait cups. Set aside for 5 to 7 minutes.
2. Put the cream in a medium-sized mixing bowl. Beat the cream until it just holds its shape. Sift the sugar over the cream and continue to beat until soft peaks form. Stir in the coffee and mix just until blended. Refrigerate until ready to serve.
3. To serve, top the pudding with equal amounts of coffee whipped cream. Served chilled. Garnish with fresh strawberries, if desired.

Strawberry Parfait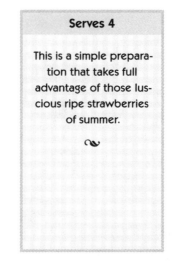

1 cup strawberries, rinsed, dried, and hulled
1½ cups nondairy whipped topping (such as Cool Whip), thawed

½ cup strawberry preserves
4 whole strawberries, for garnish
Fresh mint leaves, for garnish

Serves 4

This is a simple preparation that takes full advantage of those luscious ripe strawberries of summer.

∾

1. Slice the strawberries lengthwise and divide equally between 4 chilled martini glasses or ramekins.
2. Combine the whipped topping with the preserves in a medium-sized mixing bowl and stir until evenly blended. Dollop the mixture on top of the fruit or use a piping bag to top each with a rosette. Garnish each with a whole strawberry and a fresh mint sprig.

Chart of Blanching Times for Vegetables

Blanching vegetables before cooking helps them retain their color and flavor. For best results, cut the vegetables into uniform-sized pieces and blanch them in water that has come to a full boil. Here is a chart of blanching times for common garden vegetables.

Blanching Times for Vegetables

Vegetable Type	Blanching Time
Asparagus	2–4 minutes, depending on size
Baby carrots	5 minutes
Bell peppers	2–3 minutes
Broccoli	3 minutes
Carrots, diced	3 minutes
Carrots, whole	5 minutes
Cauliflower	3 minutes
Celery	1–1½ minutes
Parsnips	2 minutes
Snow peas	30 seconds–1 minute

Appendix B

Good Sources
of Nutrients

Good Sources of Vitamin A

Apricots
Broccoli
Cantaloupe
Carrots
Collards
Kale
Mango
Pumpkin
Spinach
Squash, winter
Sweet potato
Tomato
Turnip greens
Watermelon

Good Sources of Vitamin C

Apple with skin
Apricot, dried
Banana
Beans, lima
Broccoli
Cantaloupe
Collards
Grapefruit
Grapefruit juice
Honeydew melon
Kale
Kiwi
Orange
Orange juice
Pear with skin
Peas, green
Peppers
Potato, with skin

Spinach
Squash, winter
Strawberries
Sweet potato
Tomato
Turnip greens
Watermelon

Good Sources of Folate

Beans, dry
Black-eyed peas
Broccoli
Lentils
Mustard greens
Orange
Orange juice
Peas, green
Peas, split
Spinach
Turnip greens

Good Sources of Potassium

Apricots, dried
Banana
Beans, dry
Black-eyed peas
Cantaloupe
Grapefruit juice
Honeydew melon
Lentils
Orange juice
Peas, green
Peas, split
Plantains
Potato

Potato with skin
Prune juice
Spinach, cooked
Squash, winter
Sweet potato
Tomato

Good Sources of Dietary Fiber

Apple with skin
Apricot, dried
Banana
Beans, dry
Beans, lima
Black-eyed peas
Broccoli
Carrots
Lentils
Orange
Pear with skin
Peas, green
Peas, split
Potato with skin
Prunes
Spinach
Squash, winter
Strawberries
Sweet potato
Tomato

Note: A good source of a vitamin or mineral contributes at least 10 percent of its Percent Daily Value per serving. A good source of dietary fiber contributes at least 2 grams of dietary fiber per serving.

Appendix C

Glossary of Basic Cooking Terms

baste:

To spoon or brush a liquid over food—usually meat—during cooking. Basting prevents the food from drying out while being cooked. The basting liquid can be anything from a specially prepared sauce to the pan juices from meat that is cooking.

blanch:

To plunge vegetables and other food briefly into boiling water. Blanching seals in the color and textures of tender-crisp vegetables, such as asparagus. It's also a quick and easy way to loosen the skins on nuts, tomatoes, and other fruit, and to remove the salty flavor from foods such as ham. Blanched food that isn't going to be cooked immediately should be plunged in ice-cold water. This "shocks" the food and stops the cooking process.

boil:

To heat a liquid until bubbles form on the surface, or to cook food by placing it in liquid that is boiling. In a "rolling boil" the entire liquid is boiling, not just the surface. Stirring with a spoon won't cause the liquid to stop boiling.

braise:

To cook meat with a small amount of liquid in a tightly covered pan. Usually, the meat is browned before braising. This cooking method is an easy way to tenderize cheaper cuts of meat.

broil:

To cook food right above or under a heat source. Food can be broiled indoors in the oven or outdoors on a grill. When broiling meat, use a rack or broiling pan so that the fat from the meat can drain.

brown:

To briefly fry meat in oil until it is browned on both sides, but not cooked through. Browning the meat helps keep it tender by sealing in its natural juices.

caramelize:

To heat sugar until it becomes golden and has a syrupy texture. Meat can be caramelized by heating it in a frying pan to draw out its natural juices, which brown—or "caramelize"—on the bottom of the pan.

chop:

To cut food into small pieces, not necessarily of a uniform size. Garlic is frequently chopped before frying.

deglaze:

To add liquid to a pan or roasting pan that contains caramelized meat juices. Heating the liquid makes it easier to scrape up the hardened meat juices, which are combined with the liquid to create a sauce.

dice:

To cut food into small cubes no larger than ¼ inch.

drain:

To remove the water from blanched, washed, rinsed, or boiled food. For hassle-free draining, purchase a colander. Depending on your budget, several varieties are available, from stainless steel to inexpensive plastic.

dredge:

To coat food—usually meat or seafood—with a dry ingredient before frying. Depending on the recipe, the dry ingredient can be anything from flour or cornstarch to bread crumbs or cornmeal. Dredging provides a crisp coating and helps seal in flavor. For best results, food should be fried immediately after the coating is applied.

marinate:

To soak food in a liquid before cooking, both to tenderize it and add flavor. Most marinades contain an acidic ingredient such as lemon juice, wine, or vinegar.

mince:

To cut food into very small pieces. Minced food is cut more finely than chopped food.

sauté:

To quickly cook food in a pan in a small amount of oil, butter, or other fat.

simmer:

To cook food in liquid that is almost, but not quite, boiling.

steam:

To cook food in the steam given off by boiling water. Unlike boiling, in steaming the food never comes into direct contact with the hot water.

Index

THE EVERYTHING SERIES!

BUSINESS & PERSONAL FINANCE

Everything® Accounting Book
Everything® Budgeting Book
Everything® Business Planning Book
Everything® Coaching and Mentoring Book
Everything® Fundraising Book
Everything® Get Out of Debt Book
Everything® Grant Writing Book
Everything® Home-Based Business Book, 2nd Ed.
Everything® Homebuying Book, 2nd Ed.
Everything® Homeselling Book, 2nd Ed.
Everything® Investing Book, 2nd Ed.
Everything® Landlording Book
Everything® Leadership Book
Everything® Managing People Book, 2nd Ed.
Everything® Negotiating Book
Everything® Online Auctions Book
Everything® Online Business Book
Everything® Personal Finance Book
Everything® Personal Finance in Your 20s and 30s Book
Everything® Project Management Book
Everything® Real Estate Investing Book
Everything® Robert's Rules Book, $7.95
Everything® Selling Book
Everything® Start Your Own Business Book, 2nd Ed.
Everything® Wills & Estate Planning Book

COOKING

Everything® Barbecue Cookbook
Everything® Bartender's Book, $9.95
Everything® Chinese Cookbook
Everything® Classic Recipes Book
Everything® Cocktail Parties and Drinks Book
Everything® College Cookbook
Everything® Cooking for Baby and Toddler Book
Everything® Cooking for Two Cookbook
Everything® Diabetes Cookbook
Everything® Easy Gourmet Cookbook
Everything® Fondue Cookbook
Everything® Fondue Party Book
Everything® Gluten-Free Cookbook
Everything® Glycemic Index Cookbook
Everything® Grilling Cookbook

Everything® Healthy Meals in Minutes Cookbook
Everything® Holiday Cookbook
Everything® Indian Cookbook
Everything® Italian Cookbook
Everything® Low-Carb Cookbook
Everything® Low-Fat High-Flavor Cookbook
Everything® Low-Salt Cookbook
Everything® Meals for a Month Cookbook
Everything® Mediterranean Cookbook
Everything® Mexican Cookbook
Everything® One-Pot Cookbook
Everything® Quick and Easy 30-Minute, 5-Ingredient Cookbook
Everything® Quick Meals Cookbook
Everything® Slow Cooker Cookbook
Everything® Slow Cooking for a Crowd Cookbook
Everything® Soup Cookbook
Everything® Tex-Mex Cookbook
Everything® Thai Cookbook
Everything® Vegetarian Cookbook
Everything® Wild Game Cookbook
Everything® Wine Book, 2nd Ed.

GAMES

Everything® 15-Minute Sudoku Book, $9.95
Everything® 30-Minute Sudoku Book, $9.95
Everything® Blackjack Strategy Book
Everything® Brain Strain Book, $9.95
Everything® Bridge Book
Everything® Card Games Book
Everything® Card Tricks Book, $9.95
Everything® Casino Gambling Book, 2nd Ed.
Everything® Chess Basics Book
Everything® Craps Strategy Book
Everything® Crossword and Puzzle Book
Everything® Crossword Challenge Book
Everything® Cryptograms Book, $9.95
Everything® Easy Crosswords Book
Everything® Easy Kakuro Book, $9.95
Everything® Games Book, 2nd Ed.
Everything® Giant Sudoku Book, $9.95
Everything® Kakuro Challenge Book, $9.95
Everything® Large-Print Crossword Challenge Book
Everything® Large-Print Crosswords Book
Everything® Lateral Thinking Puzzles Book, $9.95
Everything® Mazes Book

Everything® Pencil Puzzles Book, $9.95
Everything® Poker Strategy Book
Everything® Pool & Billiards Book
Everything® Test Your IQ Book, $9.95
Everything® Texas Hold 'Em Book, $9.95
Everything® Travel Crosswords Book, $9.95
Everything® Word Games Challenge Book
Everything® Word Search Book

HEALTH

Everything® Alzheimer's Book
Everything® Diabetes Book
Everything® Health Guide to Adult Bipolar Disorder
Everything® Health Guide to Controlling Anxiety
Everything® Health Guide to Fibromyalgia
Everything® Health Guide to Thyroid Disease
Everything® Hypnosis Book
Everything® Low Cholesterol Book
Everything® Massage Book
Everything® Menopause Book
Everything® Nutrition Book
Everything® Reflexology Book
Everything® Stress Management Book

HISTORY

Everything® American Government Book
Everything® American History Book
Everything® Civil War Book
Everything® Freemasons Book
Everything® Irish History & Heritage Book
Everything® Middle East Book

HOBBIES

Everything® Candlemaking Book
Everything® Cartooning Book
Everything® Coin Collecting Book
Everything® Drawing Book
Everything® Family Tree Book, 2nd Ed.
Everything® Knitting Book
Everything® Knots Book
Everything® Photography Book
Everything® Quilting Book
Everything® Scrapbooking Book
Everything® Sewing Book
Everything® Woodworking Book

Bolded titles are new additions to the series.
All Everything® books are priced at $12.95 or $14.95, unless otherwise stated. Prices subject to change without notice.

HOME IMPROVEMENT

Everything® Feng Shui Book
Everything® Feng Shui Decluttering Book, $9.95
Everything® Fix-It Book
Everything® Home Decorating Book
Everything® Home Storage Solutions Book
Everything® Homebuilding Book
Everything® Lawn Care Book
Everything® Organize Your Home Book

KIDS' BOOKS

All titles are $7.95

Everything® Kids' Animal Puzzle & Activity Book
Everything® Kids' Baseball Book, 4th Ed.
Everything® Kids' Bible Trivia Book
Everything® Kids' Bugs Book
Everything® Kids' Cars and Trucks Puzzle & Activity Book
Everything® Kids' Christmas Puzzle & Activity Book
Everything® Kids' Cookbook
Everything® Kids' Crazy Puzzles Book
Everything® Kids' Dinosaurs Book
Everything® Kids' First Spanish Puzzle and Activity Book
Everything® Kids' Gross Hidden Pictures Book
Everything® Kids' Gross Jokes Book
Everything® Kids' Gross Mazes Book
Everything® Kids' Gross Puzzle and Activity Book
Everything® Kids' Halloween Puzzle & Activity Book
Everything® Kids' Hidden Pictures Book
Everything® Kids' Horses Book
Everything® Kids' Joke Book
Everything® Kids' Knock Knock Book
Everything® Kids' Learning Spanish Book
Everything® Kids' Math Puzzles Book
Everything® Kids' Mazes Book
Everything® Kids' Money Book
Everything® Kids' Nature Book
Everything® Kids' Pirates Puzzle and Activity Book
Everything® Kids' Princess Puzzle and Activity Book
Everything® Kids' Puzzle Book
Everything® Kids' Riddles & Brain Teasers Book
Everything® Kids' Science Experiments Book
Everything® Kids' Sharks Book
Everything® Kids' Soccer Book
Everything® Kids' Travel Activity Book

KIDS' STORY BOOKS

Everything® Fairy Tales Book

LANGUAGE

Everything® Conversational Chinese Book with CD, $19.95
Everything® Conversational Japanese Book with CD, $19.95
Everything® French Grammar Book
Everything® French Phrase Book, $9.95
Everything® French Verb Book, $9.95
Everything® German Practice Book with CD, $19.95
Everything® Inglés Book
Everything® Learning French Book
Everything® Learning German Book
Everything® Learning Italian Book
Everything® Learning Latin Book
Everything® Learning Spanish Book
Everything® Russian Practice Book with CD, $19.95
Everything® Sign Language Book
Everything® Spanish Grammar Book
Everything® Spanish Phrase Book, $9.95
Everything® Spanish Practice Book with CD, $19.95
Everything® Spanish Verb Book, $9.95

MUSIC

Everything® Drums Book with CD, $19.95
Everything® Guitar Book
Everything® Guitar Chords Book with CD, $19.95
Everything® Home Recording Book
Everything® Music Theory Book with CD, $19.95
Everything® Reading Music Book with CD, $19.95
Everything® Rock & Blues Guitar Book (with CD), $19.95
Everything® Songwriting Book

NEW AGE

Everything® Astrology Book, 2nd Ed.
Everything® Birthday Personology Book
Everything® Dreams Book, 2nd Ed.
Everything® Love Signs Book, $9.95
Everything® Numerology Book
Everything® Paganism Book
Everything® Palmistry Book
Everything® Psychic Book
Everything® Reiki Book
Everything® Sex Signs Book, $9.95
Everything® Tarot Book, 2nd Ed.
Everything® Wicca and Witchcraft Book

PARENTING

Everything® Baby Names Book, 2nd Ed.
Everything® Baby Shower Book
Everything® Baby's First Food Book
Everything® Baby's First Year Book
Everything® Birthing Book
Everything® Breastfeeding Book
Everything® Father-to-Be Book
Everything® Father's First Year Book
Everything® Get Ready for Baby Book
Everything® Get Your Baby to Sleep Book, $9.95
Everything® Getting Pregnant Book
Everything® Guide to Raising a One-Year-Old
Everything® Guide to Raising a Two-Year-Old
Everything® Homeschooling Book
Everything® Mother's First Year Book
Everything® Parent's Guide to Children and Divorce
Everything® Parent's Guide to Children with ADD/ADHD
Everything® Parent's Guide to Children with Asperger's Syndrome
Everything® Parent's Guide to Children with Autism
Everything® Parent's Guide to Children with Bipolar Disorder
Everything® Parent's Guide to Children with Dyslexia
Everything® Parent's Guide to Positive Discipline
Everything® Parent's Guide to Raising a Successful Child
Everything® Parent's Guide to Raising Boys
Everything® Parent's Guide to Raising Siblings
Everything® Parent's Guide to Sensory Integration Disorder
Everything® Parent's Guide to Tantrums
Everything® Parent's Guide to the Overweight Child
Everything® Parent's Guide to the Strong-Willed Child
Everything® Parenting a Teenager Book
Everything® Potty Training Book, $9.95
Everything® Pregnancy Book, 2nd Ed.
Everything® Pregnancy Fitness Book
Everything® Pregnancy Nutrition Book
Everything® Pregnancy Organizer, 2nd Ed., $16.95
Everything® Toddler Activities Book
Everything® Toddler Book
Everything® Tween Book
Everything® Twins, Triplets, and More Book

PETS

Everything® Aquarium Book
Everything® Boxer Book
Everything® Cat Book, 2nd Ed.
Everything® Chihuahua Book
Everything® Dachshund Book
Everything® Dog Book
Everything® Dog Health Book
Everything® Dog Owner's Organizer,
$16.95
Everything® Dog Training and Tricks Book
Everything® German Shepherd Book
Everything® Golden Retriever Book
Everything® Horse Book
Everything® Horse Care Book
Everything® Horseback Riding Book
Everything® Labrador Retriever Book
Everything® Poodle Book
Everything® Pug Book
Everything® Puppy Book
Everything® Rottweiler Book
Everything® Small Dogs Book
Everything® Tropical Fish Book
Everything® Yorkshire Terrier Book

REFERENCE

Everything® Blogging Book
Everything® Build Your Vocabulary Book
Everything® Car Care Book
Everything® Classical Mythology Book
Everything® Da Vinci Book
Everything® Divorce Book
Everything® Einstein Book
Everything® Etiquette Book, 2nd Ed.
Everything® Inventions and Patents Book
Everything® Mafia Book
Everything® Philosophy Book
Everything® Psychology Book
Everything® Shakespeare Book

RELIGION

Everything® Angels Book
Everything® Bible Book
Everything® Buddhism Book
Everything® Catholicism Book
Everything® Christianity Book
Everything® History of the Bible Book
Everything® Jesus Book
Everything® Jewish History & Heritage Book
Everything® Judaism Book
Everything® Kabbalah Book
Everything® Koran Book
Everything® Mary Book

Everything® Mary Magdalene Book
Everything® Prayer Book
Everything® Saints Book
Everything® Torah Book
Everything® Understanding Islam Book
Everything® World's Religions Book
Everything® Zen Book

SCHOOL & CAREERS

Everything® Alternative Careers Book
Everything® Career Tests Book
Everything® College Major Test Book
Everything® College Survival Book, 2nd Ed.
Everything® Cover Letter Book, 2nd Ed.
Everything® Filmmaking Book
Everything® Get-a-Job Book
Everything® Guide to Being a Paralegal
Everything® Guide to Being a Real Estate
Agent
Everything® Guide to Being a Sales Rep
Everything® Guide to Careers in Health
Care
Everything® Guide to Careers in Law
Enforcement
Everything® Guide to Government Jobs
Everything® Guide to Starting and Running
a Restaurant
Everything® Job Interview Book
Everything® New Nurse Book
Everything® New Teacher Book
Everything® Paying for College Book
Everything® Practice Interview Book
Everything® Resume Book, 2nd Ed.
Everything® Study Book

SELF-HELP

Everything® Dating Book, 2nd Ed.
Everything® Great Sex Book
Everything® Kama Sutra Book
Everything® Self-Esteem Book

SPORTS & FITNESS

Everything® Easy Fitness Book
Everything® Fishing Book
Everything® Golf Instruction Book
Everything® Pilates Book
Everything® Running Book
Everything® Weight Training Book
Everything® Yoga Book

TRAVEL

Everything® Family Guide to Cruise Vacations
Everything® Family Guide to Hawaii

Everything® Family Guide to Las Vegas,
2nd Ed.
Everything® Family Guide to Mexico
Everything® Family Guide to New York City,
2nd Ed.
Everything® Family Guide to RV Travel &
Campgrounds
Everything® Family Guide to the Caribbean
Everything® Family Guide to the Walt Disney
World Resort®, Universal Studios®,
and Greater Orlando, 4th Ed.
Everything® Family Guide to Timeshares
Everything® Family Guide to Washington
D.C., 2nd Ed.
Everything® Guide to New England

WEDDINGS

Everything® Bachelorette Party Book, $9.95
Everything® Bridesmaid Book, $9.95
Everything® Destination Wedding Book
Everything® Elopement Book, $9.95
Everything® Father of the Bride Book, $9.95
Everything® Groom Book, $9.95
Everything® Mother of the Bride Book, $9.95
Everything® Outdoor Wedding Book
Everything® Wedding Book, 3rd Ed.
Everything® Wedding Checklist, $9.95
Everything® Wedding Etiquette Book, $9.95
Everything® Wedding Organizer, 2nd Ed.,
$16.95
Everything® Wedding Shower Book, $9.95
Everything® Wedding Vows Book, $9.95
Everything® Wedding Workout Book
Everything® Weddings on a Budget Book,
$9.95

WRITING

Everything® Creative Writing Book
Everything® Get Published Book, 2nd Ed.
Everything® Grammar and Style Book
Everything® Guide to Writing a Book
Proposal
Everything® Guide to Writing a Novel
Everything® Guide to Writing Children's
Books
Everything® Guide to Writing Research
Papers
Everything® Screenwriting Book
Everything® Writing Poetry Book
Everything® Writing Well Book